Patching Development

MODERN SOUTH ASIA

Ashutosh Varshney, Series Editor
Pradeep Chhibber, Associate Series Editor

The Other One Percent
Sanjoy Chakravorty, Devesh Kapur, and Nirvikar Singh

Social Justice through Inclusion
Francesca R. Jensenius

Dispossession without Development
Michael Levien

The Man Who Remade India
Vinay Sitapati

Business and Politics in India
Edited by Christophe Jaffrelot, Atul Kohli, and Kanta Murali

Clients and Constituents
Jennifer Bussell

Gambling with Violence
Yelena Biberman

Mobilizing the Marginalized
Amit Ahuja

The Absent Dialogue
Anit Mukherjee

When Nehru Looked East
Francine Frankel

Capable Women, Incapable States
Poulami Roychowdhury

Farewell to Arms
Rumela Sen

Negotiating Democracy and Religious Pluralism
Karen Barkey, Sudipta Kaviraj, and Vatsal Naresh

Cultivating Democracy
Mukulika Banerjee

Patching Development
Rajesh Veeraraghavan

Patching Development

Information Politics and Social Change in India

RAJESH VEERARAGHAVAN

OXFORD
UNIVERSITY PRESS

Oxford University Press is a department of the University of Oxford. It furthers the University's objective of excellence in research, scholarship, and education by publishing worldwide. Oxford is a registered trade mark of Oxford University Press in the UK and certain other countries.

Published in the United States of America by Oxford University Press
198 Madison Avenue, New York, NY 10016, United States of America.

Library of Congress Cataloging-in-Publication Data
Names: Veeraraghavan, Rajesh, author.
Title: Patching development : information politics and
social change in India / Rajesh Veeraraghavan.
Description: New York, NY : Oxford University Press, [2022] |
Series: Modern South Asia | Includes bibliographical references and index.
Identifiers: LCCN 2021034890 (print) | LCCN 2021034891 (ebook) |
ISBN 9780197567821 (paperback) | ISBN 9780197567814 (hardback) |
ISBN 9780197567845 (epub)
Subjects: LCSH: National Rural Employment Guarantee Scheme
(India)—Appropriations and expenditures. | Rural
poor—Employment—India. | Social accounting—India.
Classification: LCC HD5710.85.I4 V44 2022 (print) | LCC HD5710.85.I4
(ebook) | DDC 331.12/0420954—dc23
LC record available at https://lccn.loc.gov/2021034890
LC ebook record available at https://lccn.loc.gov/2021034891

DOI: 10.1093/oso/9780197567814.001.0001

1 3 5 7 9 8 6 4 2

Paperback printed by Marquis, Canada
Hardback printed by Bridgeport National Bindery, Inc., United States of America

For Vidhya

Contents

Acknowledgments	ix
Abbreviations	xiii
Map	xv
1. Introduction	1
2. The Genesis of Rights-Based Governance	28
3. Patching Technologies of Control	49
4. Patching Institutions	68
5. Public Meetings at the Last Mile	91
6. Reading and Writing State Records	114
7. Caste, Class, and Audits	136
8. Conclusion: Patching the Balance of Power at the Last Mile	162
Appendix 1. Methodology: Using Ethnography to Study Political Economy of Information	179
Appendix 2. Explanatory Note on Comparing NREGA Performance across States	183
Notes	185
References	205
Index	225

Acknowledgments

Many people have contributed to the life of this book. I am grateful to all of you and for this opportunity to express my indebtedness and appreciation.

I want to thank the NREGA workers (in Andhra Pradesh and Bihar), government officials, and activists for their generosity in making the book possible. Unfortunately, I am not able to name all of them, as I am committed to protecting their identity. My deepest gratitude is to Raj Kumar, who traveled with me for part of my fieldwork. He served not just as translator, but also as a boon companion who got me (and himself) in and out of trouble during my fieldwork! I want to thank Prakashgaru and his family for hosting me and particularly for taking care of me when I was seriously ill during fieldwork. Thank you Pedamma for letting me stay at your house. I want to thank Sudhesh and his parents for hosting me for a part of the fieldwork. I want to thank my aunt and uncle in Hyderabad for hosting me while I was there in the city. I also want to thank Sowmya, Kavitha, and Hiran for making my Hyderabad stints pleasant. And special thanks to all those who let me intrude in your lives without anything to offer in return.

My interest in development was a direct result of my volunteer work through AID (Association for India's Development). While there are many great friends and activists who helped sensitize me to issues of the marginalized in India, I want to single out Balaji Sampath, Michael Mazgaonkar, Swati Desai, Anand Mazgaonkar, Ravi Kuchimanchi, Aravinda Pillalamarri, Kiran Kumar Vissa, Nityanand Jayaraman, Leo Saldanha, and Prashant Jawalikar, whose work, activism, and friendship has had a deep impact on me over the last twenty-plus years. I thank Kentaro Toyama for being my mentor at Microsoft Research India, encouraging me to pursue a PhD, and for continuing to support throughout my career. I also want to thank Eric Brewer, whose research talk introduced me to the field of information and communication for technology and development. My first taste for ethnography came from Balaji Parthasarthy of IIIT Bangalore and Ken Keniston from MIT, who welcomed me into their summer research group to study the effect of information and communication technology projects in development. I want to thank my friends and colleagues at Microsoft Research India and at the Technology for Emerging Markets group in Bangalore, India, who lured me into the life of research, as well as Rikin Gandhi for helping bring forth one of my research projects, Digital Green, to such scale and heights. The Digital Green project showed me the impact that research could have.

The origins of this book project started from hearing about the right to information and the work of Aruna Roy, Nikhil Dey, and Shankar Singh in AID circles and in the media. I was at the School of Information at Berkeley, and their struggle to make information a right resonated with me. An email from activists Ashish Jha and Kamayani Swami, both of whom were AID Saathis and organizers of the agricultural workers union in Arara, Bihar, asking for volunteers to be part of the social audits (which was a result of the RTI act) immediately led me to spend a summer volunteering with them, which ultimately led to my dissertation and this book. I also want to thank the many volunteers who were part of the social audit volunteer team with me—in particular, Vibhore Vardhan, for his friendship over the years.

I want to thank Jean Drèze and Reetika Khera for asking me to take seriously NREGA's implementation by the state government in Andhra Pradesh, which ultimately became the central focus of this book. Their scholarship and public action continue to be an inspiration. Sowmya Kidambi, who was the director of Social Audits in Andhra Pradesh, graciously sat for many interviews, and facilitated my access to the NREGA bureaucracy and the rest of the audit team. Senior bureaucrats K. Raju, Reddy Subramanian, and A. Murali also lent extraordinary support. Thanks to Aruna Roy and Nikhil Dey and other activists from the MKSS for spending time with me in Delhi, as well as for their critical optimism. Among the many activists I met with in Andhra Pradesh, I want to thank P. Sainath and P. S. Ajay Kumar for teaching me about rural Andhra Pradesh and for their journalism and activism to bring attention to the marginalized.

Many of the intellectual arguments I have made in this book had their genesis in coursework at UC Berkeley. I want to thank AnnaLee Saxenian (Anno) for accepting me as a PhD student at the School of Information and for being a generous, warm champion and a constant source of optimism about my growth as a scholar. I had the great privilege of learning from my advisors Peter Evans, Paul Duguid, AnnaLee Saxenian, and Michael Burawoy.

My deepest gratitude is for Peter Evans's and Paul Duguid's exceptional mentorship and guidance, reading multiple drafts, and going beyond the "call of duty" to help me write this book. I also want to thank Peter for instilling in me the desire to look for examples for transformation and reform to understand what it takes to shift power in state-society relations and for helping me refine this work over the years. I want to thank Paul for helping me develop the sociotechnical imagination when I was willing to abandon the technical for the social. He patiently, persistently, and wisely sought to retain the balance between them. I also enjoyed the banter about cricket with him.

I want to thank Michael Burawoy and Gill Hart for teaching me social theory, and for instilling in me a critical sensibility to questions of development. I want to thank Jenna Burrell, Tapan Parikh, Coye Cheshire, Geoffrey Nunberg, John

Chuang, Raka Ray, Isha̩ Ray, Alan De Janvry, and Elizabeth Sadoulet for their classes and mentorship. My friends and fellow graduate students at Berkeley provided the rich intellectual milieu for this project. I want to thank Bob Bell, Neha Kumar, Janaki Srinivasan, Robert On, Becky Tarlau, Yuri Takhteyev, Dilan Mahendran, Elisa Oreglia, Josh Blumenstock, Megan Finn, Ashwin Mathew, Melissa Ho, Daniela Rosner, Christo Sims, Rabin Patra, and Zachary Levenson, among many others who supported me.

Vivek Srinivasan has provided invaluable advice throughout every stage of this project, and his book on public services in Tamil Nadu has been a great inspiration for me to understand the role of decentralized collective action in getting the state to respond to the needs of the poor. I thank him for his friendship, and numerous conversations (and arguments) over the years to develop a nuanced view of what the state can do to respond to marginalized citizens. I want to thank Bob Bell, who has been my friend and accountability buddy for writing and meditating, for being my mentor over the years. Bob has been an invaluable ally in helping me find my own voice through our regular discussions for the last ten years. I cannot thank him enough. I want to thank Atul Pokharel for his friendship, support, and his constant prodding to focus on one sentence at a time. I thank Atul for helping me refine the concept of patching through several discussions, as well as for being an accountability partner and supporting me during the writing process.

A number of people have labored and commented on the entire manuscript: Peter Evans, Paul Duguid, Patrick Heller, Jonathan Fox, Kentaro Toyama, Irfan Nooruddin, Rachel Brulé, Vivek Srinivasan, Bob Bell, Janaki Srinivasan, Rina Agarwala, Silvia Masiero, Bhawani Buswala, Adam Auerbach, and Anindita Adhikari. I thank Kate Babbitt and Jody Hauber for being such fantastic editors at different stages of the project. A number of individuals provided many comments on one or several chapters: Jean Drèze, Reetika Khera, Michael Burawoy, Joel Simmons, Chuck Weiss, Emily Mendenhall, Elisa Oreglia, Poulami Roychowdhury, Paromita Sanyal, Gowri Vijayakumar, Rajendran Narayanan, Michael Levien, Suchi Pande, Ranjit Singh, Anya Wahal, Divjot Bawa, Atul Pokharel, Kate Chandler, Chakradhar Buddha, Rebecca Tarlau, Sakina Dhorajiwala, Kristen Looney, Milan Vaishnav, Sharan Mamidipudi, Vijayendra (Biju) Rao, Tim Davies, Aashish Gupta, Vibhore Vardhan, Sowmya Kidambi, Sky Colloredo-Mansfeld, Kari Hensley, Anjali Britto, Brendan Halloran, Jeffrey Witsoe, AnnaLee Saxenian, Rakshita Swamy, Aditya Johri, Jenna Burrell, and Yamini Aiyar. Several chapters received feedback at the Watson Institute of International Affairs at Brown University, the political economy workshop by the Carnegie Endowment for International Peace at Washington, DC, the Unpacking Participatory Democracy workshop organized at the Institute for the Study of International Development at McGill University, a book workshop organized by the Annual Conference on South Asia at the University of Wisconsin Madison, the Stanford Seminar on Liberation Technologies, the Michigan State University seminar on Technology and Development, undergraduate students in my classes at Brown University and Georgetown University, graduate students at the SAFAR at NLS Bangalore and the STS circle at the Kennedy School of Government, Harvard University. I want to thank Patrick Heller, Atul Pokharel, Sarah Besky, and Anindita Adhikari for their friendship and also for being such a rich source of intellectual stimulation and listening and reading multiple drafts at Brown University, where I was a postdoctoral fellow. The Berkman Klein center at Harvard University also initiated stimulating discussions when I was a fellow. The book was shepherded to print by David McBride at Oxford University Press; series editors Ashutosh Varshney and Pradeep Chibber; and the book's two anonymous reviewers. I want to thank Ashu for his enthusiastic support and patience for this book project.

The School of Foreign Service at Georgetown University provided the ideal intellectual environment in which to complete this project. The faculty and students, in particular at the Science, Technology and International Affairs Program, have been a great source of encouragement and support. I thank the Mortara Center at Georgetown University and the Watson Institute at Brown University and Abraham Newman for his generous support for organizing an energizing book workshop. I also want to thank Irfan Nooruddin, Scott Taylor, and Mark Giordano for being my mentors and helping me stay focused. Joanna Lewis, Carol Benedict, and Joel Hellman have also provided immeasurable leadership and support. I want to thank Joel Simmons, who first saw the potential in the idea of patching as a concept to develop further. My thanks to Aashish Gupta, Anya Wahal, and Divjot Bawa for their terrific research assistance. And special thanks to Obdulio Moronta and Whitney Tate for helping with many administrative tasks at Georgetown.

My amma, V. Hema, and my appa, K. S. Veeraraghavan (*rombha nandri, ena valathu padikavechu pathundu irukardhuku*), have loved and comforted me. I want to thank my dear brother, Sriram Veera, for being there for me through the many ups and downs of life. My aunts, uncles, and cousins, Aparna, Karthik, Gayathri, Sonia, Agastya, Bala, Mythily, Shreya, Sanjana, Prashant, Janhavi, Arya, Suku, Sritika, VTP and the Pilani Vetties, and Nandu, bring great cheer to my life. I want to thank my in-laws V. Madhuram and K. Venkataraman for all they do and in particular for their support during my fieldwork to take care of my sons. I want to thank my dear sons Dhruv and Kabir for bringing joy and meaning to all I am and do. Finally, I owe everything (personal, spiritual, and intellectual support) to my wife, Srividhya Venkataraman, without whom life would be too lonely and without love or inspiration.

Abbreviations

AID	Association for India's Development
BDO	Block development officer
BJP	Bharatiya Janata Party
CD	Compact disc
CIA	Central Intelligence Agency
CM	Chief minister
CPM	Communist Party Marxist
EC	Engineering consultant
FA	Field assistant
ICT	Information and communication technology
ICTD	Information and communication technology for development
JJSS	Jan Jagaran Shakti Sangathan
MKSS	Mazdoor Kisan Shakti Sangathan
MLA	Member of Legislative Assembly
MPDO	Mandal Parishad development officer
NGO	Nongovernmental organization
NREGA	National Rural Employment Guarantee Act
PUCL	People's Union for Civil Liberties
RTI	Right to Information
SC	Scheduled Caste
SSAAT	Society for Social Audit, Accountability and Transparency
ST	Scheduled Tribe
TA	Technical assistant
TCS	Tata Consultancy Services
TDP	Telugu Desam Party
UPA	United Progressive Alliance
YSR	Yedguri Sandinti Rajasekhara Reddy

Map

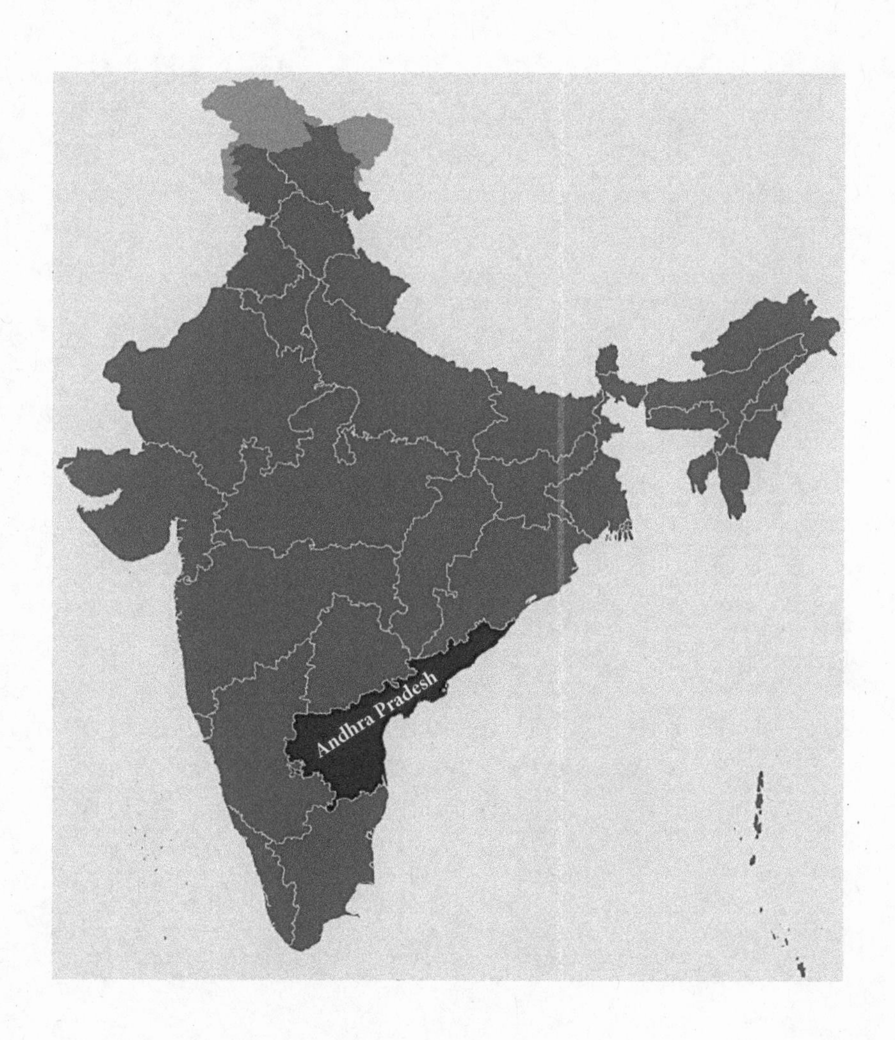

1
Introduction

One of the leading issues of modern development policy is how states can best deliver social benefits to marginalized citizens. In many countries, even well-designed programs do not deliver those benefits effectively. Political will and good policy design are critical, but they are often not enough because of resistance from local power systems. This book is concerned with understanding how states can react most effectively to the local exercise of power that often comes into play at the "last mile" of implementing a development program. How can development programs avoid being captured by either state or local power systems? I look at this question by focusing on the local implementation and adjustment of statewide programs. Can the opening of government records and the use of digital technology provide higher levels of government with better tools to effectively monitor local state action? What role can marginalized citizens and members of civil society play in strengthening these systems of accountability?

In 2005, the Indian government enacted two landmark rights-based laws: the National Rural Employment Guarantee Act (NREGA), which gave every rural citizen the right to work, and the Right to Information (RTI) Act, which granted all citizens the right to access government records. NREGA, the largest development program in the world, has two broad goals: to provide employment on demand and to build useful rural infrastructure. A coalition of civil society activists, central bureaucrats, and political party leaders worked to ensure that the social audit—a citizen oversight mechanism—was part of the original NREGA legislation (Jenkins and Manor 2017; Chopra 2011b). The rights-based social entitlements and guarantees of transparency embedded in NREGA and RTI were a fundamental departure from typical welfare programs in which citizens were passive recipients of benefits (see, for example, Drèze and Sen 2013; Khera 2011b; Drèze and Khera 2017; Hasan 2018; Jenkins and Goetz 1999; Roy 2018; Ravi and Engler 2015). These rights marked a transition to seeing the state as a force for redistribution that will improve the everyday lives of marginalized citizens. But implementation, which is left to subnational state governments, has revealed the degree to which empowering the poor both politically and economically can run up against a range of vested interests and social powers (Jenkins and Manor 2017; Sukhtankar 2016; Singh 2017).

As development economist Jean Drèze, one of the architects of NREGA, writes, there is "a deep contradiction or at least tension with NREGA: it is a proworker law implemented by an antiworker system—a system pervaded by indifference if not hostility towards marginalised people in general and rural workers in particular" (Drèze 2019, 143). Implementing an employment guarantee program can directly intervene in work relations in villages and inevitably encounters resistance from landowners who fear losing power over landless laborers who choose to work on the public program instead of working for them. Similarly, local landlords may perceive giving a landless Dalit state-paid employment at the local level as a direct threat to his dominance (Bardhan 1999). That, in turn, affects caste relations. Thus, local resistance may have economic or class-based underpinnings and may also emanate from threats to patriarchal and caste-based power structures. Programs like NREGA that cut across these intersectional categories of caste, class, and gender typically encounter the greatest resistance. The bureaucrats who are often involved in maintaining these anti-worker systems live and work in the local setting and are often hired precisely because of their links to the local power structure. Thus, development programs confront this local anti-worker system even when there is political will at higher levels to implement a program. The power system, the dense nucleus of class, caste, gender, and bureaucratic power, is often what thwarts development programs.

Patching Development focuses on understanding the mechanisms of what is often considered to be a successful case of NREGA implementation in the southern state of Andhra Pradesh.[1] It examines under what conditions and to what extent upper-level bureaucrats, who are typically seen to be complicit in this anti-worker system, can actually challenge it from within to ensure that benefits reach NREGA workers. While I do not contest the fact that indifference and apathy exist in bureaucracies,[2] this book is a case study of bureaucrats who were not indifferent. Under certain conditions, they were able to play an important role in effecting social change while consciously and diligently working to address the traditional shortcomings of the bureaucracies they were part of (see Tendler 1998; Evans 2012). Certainly there are enough reasons to believe that the bureaucrats do not care, but there are also cases of committed bureaucrats who are focused on the poor (Tendler 1998; McDonnell 2020; Pires 2011; Coslovsky et al. 2017; Lipsky 1980; Gay 2005). As sociologist Peter Evans notes, "It is always fun and often useful to expose the perfidies of public sector actors, this kind of news is already in oversupply. What is needed is more research on positive cases" (Evans 1996, 1131).[3]

The attempts of bureaucrats to move beyond the state's history of bias and failure to overcome anti-worker resistance is at the heart of the struggle to successfully implement NREGA. The national government controls the funding of NREGA but largely leaves the implementation to subnational governments. This book focuses on the struggles of upper-level bureaucrats in Andhra Pradesh to implement NREGA. In particular, I focus on the last mile of implementation through an ethnography of the everyday practices of bureaucrats in Andhra Pradesh and the technologies they use to oversee NREGA.

In this book, I refer to the administrators of NREGA in Andhra Pradesh as upper-level bureaucrats, and government employees who carry out NREGA implementation at the last mile as lower-level bureaucrats. These two layers of authority matter because they are often at odds with each other. Lower-level bureaucrats are often part of (or have to deal with) the local power system that seeks to subvert the distribution of state goods and services to citizens.[4] Similarly, while upper-level bureaucrats were determined to implement the program to its specifications, they also were constrained structurally and politically in ways that limited the success of the program. Lower-level bureaucrats are often caught between demands from upper-level bureaucrats and the local power system that they both benefit and suffer from.

A few upper-level bureaucrats in Andhra Pradesh took inspiration from the Dalit leader Bhimrao Ramji Ambedkar, the architect of India's constitution, who asked, "What is the village but a sink of localism, a den of ignorance, narrow-mindedness and communalism?"[5] Under the oppressive conditions of hierarchical caste order, Ambedkar did not have faith that decentralized politics would necessarily help Dalits and other marginalized people.[6] He argued instead that the state should erect safeguards against social oppression at the local level. In Andhra Pradesh, upper-level bureaucrats agreed with the Ambedkarite vision of using state action to neutralize the local power nexus in the villages with the support of civil society activists and NREGA workers.

The upper-level bureaucrats in Andhra Pradesh did two things: they increased the transparency of state practices, as the NREGA law mandated, and they worked to neutralize local power nexuses. This was done through using technology and democratizing access to public records. However, this opening up of state practices was limited to NREGA and did not cover bureaucratic processes in other programs.[7]

While upper-level bureaucrats in Andhra Pradesh sought to centralize power to prevent local resistance, they had to overcome the problems of centralized state bureaucracies, which often do not respond to local information and implementation failures. This involved going beyond technocratic fixes to create "participatory bureaucratic" institutions with the capacity to solicit participation from NREGA workers to monitor the program, building technology to cope with resistance at the last mile, and finding a way to resolve discrepancies by adjudicating disputes (Moffitt 2014).

The information infrastructure that upper-level bureaucrats in Andhra Pradesh assembled was a series of densely intertwined systems that monitored and provided feedback about everyday state actions structured both from the top down and just as powerfully from the bottom up. This meant focusing on changing processes that directly affected NREGA: using upper-level bureaucrats rather than local leaders to recruit frontline workers, giving the public access to NREGA documents, and conducting social audits to discuss the everyday practices of the state with marginalized citizens. However, the story I tell here is about more than finding the appropriate and efficacious institutions and technology. While these were necessary, they alone were not sufficient. The bureaucrats in charge of implementing NREGA in Andhra Pradesh realized that the actors in the local power system were actively involved in blocking initiatives and working around systems of governance (Aiyar et al. 2011). They needed to create a dynamic strategy that constantly countered such interference. If NREGA were to succeed, each aggression had to be met with an opposing action.

Reformers do not possess the capacity to fundamentally change this power axis through direct confrontation with local elites. Instead, they have to rely on a continuous series of responses, responding to information that flags problems with implementation at the local level. I call this process *patching development. Patching*, a term I borrow from software, is a metaphor for the process of replacing a problematic set of commands and rules with a new set of instructions. While software patches require only technical changes, the process of altering the rules of a government program requires both technical patches and the political wisdom to diagnose and respond to local conditions.

Patching, as used here, applies to processes that involve changes in institutions, changes in technology, and changes in documents and processes that control implementation of a public program. An example of patching is the constant adjustments upper-level bureaucrats made in how public NREGA meetings were conducted to maximize worker participation and minimize the power of local elites. Although the process of patching in Andhra Pradesh is mostly focused on making small changes, it is really about changing power equations. The local system of power is hard to transform, not because of inertia but because of counter-strategies from powerful actors at the local last mile. Patching is about the fight over power at the last mile, the untidy realities and the back-and-forth struggles over how work relations are managed within the NREGA bureaucracy with the participation of marginalized citizens to the patching process in ways that ultimately lead to patching development itself.

But I get ahead of myself. Let me start at the beginning.

In the summer of 2010, I was sitting in a hot, open field in the remote countryside in the state of Bihar in northern India. The occasion was a social audit hearing organized by Jan Jagaran Shakti Sanghatan (JJSS), a local agricultural laborers' union that had recently formed to support the workers' struggle for employment. I and many student volunteers for the union had offered to help administer a social audit of the NREGA, which at that point had been law for five years.

A tent that had been erected for the occasion was already filled with hundreds of local residents, and people from nearby villages were also trickling in. The hearing began with organizers singing revolutionary workers' songs. Then Kamesh, one of the event organizers, stood at front of the podium and demanded, "Have you ever seen a muster roll?" (A muster roll is an attendance document taken by local government officials that records NREGA work. That, in turn, determines how much a worker is owed for her or his labor.) A loud "No!" resounded through the tent. "Have you had 100 days of employment?" Again, "No!" Kamesh explained that the purpose of the meeting was to present the results from a recent audit and inform people about their rights. These included their entitlement to 100 days of paid work under the NREGA program. It also included the right to know the contents of the program's muster roll, a document that no worker had ever seen before in that village.

Looking around the crowded tent, I thought about how, a week earlier, I had assisted volunteers as they prepared for this portion of the social audit by conducting a village survey. The survey was possible because of the recent passage of the RTI law, referred to earlier, which allowed any citizen in India to inspect and obtain certified copies of government documents. We were looking at the NREGA records for the village we were going to audit when one volunteer remarked, "This Ganjaram is on multiple muster rolls. He claims to have worked in multiple places on the same day." The following day, we visited several villages with copies of official muster rolls to track down Ganjaram, only to learn he had passed away years ago.

The villagers who told us about Ganjaram had showed us their bank passbooks.[8] Normally, these are kept by local government clerks, but the impending social audits, we were told, had prompted officials to return passbooks to the workers. However, the villagers were illiterate and could not read what was written in them. They asked me to read some of the entries aloud. To one worker, a man named Kanchi, I said, "It looks as if you worked forty days this past year, received Rs. 4,000 for it in your account, and then subsequently withdrew it." Kanchi gave me a blank look that quickly turned to one of rage. All the other passbooks indicated similar activity and the villagers became increasingly agitated. Another volunteer asked them, "Are you saying that you haven't received this money?" They replied, "No, none of it." I and the other activists realized we were witnessing and participating in a simple yet radical act by engaging in a form of politics that was bringing to light the everyday acts of government officials for the first time.

This was exactly the kind of illegal and illegitimate activity JJSS was interested in unearthing, so we asked the villagers to come to the public hearing the following week. Most hesitated but eventually agreed to come. When we asked them to sign written testimony, however, most refused. "I cannot sign this paper. I need to live here," they would say. They feared retaliation from local government officials. Later, that fear spread to the other villagers. Some who had submitted written testimonies demanded that we return them.

In the evening, we encountered Kanchi and some of the villagers having a drink and discussing the day's events. We again raised the topic of the hearing. Kanchi voiced everyone's worries: "These bastards [local elites] will kill us. I am not scared, but some people are." We assured them that JJSS would remain in the area and that we would provide support.

One week later, as the public hearing got under way, Kamesh laid out the protocol for the event: "Raise your hands if you wish to share your thoughts, and come to the microphone in the front to speak." He noted that the proceedings would be video-recorded.

The mukhiya, the president of the panchayat (village council), was the first to speak. "Everything is going well in this village," he assured Kamesh. "All the work has been done, and everybody was paid." At that point, JJSS activists read out the results from the most recent social audit, making clear the gross disparities between the NREGA's records and the social audit results.

Kanchi raised his hand to speak: "My name is Kanchi, and I am from Boratola."

Kamesh said to him, "The government records say that you worked on a project to move sand from Ram's house to Krishna's. Did you do so?"

"Yes, sir, I did work on that project."

"The government records show that you worked for forty days and were paid Rs. 4,000. Is that correct?"

"No, sir, I have not been paid that much money. I only got Rs.1,000."

Someone immediately shouted, "He is lying!"

Kanchi was livid. He pointed toward the *mukhiya* and said, "He is a crook. He and his cronies must have taken the rest of my money, all 3,000 rupees!"

The mukhiya rushed over, grabbed the microphone, and hit Kamesh on the head with the stand. An immediate uproar ensued, with workers running toward the mukhiya, shouting, "Hit him, hit him!" Suddenly sticks appeared and people were charging up to the mukhiya, who was whisked away to safety. Everybody was running and shouting and there was a minor scuffle between the mukhiya's men and some of the workers. The activists clutched their documents defensively to keep them from being snatched away in the commotion.

Before long, the organizers were able to restore order. The mukhiya returned, everybody sat down, and the meeting resumed. While the atmosphere remained tense, the scuffle had paradoxically brought the agenda into sharper focus. The testimonies continued to pile up, but the workers were careful not to be abusive.

People were clapping and cheering and backing up testimonies from anyone who had the courage to speak.

However, the lower-level NREGA bureaucrats and the village politicians who were present gave testimony that countered the evidence presented. Some workers also stepped up to support the lower-level bureaucrats' claims, attesting that they had been paid fully for their work and that there were no problems in the village. The workers often booed these testimonies.

Finally the mukhiya rose and said, "I have listened to the workers' complaints, and I now know that there are problems, but I wish that somebody had told me earlier." He promised that the workers would be given the correct wages and that he would secure employment for everyone. Then the meeting ended and the social audit documents were submitted to the mukhiya, members of the media, and a representative from the district collector's office.

The next morning I visited the village where Kanchi lived and looked around until I found him. He told me, "Mukhiya came by in his car last night and threatened the people in the village for speaking out. But," he added, looking away, "he can't do anything to me." I was uneasy because it was clear to me that Kanchi's situation in the village was precarious while the mukhiya's power was strong. He and the other local elites were fiercely motivated to maintain their power.

"What do you think will happen?" I asked.

He said, "We have been discussing that in the village; it is unclear what will change. But in the last ten years that this mukhiya has been in power, I have never seen him afraid like this." He added gleefully, "It felt good."

I have spent months with workers like Kanchi, learning from them the struggles they face, their fight to get work, their demands for a better wage for agricultural work, and observing how NREGA offers them a possibility to change their social relations in their villages. This brief glimpse into my field research illustrates how the advent of the NREGA program and freedom of information reforms can give marginalized citizens the ability to publicly question the actions of local state actors by accessing government documents. But this is not the end of the story.

After the public hearing, JJSS activists were approached by one of the contractors who had conspired with the mukhiya to swindle public money. Smiling, he said, "You have done your job and are leaving, but we will be here and we know what to do to take care of our *samaj* [society]." The contractor posed a threat to the success of NREGA and was a reminder of the staying power of local elites.

While the union organizers in JJSS found social audits to be productive tools for giving marginalized workers a voice, it was necessary to find a way to ensure that the workers' grievances, once articulated, could be addressed. This required constant vigilance to counteract resistance from obstructionist local elites. Such monitoring presented a challenge for NREGA in Bihar because it did not have the support of political parties and their leaders.

Thus, the JJSS activists used such public hearings sparingly, realizing that their ultimate effectiveness depended on state action to address their findings. I was left wondering if it was even possible to sustain such oversight across the tens of thousands of caste-dominated villages in India, each of which has its own local elite leaders. What is the role of the state and what can happen when these activist-led actions to scrutinize government have the support of upper-level bureaucrats?

The First Mile and the Last Mile

In postcolonial India, a number of development programs whose stated purpose was to improve the fortunes and well-being of citizens, particularly marginalized citizens, have failed to ensure that benefits actually reach the intended recipients. The field of development studies is littered with treatises documenting failures that are attributable to state inaction coupled with local elite capture and diversion. There are many opinions about how and why state programs flounder. The literature identifies three broad reasons for this failure.

First, politicians often do not prioritize implementing programs that benefit poor and marginalized citizens. Most analyses of this strategy focus on "first-mile" problems; that is they concentrate on understanding what can lead a state to generate the political will to develop programs that target the poor (Heller 2000; Harriss 2003; Evans and Heller 2015; Drèze and Sen 2013). As political theorist and historian Partha Chatterjee has argued, most citizens of the state are powerless and are not even seen as a part of civil society; that is, as citizens who have rights. Instead, marginalized citizens are limited to using "political society," or electoral power, to make claims on the state (Chatterjee 2004). Explanations that focus on the supply side see democratic elections as a solution and look at voting for the political party that has the power to make redistributive policies or at charismatic leaders whose political strategies are aligned with the needs of the poor (Bussell 2019; Harriss 2003; Ahuja 2019). But electoral power is intermittent and is a very limited tool for holding the state accountable for its day-to-day activities.

Explanations that focus on the demand side rely on the ability of citizens and their associations to call for services from the state (Kruks-Wisner 2018; Auerbach 2019; Sanyal and Rao 2018). In this view, citizen demands are an outcome of class-based mobilizations or decentralized collective action by citizens who make claims on the state over time (Heller 2000; Kohli 2012; Srinivasan 2015).

These accounts often assume that once political will or programmatic policy is in place in the first mile, appropriate institutions can be designed to address the challenges at the last mile (Acemoglu et al. 2001; Bates 2005; Chandra 2004; North 1991; North and Weingast 1989; Wilkinson 2004). The narratives tell a story about how social movements and/or decentralized collective action generate political will that empowers bureaucrats and gives them autonomy (Evans 2012). The assumption is that states with bureaucratic capacity will get institutions right and will implement government policies as long as there is sufficient demand-side pressure.

Second, programs are usually not designed to respond well to implementation challenges. It is tempting to think about implementation challenges related to delivery as issues that can be easily overcome with a technical fix. There is a persistent tendency among policymakers to see development failures as problems of delivery. Indeed, the phrase "last mile" conjures up a technical perspective that regards development failure as a problem of delivery. In his essay titled "The Last Cultural Mile," communications theorist Ashish Rajadhyaksha traces the prehistory of the notion of a last mile, from its use in the telecommunications industry to its use to describe contemporary problems of the state:

> Indeed, it is almost less a problem than a lament, referring typically to the notorious incapacity of delivery mechanisms in India to reach their intended beneficiaries. Whether they be Tsunami victims who never get food or clothing because some middleman has hived them off, or potential telecom users in India's villages, it has become a standard truism to say this: targeted benefits do not reach their destination, and they do not do so because of distortions at, not the sender's but the recipient's end. . . . Typically a function of cost, the last mile has been relentlessly perceived as primarily, or even exclusively, a technological problem. (Rajadhyaksha 2011)

Anthropologist Tania Li (2007) has analyzed 200 years of development projects in Indonesia. They range from those undertaken by trustees in the colonial era to contemporary World Bank projects that seek to improve landscapes and livelihoods for the poor. Her analysis shows how development projects typically default to technocratic solutions that do not tackle power issues, particularly those related to land ownership. She shows how project designs that define issues as technical omit political and/or economic problems that do not have technical fixes. Even when technical fixes are possible, political and economic problems affect outcomes in ways that lead to failure.

Third, programs that are designed to challenge local power often lack the bureaucratic willingness and capacity to successfully implement the program in the last mile (Corbridge and Srivastava 2013). Economist Lant Pritchett argues that the problem of development is attributable to inadequate bureaucratic capacity. He powerfully characterizes India as a "flailing state," by which he means that it is unable to "maintain sufficient control of the administrative apparatus" to deliver government services despite "democracy and strong capability at the state level" (Pritchett 2009, 20). The capacity question can be viewed economically as well as organizationally; that is, whether enough funds are allocated for public services and whether there are enough bureaucrats who can be fully responsible for delivering public services to the poor (Kapur 2020; Dasgupta and Kapur 2020).[9] Sociologist Patrick Heller argues that state capacity is not an organizational problem ("chain of command"), but that the problem lies in "chain of sovereignty," which is a political problem (Heller 2011). This case study illustrates how these explanations for why development programs fail (lack of political will, the absence of good design, and inadequate bureaucratic capacity) did not hold true in Andhra Pradesh. Central legislation was designed well, thanks to strong political leadership, electoral competition that resulted in a coalition government at the national level, and campaigns from civil society groups that sought to ensure that the radical agenda of increasing equality across caste and class would be realized (Drèze and Khera 2017; Hasan 2018; Jenkins and Manor 2017). Moreover, the central government provides the bulk of funding—100 percent of the wages for participating workers, 75 percent of the costs of materials, and 75 percent of administrative costs. State governments are responsible for unemployment allowances and for 25 percent of the costs of materials.

Under NREGA, states must provide the 100 days per year of guaranteed waged work that each household is entitled to whenever a worker asks for it and beginning within fifteen days after the worker applies for work.[10] If the state does not comply, it must pay an unemployment allowance. Household members must be willing to do manual labor at the government-approved minimum wage. Work occurs in groups and involves state-approved projects, ideally ones that ordinary citizens identify in local public meetings. Jobs typically consist of building agricultural bunds (earthworks), repairing canals, or other productive and measurable labor projects. Typically, a work group's output is measured weekly at the worksite. The act mandates that men and women receive the same wage, a significant advancement over previous development programs in India. Social audits were mandated in the NREGA legislation to ensure that workers in the program would have a right to examine government records.

The political will and competition crucial for the successful establishment, design, and implementation of NREGA was alive and well in Andhra Pradesh.[11] The late chief minister Y. S. Rajasekhar Reddy (YSR) gave complete autonomy to bureaucrats to control NREGA funds instead of routing them through local panchayats.[12] Political scientist Diego Maiorano writes, "In fact, that the MGNREGA [NREGA] would be a priority of the state government was clear since the very beginning, when YSR asked and obtained the national scheme to be inaugurated in Andhra Pradesh by the Prime Minister" (Maiorano 2014, 96).[13]

However, generating sufficient political will to implement government programs does not automatically solve last-mile problems with delivering material benefits to marginalized people. Local power relations and the corruption that they often produce frustrate the best-designed programs and the best intentions of bureaucrats and their political bosses. In India, as elsewhere, good policies and politics are not enough by themselves. Political scientist Jonathan Fox notes that "institutional reforms that might look 'enabling' on paper need to be unpacked and examined from below to determine their actual coverage, depth, and empowerment impacts in practice" (Fox 2007, 354). It is therefore necessary to understand how local power structures hinder, obstruct, and ultimately thwart development programs.

The Local Power System as an Anti-Worker Nexus

> Once upon a time, public employment programmes in rural India were safely in the hands of private contractors and their political masters, with a little help from corrupt bureaucrats. The game was roughly as follows. Private contractors were the direct recipients of "work orders" and the corresponding funds. They made money by submitting fudged muster rolls, with inflated employment and wage figures. A substantial part of the loot was recycled through the so-called "PC" (percentage) system, whereby various functionaries received fixed percentages of the amounts released. The contractors also had to pay tribute to their political bosses, for whom these funds came in handy during election campaigns. In return for this, the political masters helped them to get contracts and escape scrutiny. This is the sort of situation that led writer P. Sainath to say that "everybody loves a good drought"—the peak season for rural employment programmes. Labourers, for their part, worked hard and earned a pittance.
>
> —Jean Drèze (2007)

In the preceding vignette, the mukhiya's actions demonstrate how a local power system typically operates and what the sources of its power are at the last mile. The mukhiya, an elected representative who is also a landholder and a member of the dominant caste, maintains deep connections to the contractor, who is involved in the "percentage" scheme. NREGA legislation sought to eliminate this power by stipulating that work done as part of the program cannot be outsourced to contractors. However, as the vignette showed, contractors continue to be involved in the last-mile implementation. One source of this influence is class power that derives from owning agricultural land where the landless work. In theory, state employment programs offer alternative employment to workers, but such programs often operate through intermediaries who are local contractors with strong political connections and are part of the local power system.

In many parts of the world and certainly in India, the forms of social relations that repressed workers have changed and individuals are now able to sell their labor in the market. But as development economist Pranab Bardhan's classic study shows, members of the dominant landed class collude among themselves across different villages to control the "interlocking of factor markets (particularly those of land, labor and credit)" by setting uniform wages and deciding when work will be available (Bardhan 1980, 82). In other words, there is a long way to go.

The control of the landed class is far reaching and extends into social spheres (Kohli 1987). The dominant class, who are also from dominant castes, control where dominated castes like Dalits and Adivasis are able to live, where they can move about within the village, what they should wear, and whether they can visit public places and religious settings. Although this has been successfully challenged and fought in the villages through collective action, caste/class inequities continue today. For example, in Chapter 7, I describe how a Dalit youth encounters a local Reddy landlord who does not like the fact that the youth is wearing a nice white shirt. The Reddy forces the young Dalit man to do the useless work of moving a heap of cow dung from one place to the other with the simple goal of making sure his shirt gets soiled, thus putting him in his place. This form of local power creates a fundamental asymmetry in social relations (Frankel and Rao 1990). It is the reason workers are afraid to speak out on their own when programs don't work.

Further, as political scientist Guillermo O'Donnell argues, in many states, the public authority of the modern state radiates out unevenly and "the components of democratic legality and, hence, of publicness and citizenship, fade away at the frontiers of various regions and class, gender and ethnic relations" (O'Donnell 1993, 1361). However, as scholars have observed, we need to draw a distinction between the coercive arm of the state and the developmental state apparatus (Evans 1989; Kohli 2004). As I show in Chapter 7, inspecting police records made it clear to me that the coercive arm of the state apparatus (the police) was present in this village and was happy to reproduce long-entrenched local structures (Srinivasan 2015; Thachil 2020).[14] While police kept detailed accounts of their actions to maintain law and order, I could not find historical records created by local representatives of the state about issues such as who had access to water, whether Dalit children were being educated, or whether people were getting work.

In development literature, the Indian state appears as a paradox: on the one hand, it is seen as a "semi-developmental" bureaucracy that is capable of carrying out programs for the poor, and on the other hand, it is portrayed as having a dismal record of delivering goods and services to the intended recipients in its 640,000 villages (Evans 2012; Pritchett 2009; Gupta 2012; Harriss-White 2003).[15] "The state" is a broad conceptual term as it is used in the literature. Scholars use the term "state" as a shorthand that sometimes refers to bureaucrats and politicians, sometimes to the subnational state (e.g., the state of Andhra Pradesh), and sometimes to institutions.[16] Even when it is used to refer specifically to a bureaucracy, there is a tendency to refer to bureaucrats as a monolithic entity and to erase the differences that may exist among them (Scott 1998). My analysis focuses on the complexities in the relations between state and society in Andhra Pradesh instead of seeing such relations as inherently conflictual (Evans 1995; Migdal 2001; Fox 1993). This is exemplified by local bureaucrats who commonly contend with pressure from upper-level bureaucrats but live and work in the local setting and are often hired because of their links to the local power system.

Historically, local members of state institutions (police, tax collector, land) have been concerned with preserving power relations, hence the priority they give law and order over development (Dandeker 1994). In contrast, there are only a few opportunities for the poor to engage directly with the state as citizens rather than as clients or supplicants. Sociologist Patrick Heller refers to this as a limited "institutional surface area of the state" (Heller 2012, 647).

Development programs can be seen as attempts to increase the capacity of the "developmental state" (Evans and Heller 2015). As political scientist Stuart Corbridge and others point out, irrespective of whether such programs actually deliver, a development program is often the first time marginalized citizens get to encounter a state official who is concerned even nominally with their welfare, or, in other words, to "see the state" (Corbridge et al. 2005). However, some have argued that development interventions carry no guarantee of sincere interest in the welfare of the poor and merely produce "discourse of development" and unitary "technologies of rule" that lead to failures (Escobar 2011). A development program may end up contributing more to the building of bureaucracy, an "anti-politics machine" that does not serve the poor (Ferguson 1990).

Development programs in Andhra Pradesh have not been any different and appear to follow Ferguson's description. The National Food for Work program in Andhra, the predecessor of the NREGA, was often called the "loot for work" program because it had "exceptionally high misappropriation(s)" of development funds (Deshingkar et al. 2005, 576; Maiorano 2014). Here, as in other parts of India, villages are deeply divided along class and caste lines (Balagopal 2011). Historically, caste and class relations have been intertwined. Caste inequality in

Andhra Pradesh contributed to class-based inequality because of a labor system that restricted the upward mobility of workers (Bayly 2001). Farm owners exploited members of lower-caste households in order to harvest their crops. Those workers either owned marginal land or were landless (Jakimow 2014). In Andhra Pradesh, as in many states, land reforms have not been carried out fully, resulting in a social structure in rural areas that consists largely of a landed class and landless laborers (Balagopal 2011; Kohli 2004; Frankel 1978).[17]

The chief bureaucrat of NREGA in Andhra Pradesh, Koppula Raju,[18] speaking of the National Food for Work program, identified three local actors as the nexus of corruption: local politicians, engineers, and contractors. "I found three kinds of vested interests: politicians who get the works sanctioned are bringing the works to the village so that they have a share in it, engineers who implement the works and make the estimates, and contractors [who hire workers]. I have found that development programs in the past have been driven through and through by these vested interests."[19]

The capacity of these local actors to capture state programs and resources is based on their local social power, the alliances they build among themselves, and their capacity to exploit unequal access to information (Reinikka et al. 2004a; Farzana et al. 2017). The bureaucratic systems that link higher levels of government to the local government (e.g., blocks, mandals, and panchayats) are opaque to marginalized citizens, and lower-level bureaucrats tend to hoard government records that could make their actions transparent.

The local power system is predicated on this opacity and change that is hard to come by (Mander and Joshi 1999).[20] Local officials resist any attempt on the part of citizens to open up access to records and exercise the RTI, even when social movements lead such efforts (Roy 2018). This collusion at the local level maintains the status quo, leading to what anthropologist Akhil Gupta calls "structural violence" (Gupta 2012). This is why development programs designed to meet needs of the poor often fail in India.

The questions, then, are: How do you get bureaucrats to deal with local implementation failures? Is it possible to do this using the help of civil society organizations and the participation of marginalized citizens? Two strategies used by upper-level bureaucrats in Andhra Pradesh were gathering local information about the details of last-mile implementation and opening that information up to social auditors and citizens.

Bureaucracy and Local Information

This book expands the conventional wisdom that centralized state institutions can adapt to realities on the ground by leveraging local information to fix problems with the implementation of development programs without devolving power to local institutions.[21] In the long run, devolving power to local institutions is perhaps more effective and sustainable than relying on centralized state institutions. However, such decentralization requires a massive transfer of power on the part of upper-level bureaucrats and the building of accountable local institutions. Sometimes there are fortuitous circumstances when political forces and members of civil society can work together to push through structural reforms (Fox 1993). This is what happened in Kerala with the people's campaign for decentralized planning and municipalization and in Brazil's participatory budgeting (Heller 2000; Roy 2018; Baiocchi 2003).[22] But because local power systems are so entrenched and organized social groups in civil society are largely absent in places like Andhra Pradesh, any major reforms need to use different strategies in order to redistribute power.[23]

We know a great deal about the failures of centralized state bureaucracies to adapt to realities on the ground. Most scholarly accounts have not adequately addressed the question of agility or are pessimistic about the possibility that a bureaucracy can be flexible. They typically emphasize how state institutions are relatively static and cannot adequately respond to information about local conditions. Take, for instance, political scientist and anthropologist James Scott's argument that centralized high-modernist states fail spectacularly to incorporate local information ("metis") and produce disastrous results for citizens. In the state vs market debate, at the other end of the political spectrum, Hayek asserts that it is structurally impossible to adequately incorporate local information compared to the far more responsive market (Hayek 1944).

The development literature describes five main mechanisms by which a centralized state can use local information to respond to local changes: decentralization, state-society partnerships, public-private partnerships, street-level bureaucracy, and incrementalism. First, some state governments (like Kerala) are able in certain policy areas to effectively decentralize implementation to the local state (Heller 1999). This type of devolution of power is based in part on the idea that the more local the decision-making, the more feasible it is to incorporate relevant local information into the policymaking process. Community self-governance takes decentralization to the furthest extent possible, reserving optional, minimal roles for the central state (Ostrom 1990; Chambers 1994). Another version of decentralization, polycentricity (Ostrom 1994), places self-governance within a federated structure. Proponents of polycentrism assume that information relevant to users of public services will be best known to citizens alone (as opposed to state actors), so it is best to leave governance decisions to them. Devolution formally changes state institutions in order to make them more bottom up in terms of policy formulation and implementation.

Second, some states can forge institutional partnerships with civil society groups to hold bureaucrats accountable for policy decisions (Evans et al. 1996; Fox 1993). India's RTI Act (2005) is an example of this type of partnership. This type of state-society partnership is predicated on the hope that local citizens and civil society groups will use local information to put pressure on state bureaucrats, particularly at the lower levels. It requires members of higher levels of the state bureaucracy to align with civil society groups to pressure lower-level bureaucrats to implement programs from the top (the bureaucrats) and from the bottom (the citizen groups). Political scientist Jonathan Fox calls this the "sandwich" strategy (Fox 1993). This strategy is limited by the extent to which upper-level bureaucrats are able to find support in civil society groups to support their initiatives. Third, some states outsource key functions to profit-seeking private firms (Banerjee et al. 2016; Kuriyan and Ray 2009a). This assumes that a contractual division of labor between private and public actors will result in efficient, accountable implementation that incorporates local information, as reflected primarily in market prices.

Fourth, some states benefit from high levels of bureaucratic discretion, typically at the street level (Lipsky 1980). These states give a large amount of discretion to local bureaucrats because they have knowledge about local conditions and are thus well positioned to solve local problems (Pires 2011; Coslovsky et al. 2017). This mechanism requires other ways to hold bureaucrats at various levels accountable, such as through innovative program design, careful staffing of local offices, or institutional changes (Tendler 1998; McDonnell 2020).

Finally, some states practice incremental policy making by "muddling through" (Lindblom 1959; Hayes 2017) the policy process, which incidentally makes them more responsive and flexible. This type of policymaking involves making relatively small changes, or step-by-step policy departures that are aimed at achieving relatively limited policy aims or policy departures (Mangla 2018). Incrementalism concerns policy formulation and is primarily about selecting alternative policies to be considered based on what can be achieved (Hayes 2017). Incremental policymaking typically results in remedial policies.

The problem is that the requirements of the mechanisms the literature highlights may not always be possible or even necessary to make the central state more responsive to local information. The decentralization literature requires changing institutions to devolve more formal power to the local state. And harnessing street-level bureaucracy ultimately requires giving more formal or informal discretion to street-level bureaucrats. The lower-level bureaucrats are either part of the local power system or are prey to local power structures.

The framework of patching development builds on existing work by bringing together elements from each of these existing mechanisms while also extending them. It offers a different mechanism through which centralized states can incorporate and respond to local information.

Theorizing the Patching Process

The practices through which NREGA was managed in Andhra Pradesh were the result of patching development, a process of contestation within the NREGA bureaucracy and a combination of pressure and cooperation between social groups and bureaucrats.[24] I borrow the term *patching* from software programming. Software patches are bits of code designed to fix specific parts of a larger software system that are not functioning as originally planned. Patching software is a routine and continuous process.

Patching development is the ability to be flexible in responding to new situations, in this case in order to deal with attempts by powerful actors to thwart NREGA goals at the local last mile. It is about changing power equations by paying attention to the minute details of all processes associated with the program. It includes making institutional and technological changes that lead to new ways of documenting activity. All of these changes rely on the political will and capability of bureaucrats in the central government structure of the program.[25]

The idea of using patching as a metaphor for how NREGA operates in Andhra Pradesh first occurred to me as I was sitting in the office of the principal secretary of rural development in Hyderabad. He was having a brainstorming meeting with a group of software engineers from a company the Andhra Pradesh government had hired. They were presenting their latest design change to the software system. The topic was making changes to the electronic muster roll, a digital attendance register. The discussion focused on figuring out a software change that would involve making a particular field read only. They were trying to restrict who could modify that field.

The discussion was about how to eliminate entries in the muster roll that claimed that the same worker had been at multiple worksites. The strategy was to limit how often workers can change groups. Once a worker joins a group, they must remain in that group for at least a year. This restriction is intended to prevent lower-level bureaucrats from falsifying reports by moving a worker to multiple groups. The new state-issued muster rolls the software company had designed were already filled out with both the group and the worksite assignments for each worker.[26] Having previously worked at a large software company myself, I understood the technical discussions but missed the larger significance of what they were up to. Only after multiple meetings did I understand the broader meaning of their focus on such a specific part of the system.

What I came to understand is that seemingly inconsequential changes in administrative processes were central to fixing the problems of NREGA's governance of the last mile. Upper-level bureaucrats would constantly patch to maintain the program's autonomy and counteract the attempts of landowners and local members of political parties to capture the program at the last mile, as well as resistance from lower-level bureaucrats to the patching itself. Upper-level bureaucrats have focused on the granular details of the muster roll because they understand the politics of implementation at the last mile. While the actions of upper-level bureaucrats on occasion do resemble what Scott referred to as the high modernist state that is not able to understand the local, that is not the whole story (Scott 1998). This is a case where state officials understand only too well the practices by which programs are often derailed and seek to eliminate them with the enhanced supervision that digital technology makes possible.

The process of patching development has three features. First, patching is *top down*; the patch sender is at a higher level than (i.e., has jurisdiction over) the patch receiver. Second, patching is about *fine-grained changes*; patches are extremely specific and make focused alterations to policy. Third, patching is *iterative*; bureaucrats send many patches as new information about problems in the field reaches them.[27] Patches are part of a continuous cycle of fine-grained changes to the implementation.

Patches, then, are a series of incremental changes, rather than a one-time overhaul. By patching, centralized states can repeatedly change their practices and plans based on information and challenges that arise during implementation. These patches include technical fixes and incorporate detailed local information into updated plans and strategies for implementing them. It is a mechanism through which dynamic central state institutions can incorporate local information to address implementation problems.

Patching development is a political process. *Repair* is another technical term used in the science, technology, and society literature to describe fixing broken information infrastructures (Jackson et al. 2007).[28] However, while repair is often about trying to maintain an infrastructure to preserve the original intent and design, patching is about modifying an existing information infrastructure to accommodate unanticipated uses because of resistance (Veeraraghavan 2021).[29] The patching process requires high-level bureaucrats to be agile. Their work process is different from the type of flexibility that street-level bureaucrats exercise (Lipsky 2010). Street-level bureaucrats have discretion because the nature of the service they provide calls for human judgment that cannot be covered in a policy manual and for which there is no substitute (Lipsky 2010). Patches are not intended as tentative experiments that will be refined subsequently (Banerjee and Duflo 2009). Indeed, the reasons for subsequent patches are primarily unexpected demands that arise after implementation.

Patching is also different from the incrementalism the policy literature describes because it deals with the small ways power is exercised, in order to make programs that are already in place work as intended, rather than taking small steps to get the appropriate policy implemented (Lindblom 1979; Hayes 2017). Incrementalist thinkers focus on figuring out the best *plan* going forward given the constraints of a situation. Patching is an incrementalist policy process in the sense that it involves relatively small changes designed to achieve limited policy aims. However, patching is fundamentally different from incrementalism because it is about finding a way to deal with local resistance to *implementation.* In other words, patching is about redistributing power during the implementation of a policy.

Patching is also different from apolitical technocratic fixes that reduce complex development issues to technical problems for which there are solutions if only one can find the right technology. Technology critic Evgeny Morozov has used the word "solutionism" to describe the tendency to "[recast] all complex social situations either as neatly defined problems with definite, computable solutions or as transparent and self-evident processes that can be easily optimized—if only the right algorithms are in place!" (Morozov 2014, 5). Patching is a sociotechnical process that often involves no technology fixes but instead makes changes in institutions and other processes. Even when patching involves technology, it is explicitly a political process that is about more than finding the "right algorithms." The problem with solutionism or rendering complex problems as technical issues is that this approach doesn't solve the right problem and can actually worsen a situation (Singh 2019b). The implications of the inadequacy of solutionism urge us to reflect on what the problem is and what is being left out of the analysis of the situation (Khera 2018b; Singh 2020; Alkhatib and Bernstein 2019).

Drawing on bureaucrats' precise use of patching in Andhra Pradesh, I describe a politics of information and technology that includes patterns of both contestation and cooperation between members of state bureaucracy and members of civil society (Sassen 2002). Upper-level NREGA bureaucrats harnessed public commitment to the program to create a social audit institution that elicits feedback from marginalized citizens. The social audit institution, which is semiautonomous, includes members recruited from civil society and from the marginalized community.

Patching development is neither a purely technological process nor an exclusively administrative one. While each patch may have only limited local significance, the cumulative impact of continued engagement is transformative in fundamental ways and is more likely to lead to effective and just programs.

Delivering Public Services to Marginalized Citizens: Patching at the Last Mile

In Andhra Pradesh, upper-level NREGA bureaucrats sought to assemble an information infrastructure to make NREGA activities visible and to enlist participation from citizens. This involved using technology and conducting social audits. However, these activities involved a political struggle at the last mile, where institutions, meetings, and technology were sites of local power conflicts that required bureaucrats to issue frequent patches to deal with multiple kinds of resistance. It is important to note that each of the contexts of institutions, documents, and technology goes through each stage in patching—namely top-down, fine-grained changes and iteration—but in the following section, I am choosing to illustrate the elements by focusing on only one dimension for each case in the interest of brevity.

Top-Down Action: Patching Institutions

Does the state have the power to implement programs that reach the poor? A useful starting point for understanding the power of the modern state is Michael Mann's analysis of infrastructural power, which he defines as "the capacity of the state actually to penetrate civil society, and to implement logistically political decisions throughout the realm" (Mann 1984, 189). Infrastructural power is necessary in building state capacity to implement welfare schemes and deal with last-mile problems that thwart that capacity.

The state also exercises in what Pierre Bourdieu calls symbolic power by controlling state documents (Bourdieu et al. 1994; Loveman 2005). Bourdieu has theorized the symbolic power of the state as the authority to impose a system of classification on its citizens. In contrast to the Weberian idea that states have a "legitimate monopoly of violence," Bourdieu posits that the state has a "legitimate monopoly of symbolic power."[30] In Andhra Pradesh, state bureaucrats attempted to democratize state power by creating institutions that opened up the state through giving ordinary citizens access to information.

One of the goals of democracy is to give everyone an equal voice. The dominant theory used to think about openness in government assumes that an information asymmetry exists between citizens and the state (Stiglitz 2002; Lieberman et al. 2014). This theory of accountability hypothesizes that if that asymmetry is addressed by increasing the amount of information available to citizens—for example, by putting government records into the hands of the poor—more people will be able to see and question the government's mistakes and injustices (Shankar et al. 2011). Transparency expands the range of people who have access to information beyond traditional elites and powerbrokers, often the gatekeepers who ration information[31]. Over the past thirty years, many democratic countries around the world have passed legislation giving citizens the right to access information so they can monitor government actions.[32]

But, as the opening vignette from my fieldwork in Bihar showed, transparency doesn't lead to change unless someone with power causes the change.[33] This is because marginalized citizens on their own are not usually in a position to challenge local elites and state agents, even when information is available to them, because they simply are not powerful enough to use the information for that purpose (Fox 2015). Moreover, thinking about information as a causal agent often leads to tunnel vision whereby information enthusiasts mistakenly believe they can "hack it alone with only information by their side."[34] They fail to acknowledge the stake the local power system has in rationing information.

Because state-led transparency is ineffective on its own and efforts led by civil society groups are too sporadic or narrowly focused, we have good reason to closely investigate alternate models. The state must also create mechanisms through which citizens can contest the actions of the lower-level bureaucrats.[35] This is often a two-step process: making the upper-level bureaucrats aware of local power dynamics and then creating mechanisms to hold lower-level bureaucrats accountable.[36]

The question then becomes, what should be built to accomplish this? These kinds of solutions must go beyond what Peter Evans calls "institutional monocropping" (Evans 2004). Information institutions need to overcome social hierarchy and local elite capture and need to include participation from marginalized citizens.[37] How to get marginalized citizens to participate is the subject of intense debate in the current literature and, as Chapter 5 illustrates, a bedeviling thing in practice (Mansuri and Rao 2012; Baiocchi et al. 2011; Gaventa 2006). Some scholars challenge the pervasive belief that "participation" is an appropriate remedy for political exclusion and for community building (Christens and Speer 2006; Banerjee et al. 2010). Cooke and Kothari (2001) argue that participation could instead be "the new tyranny." The valorization of participation continues because its proponents have a naïve view of power: they often "essentialize and romanticize the local" and see it as the site of empowerment (Mohan and Stokke 2000, 249). However, as Mohan and Stokke point out, this perspective leads to a tendency to ignore power inequalities.

I argue that what is needed is local policies that overcome local power structures. My argument draws the distinction Bourdieu makes between *opus operatum*, the completed action, and *modus operandi*, the process of doing the task (Bourdieu 1973). Brown and Duguid's (1991, 41) analysis of understanding workplace practice invokes this distinction by defining it as "the way a task, as it unfolds over time, looks to someone at work on it, while many of the options and dilemmas remain unresolved, as opposed to the way it looks with hindsight as a finished task."

The state-society literature seems to offer an alternative by looking for synergies between state and society (Evans and Heller 2015; Lavalle et al. 2005; Mansuri and Rao 2013; Evans 1997). Synergy between state actors and a mobilized society leads them to "co-produce" desirable outcomes (Evans 1996; Ostrom 1996; Tarlau 2013). For state actors, soliciting the participation of the marginalized citizens is key, especially since the opportunities for local elites to capture a state process are so pronounced (Adhikari and Bhatia 2010; Bardhan 2002; Bardhan and Mookherjee 2006). Synergy is predicated on sufficient ties between reformist actors in state bureaucracies and in communities (embeddedness) and a certain division of labor (complementarity) (Evans 1996). State and community can be brought together through the will of the state actors or from actions of society.[38] The willingness of society groups to cooperate and of those within state bureaucracies to work for change create "sandwich" strategies that pressure lower-level bureaucrats to comply with new policies (Fox 1993).[39] Sandwich strategies are predicated on "opening from above meets mobilization from below," or semi-autonomous forms of collective action from the bottom. In Andhra Pradesh, the demands of social groups led state bureaucrats to change their priorities to focus on NREGA more seriously than bureaucrats in many other states. But upper-level bureaucrats in Andhra Pradesh used a "top-down" strategy for dealing with the local power system that was more in alignment with the Ambedkarian vision that sought to centralize power away from the local elites in the villages.[40]

The Andhra Pradesh upper-level bureaucrats whose decisions I examine agreed with the Ambedkarite top-down vision and partnered with civil society to create a semi-autonomous "participatory bureaucracy."[41] The overarching idea was to make state-level, top-down policy adaptive. The creation of the Society for Social Audit and Transparency in Andhra Pradesh was a top-down effort by activist bureaucrats with links to social movements. NREGA provides funding and oversight, but the audit team has autonomy from that bureaucracy in terms of recruitment, management, and operations.

In Chapter 4, I trace how creation of a participatory bureaucratic institution was the result of an elaborate process of institutional patching that focused on three distinct goals: recruiting auditors from and with a commitment to the marginalized citizens, gaining the trust of workers, and operating within the boundaries of what was politically feasible. The patch that the social audit institution constitutes is a result of negotiation and compromises between key activists and upper-level bureaucrats, a process that was tempered by the political realities of Andhra Pradesh. Andhra bureaucrats sought a direct relationship with marginalized citizens and controlled how they partnered with civil society.[42] In addition, questions of caste and class representation were integral to the process in terms of who was hired to be the field assistant and the village social auditor. The connections of the people who occupied these two positions to political power mattered. One of the strengths of the social audit institution is the contestation of perception and how it is seen differently by different actors. I argue that the social audit institution in Andhra Pradesh had to be constantly patched to occupy an interstitial position in how it was perceived by different actors (Tarlau 2019). However, although state-level bureaucrats meticulously constructed this top-down institution and mechanisms targeted at the specific context, it was *still* not enough to eliminate last-mile problems.

Controlling Bureaucratic Practices: Patching Documents

In addition to the infrastructural power the state has, it exercises symbolic power through its production and circulation of documents. Recently, anthropologists who analyze how bureaucracies' function have argued that the writing of documents is a particularly significant practice in terms of how power is exercised (Hull 2012a). Anthropologist Akhil Gupta goes even further, writing that "one has to shift attention away from writing's instrumental function in helping run the government to its constitutive role as that which defines what the state is and what it does" (Gupta 2012).[43] Anthropologist Nayanika Mathur defines bureaucratic writing as "a process that requires the hard labour of writing, interpreting, reading, drafting, redrafting. . . . Performance of this labour is critical for the state and its project of welfare to remain alive" (Mathur 2015 115). According to anthropologist Mathew Hull, who writes about the contemporary government in Pakistan, "if you want to understand bureaucratic activities, follow the paper" (Hull 2012b, 22).[44]

Writing and production of documents, these scholars argue, is what actually constitutes the state. In theory, state documents are static, a self-representation of stateness. Following Bourdieu, documents become mechanisms through which states exert their power because citizens see them as legitimate. Recent critical work on governmental transparency argues that in order to understand how information promotes transparency, we must examine power in the context of social relations and how documents could generate public action (Benjamin et al. 2007; Fung et al. 2007; Hetherington 2011; Srinivasan 2011).

In this book, I study the evolution of state power by looking at how the production of government documents is a process that the actions of both state employees and members of the public challenge. In order to fully comprehend this process, I have mapped out the routes by which everyday government documents are actually produced instead of relying on what planning documents say about how they should be generated (see, e.g., Hull 2012).

My analysis focuses on how expanding access to government documents democratizes symbolic power, both within the state bureaucracy and at the local level, by giving marginalized workers access to information about their participation in NREGA during the social audit. This is why the social audit and the public meeting detailed in the opening vignette were so "radical" to me and the other JJSS activists: we were witnessing the government being held accountable from the bottom up (Abers 2001). For the first time ever, a public works project had mandated an open meeting process that enabled ordinary citizens to inspect official records and confront lower-level bureaucrats in attendance about them. In Andhra Pradesh, this democratization had been initiated by the upper-level bureaucrats themselves, who had created not only the infrastructure to make it possible, but also the independent, participatory bureaucracy.

The ambition of the social auditors goes beyond merely disseminating existing government documents; they want to help the poor write new documents that question state accounts and create the possibility for citizens to be directly involved in how the state is accountable to them. The question then becomes, to what extent does the presence of outside social auditors allow NREGA workers to realistically overcome power differentials and openly speak out and write new documents?[45] The struggle to make NREGA administrators fully accountable centers on questions of who has "read" access to NREGA records and who has "write" access to them. How do upper-level bureaucrats facilitate and ultimately limit this rewriting?

Furthermore, it is also possible that conditions for marginalized citizens could worsen if they speak out, a dynamic I analyze in Chapter 5 by comparing different public meetings. Another danger is that creating a third party to conduct social audits may have negative consequences. The third-party institution might have its own interests to which it is beholden. It is also possible to imagine that the government could effectively co-opt the existence of the participatory auditory mechanism by pressuring it to turn away from thorny issues of corruption instead of exposing and confronting them. The government could contend that it has made information available for people and thus has fulfilled its duties of transparency. The many possible outcomes and consequences of social audits demonstrate that the notion that information empowers is simplistic and that we need to take seriously the dynamics of power in all possible manifestations.

Iteration: Patching Technology to Address Local Resistance

Patches deal with the continuous exercise of power. For example, there is no one "right" institutional structure for conducting a participatory meeting to solicit feedback from workers as part of a social audit. Those who plan such interventions have to contend with resistance at every stage and level of the process and must neutralize that resistance by taking further action. Thus, iteration is an important aspect of patching. While iteration applies to institutions, public meetings, and technology, it is illustrative to look at the iterative use of digital technology to counter local resistance.

Digital technology is seen as a potential solution for many development problems. Some researchers treat technology as a black box, freezing their analysis at the moment of implementation by arguing that a use of technology was successful, regardless of difficulties or setbacks (Muralidharan et al. 2014b). Conversely, some analysts document only the conspicuous failures of the use of digital technology.[46] For example, a study that focused on Bangalore found that digitizing land records for the purpose of eliminating corruption and making it easy for the poor to access the state often seems to actually increase bribery and drastically reduce local access to the state while commodifying the land market and opening it up for speculation, making it easy for the rich to invest from a far distance (Benjamin et al. 2007). Studies of the impact of technology find it to be the explanation for the success or failure of interventions. Most studies of technology-based development projects seek to measure outcomes; they rarely pay attention to the iteration of technological processes that have the potential to both advance and impede project goals. Often, iterations of technologies are also done in a haphazard manner without any pilots and without any consultation leading to worse outcomes.

Iteration is more than a simple a technological repetition of the sort Silicon Valley's technology entrepreneurs valorize under the rubric of "fail fast, fail often."[47] Focusing only on the technical iterations of a system or only on policy decisions misses the critical way these two dimensions interact and could lead to what information scholars John Seely Brown and Paul Duguid have called "Moore's law solutions," in which a new revision of technology is created to solve problems that may have been created by the technology in the first place (Brown and Duguid 2017, 15).[48]

Most promisingly, the field of Information and Communication Technologies for Development (ICTD) has emerged where computer scientists and social scientists have critically examined the use of technology to address problems in development.[49] These researchers urge us to pay attention not just to the intentions and capacities of the actors, but also to how incentives are embedded in technology and its unintended adaptations.[50] The digital technologies NREGA bureaucrats adopted involved political relations—between upper- and lower-level bureaucrats and between lower-level bureaucrats and NREGA workers. In order to understand how those contestations played out, this book looks at how the use of technology within NREGA evolved in response to iterations in the exercise of power (Veeraraghavan 2013).

Patching Development shows how, in the daily process of state-making, patching is key for understanding how Andhra Pradesh bureaucrats sought to build a democratic state. The last-mile solution is messy and will remain so until the problematic core conditions change. This requires bringing politics—contesting rights—out of formal institutions and down to the microlevel of informal, intra-village politics (Helmke and Levitsky 2004; Prillaman 2018; Khan 2019; Brulé 2020b; 2020a).

Patching Development is also an account of the informational politics of resistance and conflict that are central to building and sustaining participatory bureaucracy wherever it flourishes. The central story is how the interventions involved power dynamics. Upper-level bureaucrats increased their power over the lower-level bureaucrats while decreasing the power of local elites over the workers. If this account of the complex saga of NREGA implementation in Andhra achieves its goal, it should expand current thinking on how states might more effectively deliver social benefits to marginalized citizens.

Methods and Chapter Overview

Patching Development is primarily based on an ethnographic investigation of government implementation of NREGA.[51] My fieldwork was done in two states, Andhra Pradesh and Bihar, but I spent the majority of my time in Andhra Pradesh. I used a variety of approaches to collect data, including participant observation, unstructured and semi-structured interviews, a survey administered in fifteen villages, content analysis of documents, and archival work in the assembly archives in Andhra Pradesh. The fieldwork was conducted over eighteen months in 2011 and 2012, with follow-up visits in 2016 and 2017. During this time, I lived with and "worked" as an unpaid daily wage laborer and interviewed a large number of workers and other residents in each village. I also attended the social audits in the village and retrieved documents from the Andhra Pradesh legislative assembly to analyze how the legislators discuss NREGA in their meetings. I conducted over 100 semi-structured interviews with individuals working at the village, regional, state, and national levels.

In Chapter 2, I explain the political context that set the stage for passing the radical legislation of NREGA and India's RTI laws, and I trace the historical roots for the political support for NREGA in Andhra Pradesh. Chapter 3 focuses on how digital technology mediates the contestations between the upper-level bureaucrats and the lower-level bureaucrats and politicians. Chapter 4 explains the process of institutional patching as a result of struggle for control between the politicians, upper-level bureaucrats, and civil society in Andhra Pradesh that led to the creation of the social audit institution. Chapters 5 and 6 explain how the structure of the social audit public meetings were further shaped by local struggles during the implementation of the new institution in Andhra Pradesh. Chapter 7 focuses on how the NREGA process unfolded in a village that is divided by caste and class relations. Chapter 8 concludes with implications of my findings.

2
The Genesis of Rights-Based Governance

In 2005, the Indian government enacted two landmark rights-based laws: the National Rural Employment Guarantee Act (NREGA), guaranteeing every rural citizen the right to work, and the Right to Information (RTI) Act, which granted all citizens the right to access government records. The rights-based turn and guarantees of transparency embedded in these laws represented a fundamental departure from typical welfare programs, in which citizens are passive recipients of benefits (Nilsen 2018). In so doing, they created the potential to change the Indian state's relationship with ordinary citizens in radical ways (Pande 2014).

This chapter asks two questions: First, what led to the passage of the NREGA and the RTI in India? Second, what contributory factors explain the Andhra Pradesh government's prioritizing of NREGA's implementation and being the only state to implement social audits, a key component of transparency and citizen participation? Andhra Pradesh's achievement was unusual in that the state did not have a notable history of effectively delivering welfare schemes (Bernstorff 1973; Mukherji and Zarhani 2020). Nonetheless, a set of distinct factors converged; as a result, Andhra Pradesh's implementation is regarded as a model for other states (Maiorano 2014; Mukherji et al. 2018). This is significant because NREGA itself is unique in Indian development (Drèze et al. 2006). First, it is based on the concept of rights. It is also the first national program since India gained independence in 1947 that guarantees employment to any rural citizen willing to work on public works projects (Khera 2011b). Additionally, NREGA created the opportunity for ordinary citizens to inspect government records for the first time through the social audit process (Aakella and Kidambi 2007b).

While NREGA is legislated to be nationwide, individual states are responsible for their own implementation. Current research has shown a tremendous diversity in how these programs are implemented in different states (Sukhtankar 2016). By identifying and examining the disparate elements and influences that coalesced to make NREGA's success in Andhra Pradesh possible, we come to understand how groundbreaking legislation can be implemented so that it realizes its optimal capability to enlarge democracy and change lives.[1]

Basic Tenets of NREGA: Compromises and Advances

Rob Jenkins, a political scientist, summarizes NREGA best: "NREGA is both revolutionary and modest; it promises every rural household one hundred days of employment annually on public-works projects, but the labor is taxing and pays minimum wage, at best" (Jenkins 2016). As mentioned earlier, NREGA was the first program in the world of its size that offered guaranteed employment to citizens (Jenkins and Manor 2017). However, instead of providing unlimited work for those who want it, the legislative process resulted in a compromise, limiting participation to 100 days per family per year, and only in rural areas (Khera 2011b).

NREGA has two broad goals: to provide employment on demand and to build useful infrastructure. The 100 days per year of guaranteed waged work must be provided by the state whenever the worker asks for it, and within fifteen days of receiving an application. If the state does not comply, it must pay an unemployment allowance. Work occurs in groups and involves state-approved projects. Household members must be willing to do manual labor at the government-approved minimum wage.

Additionally, NREGA gives ordinary citizens a voice in identifying local public works. Jobs typically consist of building agricultural bunds (earthworks), repairing canals, or other productive and measurable labor projects on public lands. Workers are supposed to be paid bimonthly on a piece-rate basis. Typically, a work group's output is measured weekly at the worksite. The act mandates that men and women receive the same wage, a significant advancement over previous development programs in India. The central government provides the bulk of funding—100 percent of the wages for participating workers, 75 percent of the costs of materials, and 75 percent of administrative costs. State governments are responsible for unemployment allowances and 25 percent of the costs of materials (Khera 2011b).

NREGA emphasizes labor-intensive projects and prohibits the use of contractors and machines. This practice also represents a radical departure from other rural work programs, which are typically controlled by contractors (Jenkins and Manor 2017). Since the objective is to provide jobs, manual labor is the mode of employment.

NREGA's budget is approximately US$5.5 billion per year (Muralidharan et al. 2014a). In 2013–2014, the program employed nearly 48 million people, a figure that corresponds to 24.4 percent of all rural households (Desai et al. 2015). Dalits and Adivasis constitute 49.5 percent of NREGA workers, while women account for 47.5 percent. a significantly higher proportion than in most other development programs in India (Sukhtankar 2016).

Origins of the Rights-Based Approach to Development Programs

The rights-based approach in development programs can be traced to India's constitution, particularly the Directive Principles of State Policy (Drèze 2004).[2] From its inception, the Indian constitution codified a distinction between fundamental rights and rights that are guidelines for forming state policy. While fundamental rights were enforceable in a court of law, the Directive Principles laid down ideals for the Indian state to work toward, but stopped short of ensuring that these rights would be made into law.[3] The Directive Principles are an embodiment of Bhimrao Ramji Ambedkar's radical view of democracy, which linked political rights with economic and social rights (Drèze 2004; Bhatia and Bhabha 2017).

The rationale for this link between political and economic democracy was provided by Ambedkar himself during debates in the constituent assembly:

> Our object in framing the Constitution is really two-fold: (i) To lay down the form of political democracy, and (ii) To lay down that our ideal is economic democracy and also to prescribe that every government whatever is in power shall strive to bring about economic democracy. The Directive Principles have a great value, for they lay down that our ideal is economic democracy. (Constituent Assembly Debates 1948, quoted in Drèze 2004, 1723)

For decades, these Directive Principles remained ideals, while various civil society groups pressured the state to legislate them into law (Drèze 2004). With the passage of NREGA, nearly a half century after the initial constitutional seed was planted, the national government passed an economic law based on the concept of rights, bringing the Directive Principles full circle from vision to reality.

Right to Work Legislation

In April 2001, the People's Union for Civil Liberties (PUCL) filed a petition with the Indian Supreme Court invoking the right to food (Srinivasan 2010).[4] The petition was in response to severe drought in several parts of the country,[5] while at the same time, food grains were stored in government warehouses (Drèze 1995; Drèze 2019).[6] Civil society groups framed the situation as "hunger amidst plenty" (Srinivasan and Narayanan 2009, 3). As the right to food activists noted, "It was also a time of absurd paradox. Even as parts of the country were reeling from the severe stress of drought for the third consecutive year, foodgrain stocks held by the government exceeded 50 million metric tons. This level was far above the norms set by the government for buffer stocks. In fact, government warehouses were overflowing, and with storage capacity filled, mounds of grain were left out in the open" (Srinivasan and Narayanan 2009, 2). While civil society groups made the case that food shortages were a result of political priorities and bureaucratic choices rather than natural disasters, the PUCL petition went a step further, connecting the right to food to a guaranteed right in the constitution—the right to life—which, it argued, the states had failed to provide. The media work of the campaign made it difficult for the government to assert it did not have resources to remedy a food shortage (Srinivasan and Narayanan 2009; Waldman 2002).[7]

After hearing the case, the Supreme Court demanded a response from state governments. State bureaucrats countered with a list of actions they had already undertaken to deal with droughts. The PUCL petition pointed out that these programs had indeed been well implemented. The Supreme Court thus issued an interim order mandating that state governments regard the programs they had begun as legally required.[8] As a result of the Court's intervention, various state drought relief programs became law, and states could not withdraw support from these programs.

The Court's order also empowered civil society groups to escalate their efforts to force the states to act. Most notably, the groups that had come together under the right-to-food campaign began to put greater pressure on state governments.[9] The right-to-food campaigns were highly networked and able to quickly mobilize protest actions in 1,000 villages spread over ten states (Srinivasan and Narayanan 2009). These protests demanded state action to implement relief programs.

Separately, the Supreme Court continued the pressure and summoned representatives of state governments to appear before it for regular updates on their progress. Ultimately, these actions resulted in an order from the Court to regularize a program providing free midday meals in every rural school. That Supreme Court order became the template for future legislation, including that which created NREGA.

In 2004, at the first national convention of the right-to-food campaign, activists presented a seminal draft of legislation guaranteeing the right to employment. In 2005, this would become the National Rural Employment Guarantee Act (NREGA) (Khera 2005).[10]

As background, several studies have pointed to the critical role of Sonia Gandhi, the leader of the Congress Party (MacAuslan 2008; Maiorano 2014; Sharma 2015), in creating the political will and muscle to pass the first right to work act in India. Gandhi's strong support ensured that NREGA was a key component of the election manifesto of the Congress Party in 2004, which focused on rural voters' social and economic malaise. By contrast, the opposition political party in Andhra Pradesh, the Telugu Desam Party (TDP) headed by

Chandrababu Naidu, focused its campaign on urban areas (TDP was part of the National Democratic Alliance at the center, where the Bharatiya Janata Party [BJP] was the lead party). Naidu made use of the party's slogan, "India Shining," in his campaign (Ahmed and Varshney 2012, 36). This phrase was designed to promote international trade with India and emphasized capitalism-centered economic growth (or potential growth) at a time when many Indian people were suffering, particularly rural residents. Naidu's Congress Party (Indian National Congress; INC) opponent won in a landslide in Andhra Pradesh, and the INC also won a majority in Parliament (Ahmed and Varshney 2012; Ramesh 2004). The Congress Party relied on a coalition of parties known as the United Progressive Alliance (UPA) to form the new government. Parties on the left gained a historic number of the parliamentary seats that year, and their members lobbied heavily to ensure that NREGA was on the governance agenda. The political parties in the UPA organized a set of demands called the National Common Minimum Program, and NREGA was one of the central items on that list.

The new government created a National Advisory Council, chaired by Sonia Gandhi, to facilitate consultation about legislation and policy (McCartney and Roy 2016). The council was responsible for developing a draft of NREGA. Energized by this success, the right-to-food campaign began to push for outside support for the bill. Within a short time, they collected over one million signatures from 400 districts in the country on a petition asking Parliament to pass the right-to-work legislation (Srinivasan and Narayanan 2009). The initial draft was subject to numerous changes, but in the end, thanks to a motivated coalition of disparate, galvanizing forces, it became the transformational National Rural Employment Guarantee Act of 2005 (Khera 2011b; Chopra 2011a; Dreze 2010).

Origins of the Right-to-Information Movement

The RTI law in India has its origins in the struggles of the Rajasthan group Mazdoor Kisan Shakti Sangathan (MKSS). The MKSS was founded in 1990 in response to corruption in public works projects. Its initial goal was to ensure that workers be paid proper wages (Singh 2005) and the tool it used to question the state's actions came to be known as the social audit.

Aruna Roy, one of the founders, traces the origins of MKSS audits to a 1994 interaction with a village elder in Devdungri who worked in a state-funded drought relief program:

> He came with a complaint of non-payment of full minimum wage. But unlike most others, he had additional information. He had seen the muster roll, which

> had an entry for Rs. 22 per day, but all the workers were being paid only Rs. 11 per day. He had asked the overseer why he was being paid less than what was entered. The answer was that he alone would be paid Rs. 22, but that he should refrain from telling other workers what he had seen, or even mention that he had been paid more than them. (Roy and MKSS Collective 2018, 98)

MKSS realized that rhetoric and media campaigns would not be enough to ensure that workers received their full wages. For that to happen, workers needed to access government records, which at the time were not available to the public. These documents recorded misappropriation associated with public works projects that had not been completed or in some cases even started. Roy writes, "In one instance of misappropriation of funds, Rs. 36 lakh (3.6 million) was paid to a fraudulent company called Bhairon Nath and Sons" (Roy and MKSS Collective 2018, 98).

MKSS demanded access to state documents. Up to that time, the only people who had such access were state bureaucrats. Partly because of protests and partly because of luck, the group acquired the attendance registers of public work projects, which group members copied by hand (Roy and MKSS Collective 2018; Sharma 2015; Srinivasan 2011). To verify accuracy, MKSS did something no one had done before: they showed the documents to the workers. Since the workers were not literate, MKSS activists read them aloud. This process revealed numerous discrepancies. The documents listed the names of village leaders who had never gone to a worksite, names of worksites that didn't exist, inflated wage rates, and other fabrications. In response to these revelations, worker protested in several villages where MKSS was organizing and, with the help of MKSS, mobilized to demand their full wages.

The group's initial tactic was a hunger strike, which was not effective, because, as Roy explains, the strategy offered only "platforms for one-sided communication of one's own understanding and demands" (Roy and MKSS Collective 2018, 98). It did not create opportunities to engage with government officials or to gain responses from them. As a result, Roy and her group moved to a new, tactically shrewder mode of protest, the public hearing:

> Unlike earlier protests, the issues of corruption and arbitrary use of power had to hear evidence and facts. This was to be placed in the public domain and in an open-ended space where people who differed could come and state their differences. The panel [of independent observers] examined the evidence on both sides and came to a conclusion. (Roy and MKSS Collective 2018, 98)

This search for a more neutral and open interactive platform for democratic expression and deliberative debate led to the idea of village-based public hearings called *jan sunwais*. As Jean Drèze notes, the idea of public hearing has deeper roots, "Jotirao Phule, who was apparently checking muster rolls more than a century before Mazdoor Kisan Shakti Sangathan" (Drèze 2004, 1729). More recently a precedent for such public hearings also existed under the Environmental Protection Act, but the meetings were not mandatory. Roy and the MKSS borrowed the structure and implemented it as a means of creating oversight for public works projects (Roy and Dey 2001, 3). Organizing public hearings was new territory for the MKSS; in the past, the group had organized only meetings, rallies, and protests. As a result, leaders were somewhat apprehensive about how the new model of public hearings would be received and understood. They wondered whether people would turn up, how to make it easy for ordinary citizens to speak out, and whether the process would gain the legitimacy required to expose and address specific instances of corruption. Most importantly, it remained to be seen whether an atmosphere could be created in which people would find the courage to speak out openly against the state officials who had been exploiting them.[11]

To their surprise, MKSS activists found that people not only spoke out in these meetings, but that the act of speaking had a "multiplying effect, like a predictable chemical reaction" (Roy and MKSS Collective 2018, 98).

Public meetings had a long history in India, but the MKSS had initiated something radical and unique: public meetings where citizens had access to government documents and could publicly question state officials. MKSS continued to hold these hearings in different districts. The process was that MKSS activists would gain access to documents that historically had been closed. They would then take the documents to workers to ascertain whether they were accurate. Finally, they would discuss their findings in *jan sunwais* that activists, students, and volunteers who traveled to the villages helped facilitate. Volunteers checked the documents by going door-to-door and verifying details with workers, visiting worksites, and generating written reports. MKSS used the reports to demand that local state officials explain the discrepancies. The results were mixed. Social audits often led to backlash because the *sarpanches* (elected village council leaders) did not want their actions to be monitored. But the strategy also led to success as well, and sometimes workers were paid the back wages owed to them.

On a national level the story ended in triumph: the MKSS secured the right for everyone to see government documents. It certainly helped that the movement's leading activists were former bureaucrats with a deep knowledge of and access to state bureaucracies (Sharma 2015). In 2005, their efforts culminated in passage of the Right to Information (RTI) Act (Baviskar 2013; Roy and MKSS Collective 2018).

Furthermore, the provisions that the RTI Act enshrined into law became an integral part of a government program when NREGA was passed (Baviskar 2013;

Jenkins and Manor 2017). The program mandated social audits, a legal framework for operationalizing the RTI Act. For the first time, a public works project mandated an open process that enabled ordinary citizens to inspect public records. The law requires a biannual social audit and offers guidelines to govern the audit process. These guidelines delineate procedures for conducting social audits: how to collect information, how to prepare documents for the audit, and how to publicize social audit public meetings. While the basic processes of NREGA social audits came from the MKSS manual, the law left it up to state governments to decide who should conduct them, who could participate in them, and the effects social audits would have on how state bureaucrats administered the NREGA. Taken together, NREGA and the RTI Act advanced the rights of ordinary citizens to participate in government in groundbreaking ways by bringing together the right to work, the right to inspect documents and have their voices heard in agreement or objection, and the right to be fairly paid for their labor.

Relative Comparison of NREGA Outcomes

NREGA has had a profound impact on the lives of India's rural villagers, particularly women, by giving them an alternative source of employment. The India Human Development Survey shows that from 2004–2005 to 2011–2012, there was a 45 percent increase in female workers in the labor force. This is attributed to the introduction of NREGA in 2005 (Sukhtankar 2016). This is a remarkable success, especially when compared to the history of Indian development programs that have failed to achieve their goals, particularly in Andhra Pradesh (Deshingkar et al., 2005). NREGA also generated the unexpected benefit of increasing the bargaining power of landless laborers. As a result, agricultural wages rose. A recent study found that in Andhra Pradesh, NREGA increased the mean income of NREGA workers by 12.7 percent and that 90 percent of that increase came from rising agricultural wages (Muralidharan et al. 2019).

Although a national program, NREGA's administration was entrusted to each individual state. As a result, there are marked variations in performance across states and districts. However, despite the great diversity (Sukhtankar 2016), Andhra Pradesh is regarded as a model example of how to put the program into practice. Economists Clément Imbert and John Papp refer to it as a "star" state (Imbert and Papp 2012). Numerous sources identify the implementation of this program in Andhra Pradesh as a model to be imitated (Aiyar and Samji 2009; Imbert and Papp 2015; Maiorano 2014; Dasgupta et al. 2017 Mann et al. 2012; Muralidharan, Niehaus, and Sukhtankar 2016; Deininger and Liu 2013) and Andhra Pradesh's implementation of NREGA consistently ranks near the top among the states.

As Table 2.1 shows, Andhra Pradesh has consistently ranked among the best-performing states on the ability of the program to respond to demands from workers, the number of workers who completed 100 days of work, and the participation of three traditionally underrepresented groups—women, Dalit, and Adivasi groups—in its workforce. Andhra Pradesh's performance in NREGA outperforms most states in India. Tables 2.1 and 2.2 show the performance in three categories: expenditure, participation, and inclusion.

As Tables 2.1 and 2.2 show, Andhra Pradesh spends on average three times the administrative cost to run NREGA as compared to other states. While administration cost is sometimes viewed as overhead and a sign of bureaucratic

Table 2.1 Performance of NREGA in Andhra Pradesh from a Comparative Perspective, 2013–2014

Indicator	Andhra Pradesh	All-India	AP's Rank among 20 Major States
Expenditure			
Proportion of expenditure on wages (%)	70.7	73.4	7
Wage expenditure per rural person (Rs.)	599.9	314.6	5
Proportion of expenditure on administration (%)	11.0	6.1	1
Administrative expenditure per rural person (Rs.)	104.8	27.9	1
Participation			
Job cards as a proportion (%) of rural households	106.3	76.9	1
Employment generated per rural household (days)	21.1	12.6	6
Proportion of rural households who worked 100 days (%)	5.3	2.7	4
Inclusion			
Proportion of workdays by women (%)	58.6	52.8	5
Average employment for a rural Dalit person (days)	6.4	3.2	3
Average employment for a rural Adivasi person (days)	8.4	4.1	1

Note: Andhra Pradesh figures include Telangana. The major states included in the calculation of the rank (apart from Andhra Pradesh) are Assam, Bihar, Chhattisgarh, Gujarat, Haryana, Himachal Pradesh, Jammu and Kashmir, Jharkhand, Karnataka, Kerala, Madhya Pradesh, Maharashtra, Odisha, Punjab, Rajasthan, Tamil Nadu, Uttar Pradesh, Uttarakhand, and West Bengal. Rural households are for 2013–2014, estimated from National Population Projections. Rural Dalit and Adivasi proportion used to calculate average employment per rural Adivasi or Dalit person is as per Census 2011.

Table 2.2 Performance of NREGA in Andhra Pradesh from a Comparative Perspective, 2019–2020

Indicator	Andhra Pradesh	All-India	AP's Rank among 20 Major States
Expenditure			
Proportion of expenditure on wages (%)	84.6	70.5	1
Wage expenditure per rural person (Rs.)	889.3	380.3	3
Proportion of expenditure on administration (%)	5.1	4.4	8
Administrative expenditure per rural person (Rs.)	53.3	23.5	3
Participation			
Job cards as a proportion (%) of rural households	104.7	73.6	2
Employment generated per rural household (days)	18.5	9.8	4
Proportion of rural households who worked 100 days (%)	2.0	0.6	2
Inclusion			
Proportion of workdays by women (%)	60.5	55.8	5
Average employment for a rural Dalit person (days)	5.3	2.2	3
Average employment for a rural Adivasi person (days)	6.8	3.2	2

Note: Andhra Pradesh figures include Telangana. The major states are included in the calculation of the rank (apart from Andhra Pradesh) are Assam, Bihar, Chhattisgarh, Gujarat, Haryana, Himachal Pradesh, Jammu and Kashmir (including Ladakh), Jharkhand, Karnataka, Kerala, Madhya Pradesh, Maharashtra, Odisha, Punjab, Rajasthan, Tamil Nadu, Uttar Pradesh, Uttarakhand, and West Bengal. Rural households are for 2019–2020, estimated from National Population Projections. Rural Dalit and Adivasi proportion used to calculate average employment per rural Adivasi or Dalit person is as per Census 2011.

bloat, in this case, Andhra Pradesh spends about two to four times more than the rest, which is one indicator that bureaucratic administration is focused on optimizing implementation of the program. To put the figures of three times the cost in context, the state bureaucracy in Andhra Pradesh uniquely has created an independent social audit unit and has invested heavily in technologies to monitor performance. In the participation category, Andhra Pradesh performs near the top in participation of workers as measured by the job cards as a proportion of rural households. NREGA aims to help the marginalized, and under the inclusion category, Andhra Pradesh ranks near the top in the number of workdays generated for women, Dalits, and Adivasis.

Until 2013, Andhra Pradesh was the only state to implement social audits. At that time, the state split into Andhra Pradesh and Telangana, with both continuing the audits. Since then, there has been a push by the central government for other states to follow suit. As of this writing, only a few states possess the essential requirement for successful social audits: strong political underpinnings. Such support does not appear out of thin air. It is the outcome of sustained struggle, often by marginalized people, to achieve a foothold of power (Dreze 2004). The following section traces the origin of the political will and priority to implement NREGA effectively in Andhra Pradesh.

Dalit Mobilization and the Political Road to NREGA in Andhra Pradesh

In Andhra Pradesh, as in other parts of India, villages are deeply divided along class and caste lines (Balagopal 2011). In the past few decades, exploitative relations between landowners and the landless class have come under pressure due to low-caste groups in Andhra Pradesh mobilizing politically (Byres et al. 2013; Jakimow 2014). Moreover, marginalized people have acquired a greater voice in shaping policy in recent decades as the capacity of dominant castes to influence the political behavior of marginalized people has gradually declined. This loss of influence has led to identity-based politics that are transforming the rural countryside (Balagopal 2011; Kohli 1998). Scholars have characterized the phenomenon as a "deepening of democracy," a "transformation of rural authority," and a "silent revolution" that has fundamentally changed social and political relations in India (Jaffrelot 2003; Mendelsohn 1993; Varshney 2000).[12] As activist and scholar Vivek Srinivasan notes, these struggles often take the form of "decentralized collective action" on the part of common people who demand public services that eventually result in change (Srinivasan 2015, 44). The most studied and celebrated case in India is that of Kerala, where an alliance between an organized worker movement and a parliamentary communist party resulted in a pact with the state that led to improving the welfare of the poor (Heller 2000).

In Andhra Pradesh, marginalized groups increased their social and political power through a number of social movements. Historically, communist parties in rural areas have focused on the issue of land redistribution (Appu 1997). With some exceptions, land reforms have been incomplete or mostly a failure (Herring and Edwards 1983; Appu 1997). Andhra Pradesh is one of the few states in India with strong extra-parliamentary armed communist movements (Maoist) that are opposed to the state (Balagopal 2006). These groups operate mainly in the Adivasi areas, and the state has heavily opposed them in Andhra Pradesh. However, as Balagopal (2011) notes, from the 1980s onward, the stronger social movements in Andhra Pradesh have been focused on identity rather than land: for example, issues of concern to Dalits, Adivasis, and women. Furthermore, these movements developed independently of communist campaigns (Balagopal 2011) and often centered on specific areas of contestation. For example, the anti-arrack moment was a struggle by rural women that became a movement to prohibit liquor consumption (primarily by men) (Reddy and Patnaik 1993).[13]

The Dalit movement emerged out of "decentralized collective action" over several years to achieve greater dignity (Srinivasan 2015, 44). Its participants demanded equal access to public spaces, water, and temples; the freedom to celebrate their own festivals; and the ability to go anywhere they wanted in the village (Srinivasan 2015). Until recently, this growing assertiveness was met with brutality. A pivotal massacre, part of the documented history of such indiscriminate killing, was the notorious incident in the village of Karamchedu, in Prakasam district, where six Dalits were brutally murdered and many more seriously injured on July 17, 1985. Dalits from Karamchedu fled to a nearby village, where Dalits from other villages joined them to demand that state action be taken against such atrocities (Balagopal 2011). Extensive media coverage of this incident led to a mass organization of Dalits in the group Dalit Mahasabha in Andhra Pradesh. The Dalit Mahasabha leadership emerged organically and was not associated with any political party.[14] Caste consciousness was the central focus, distinct from the class-based movements. Ambedkarism became the guiding ideological force underpinning this "new Dalit democratic revolution" (Rao 2015, 129).

Unfortunately, Dalit assertiveness provoked further attacks on them by upper-caste groups. The National Human Rights Commission has documented massacres occurring between 1985 and 1991 (Balagopal 2011).[15] Such barbarity shaped the Dalit movement's agenda, political discourse, and strategy over the years (Ratnam 2008; Rao 2015).

Their protests took multiple forms, including blocking roads, burning effigies, engaging in collective bargaining, refusing collectively to accept wages, cutting trees, fasting, taking legal action, writing letters, locking government offices, staging mock funerals, gathering signatures on petitions, breaking pots, organizing processions, picketing, and setting up supplementary tuition centers for Dalit students (Srinivasan 2015, 73–76).

While forged in violence and blood, over time, these public actions by Dalits led to political capacity that was strong enough to influence and make claims on the state of Andhra Pradesh to formulate new policies to benefit the marginalized, including Dalits (Mooij 2002; Kruks-Wisner 2018).[16]

In the 1980s, the Telugu Desam Party under N. T. Rama Rao came to power in Andhra Pradesh, overthrowing the Congress Party's monopoly in the state in part because Rao promised to deliver a food subsidy program called the "Rs. 2 per kilo of rice" scheme (Mooij 2002, 26). The rice subsidy was enormously popular among the rural poor and became part of the state's policy for several years. The TDP's focus on the rural poor led to its dominance over Congress in 1983, but over time its priorities shifted, and by 2004, the election year that was critical for implementing NREGA in Andhra Pradesh, TDP's emphasis was on urban industrial growth and the "India Shining" campaign to modernize Andhra Pradesh. During the previous five years, non–Congress Party governments had ruled at both the central and state levels, but in 2004 one particularly astute and charismatic Congress Party politician, Y. S. Rajasekhar Reddy (popularly referred to as YSR), campaigned vigorously to become chief minister of Andhra Pradesh on the promise that he would focus on the rural poor. His theme of condemning rural neglect resonated in Andhra Pradesh, where drought was widespread, and the previous government had been responsible for a famously corrupt Food for Work program. YSR even undertook a *padayatra* (journey on foot) across the poorer districts in Andhra for forty-five days in the hot summer.

YSR's focus on the rural poor not only propelled him to victory in the election in 2004, but it also played a crucial role in getting the Congress Party elected to power nationally. The TDP lost badly, primarily because of its neglect of rural areas. YSR had been a prominent politician in Andhra Pradesh and in the Congress Party since the 1980s. YSR's rise in politics "has been accompanied by more bloodshed than that of any other politician in this state. Not bloodshed for some avowed 'higher cause,' but bloodshed for the narrowest possible cause—the rise of one individual to political power and prominence" (Balagopal 2011, 327). Yet, YSR decided to focus on developmental programs that benefit the rural poor (Srinivasulu 2009).[17] The 2004 sweep made him particularly important with the Congress Party leadership,[18] and he wielded a degree of power other Congress Party chief ministers did not enjoy at that time, either in their states or at the national level. Because Andhra Pradesh was the only major state governed by the ruling Congress Party at that time, the party was keen to see NREGA find a firm footing there.

At the time, many people wondered why YSR, an upper-caste person and a landowner, would take such pains with a program that would largely benefit landless laborers rather than farmers.[19] Maiorano argues that the genesis of political support in Andhra Pradesh for NREGA can be attributed to three factors: (1) landless laborers constituted a significant voting block; (2) the perception of Congress Party representatives was that 100 days of work per family would not directly or significantly affect the interests of the farming class; and (3) people underestimated the extent to which this program would raise the minimum wage in the countryside (Maiorano 2014).[20]

Andhra Pradesh had the political clout and priority to implement NREGA well because the Congress Party needed it to be successful in order to showcase the program nationally. YSR had campaigned on big promises to rural landless workers, and he was a charismatic and ruthless leader who could discipline his political party members, so they did not meddle with his prize plan. In addition, YSR sent a strong message to his political party members to not use NREGA and other welfare schemes to amass wealth (Maiorano 2014).[21]

Bureaucratic Autonomy and Andhra Pradesh's Centralized Model of Governance

While generating political support is a necessary condition for the proper implementation of government programs, it is not sufficient. Ultimately, programs must be designed, managed, and monitored by bureaucrats. This process is particularly difficult in a context where contractors and local politicians have had undue influence. Further, bureaucrats are often themselves involved in "percentage schemes" in which they skim money from every payment a government program makes (Drèze 2007). It is also true that India has a tradition of committed bureaucrats dedicated to implementing programs fairly. In Andhra Pradesh, the most notable member of this latter group was the late S. R. Sankaran, who inspired many bureaucrats to have a pro-poor focus.[22]

Because YSR was keen on implementing NREGA well, he chose a top Indian administrative officer, Koppula Raju, to head the rural development department.[23] Raju had made his name by administering several successful programs in Andhra Pradesh.[24] According to Raju, YSR told him to ensure that the program was well implemented and gave him full autonomy with regard to recruitment of employees. He also warned Congress Party members not to interfere with the implementation of the NREGA at the local level. He gave bureaucrats the power to control NREGA funds, instead of having the funds routed through the panchayat system of elected local representatives.[25] He warded off criticism from the Members of the Legislative Assembly (MLAs) in the party by telling them to keep away from this program, he would find other ways for them to make money. As Maiorano notes: "The chief minister's actions were crucial to chang[ing] the very perception of the state's welfare schemes, from a way to amass wealth by powerful actors, to a device for re-election" (Maiorano 2014, 102). These actions set the stage for the bureaucracy to control the implementation of the program.

They also marked a fundamental shift in the governance of Andhra Pradesh. Centralization of programs was not new to Andhra Pradesh, as the elites of political party and in particular chief ministers always wanted direct control of programs.[26] But with YSR, there was greater (if not complete) autonomy given to the bureaucracy to implement the program, making it closer to the Weberian idea of bureaucratic autonomy.

Andhra Pradesh, like all Indian states, is administered through the hierarchy. The state is divided into districts. Within each district there are mandals. (In other states, the districts are divided into administrative blocks.[27]) The mandals are further divided into gram panchayats and then into villages. Finally, within villages are habitations, which are often segregated by caste.

Figure 2.1 shows the hierarchy of the implementing bodies for the NREGA program in Andhra Pradesh. The administration of NREGA operates at different levels of the hierarchy. The four tiers of administration are the state, district, mandal, and village levels. In Andhra Pradesh, there has been an effort since the late 1990s to outsource the work of the state to outside agents and contractors (Manor 2007; Kuriyan and Ray 2009a). The NREGA bureaucracy continued that trend of employing contract labor.

With the exception of the mandal program development officer (MPDO), the entire bureaucracy at the mandal level is a temporary workforce. Frontline bureaucrats are not recruited through the civil service. While there has been a struggle to unionize the bureaucrats and to fight for permanent status, there has also been a strong pushback from the upper-level bureaucrats, and ultimately the politicians, against yielding that power. Village-level agents are controlled at the

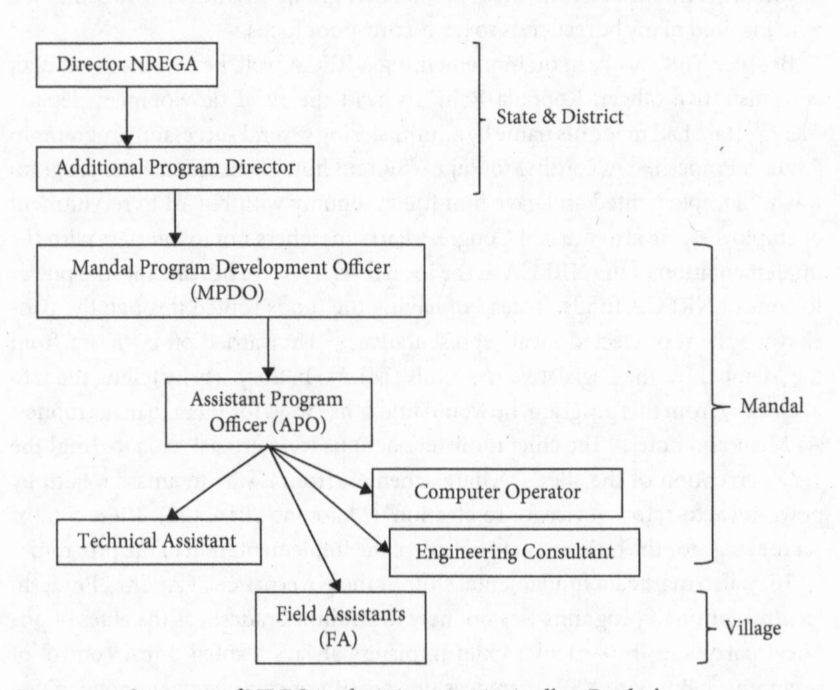

Figure 2.1 Structure of NREGA administration in Andhra Pradesh.

mandal level. The NREGA bureaucracy has no offices at the village level. There is a district office with administrators, but their role is limited to storing documentation and rubber-stamping projects that come up and down the hierarchy.

Decisions about projects are made at the mandal level. The mandal has an office that is sometimes called the MPDO office. Each village typically has a field assistant (FA), who assigns work, maintains attendance registers, and makes all key decisions at the field level. Field assistant is an important position at the village level; it is an administrative position and is not part of the village panchayat.

The technical side of the program, planning the actual work, is done by two other administrative positions at the mandal level, the technical assistant (TA) and the engineering consultant (EC). Appointments to these two positions are made at the state level, again to ensure independence from local political influences. The people who fill them are also temporary contract employees and often have a diploma and in some cases engineering degrees.

Although NREGA work is standard and "simple," the technical assistants and engineering consultants still need to know how to read engineering diagrams. Their role is to plan projects and take measurements. Engineering consultants handle projects that require technical expertise and focus more on the planning aspect of the work. Technical assistants measure the work done on job sites. This occurs because the NREGA pays workers based on the amount of work they do, rather than the number of hours they work. However, they are expected to stay the entire day at the worksite.[28] The technical assistants maintain measurement books that document the dimensions of the work. In effect, they do the job contractors used to do before NREGA.

The most critical actor at the mandal level is the computer operator. He or she is responsible for digitizing all the records and plays a critical role in the implementation of NREGA in Andhra Pradesh, which relies on information technology to control program implementation. In sum, NREGA governance at the last mile is a highly systemized hierarchy administered from the top to tightly control oversight and practices. However, as we will see, various local forces are constantly pushing against that, creating a fluid dynamic that requires adaptation and adjustment.

In 1992, there was a move to decentralize control nationwide in order to solve the problem of lack of power at the lower levels of government. As a result, elected governments in villages began undertaking development work. The 73rd Amendment to the Indian Constitution gave village councils, or gram panchayats, an increased role in rural governance (Baviskar 2013). Decentralization did not automatically bring greater accountability, however. In the eyes of bureaucrats who operate at the state level, like Raju, the new system simply introduced new possibilities for bureaucrats below them to subvert the spirit of the amendment.

The Food for Work program in Andhra, the predecessor of the NREGA, was often called the "loot for work" program because it had "exceptionally high misappropriation(s)" at the local level (Deshingkar et al. 2005, 576; Maiorano 2014). Local officials embezzled funds by forging muster rolls (attendance registers), paying daily wages that were lower than the prescribed minimum wage, and taking bribes in exchange for allotting work (Deshingkar et al. 2005). As geographer and policy researcher Priya Deshingkar and colleagues, who studied India's Food for Work program, noted, "one of the most disturbing findings that emerges from this research is that almost everywhere we studied, panchayat officials and sarpanches were instrumental in the corruption of Food for Work" level (Deshingkar et al. 2005, 589).

In contrast to the Food for Work program, Raju and other bureaucrats at the top responsible for rolling out NREGA solved this problem by taking away power from implementing bodies at the local level and assuming central control of the everyday governance of NREGA. Raju wanted total control of the daily practices of the program.

> So I realized that if NREGA is to run, we have to keep these three fellows out. We need to have a totally different business process. The same business process just will not work. Willy-nilly, these people will come in and position themselves. We need to turn the whole thing upside down, and only then will things move. We need to take away the powers from *everyone*[29] [my emphasis].

It should be noted that Raju's conception of "everyone" was restricted to everybody at the local level. There were no provisions to allow scrutiny of actions of the upper-level bureaucrats.

To assure the higher-level bureaucrats' complete control, Raju immediately looked to technology and hired the services of Tata Consultancy Services, a private software company. Chandrababu Naidu, YSR's predecessor in Andhra, had prioritized the use of technology in order to improve government efficiency and centralize control of the bureaucrats (Manor 2007).[30] He aggressively promoted modernization of the state through the use of computers and was often portrayed in the media working on his laptop. Naidu had also pioneered the use of computers and networking technology as a means of communicating directly with bureaucrats at all levels. He would appear on videoconferencing calls, deliver instant reports from the field, and review performance of programs. His emphasis was so impactful that there was resentment among government bureaucrats (particularly at the lower levels) about direct oversight of them via technical means.

With widespread exposure to the use of computing tools already in place within the bureaucracy in Andhra Pradesh, Raju, with the political backing of his boss YSR, sought to set up an elaborate computing infrastructure to control the daily practices of NREGA bureaucrats. To increase the transparency of NREGA processes, the enabling legislation had required all states to conduct social audits. The law stipulated that the *gram sabha* (village meetings) conduct regular social audits every six months.[31] The state government of Andhra Pradesh went a step further by creating a new institution called the Society for Social Audit, Accountability and Transparency (SSAAT), a story I relate in Chapter 4. The Andhra Pradesh model of governance is distinctive because it combines heightened administrative monitoring using digital technology with the opening up of records to workers through the audit process to create accountability. This dual process is unusual; most approaches that use digital technology omit face-to-face interactions. Figure 2.2 shows the schematic of the Andhra Pradesh model of governance, with two steps.

The first step was the use of digital technology within the bureaucracy. The fundamental premise of that strategy was that if higher-level bureaucrats could monitor subordinates, the subordinates would increase their level of compliance with the rules of the system. Higher-level bureaucrats wanted to build a system that used technology such as computerized databases, text messages, mobile phones, and geotracking to monitor the work practices of lower-level bureaucrats. Two principles guided the use of digital technology: it would increase the visibility of work done at every level of the bureaucracy, and it would enable state-level bureaucrats to control practices at the field level.

The second step was a vertical governance strategy that involved the creation of an audit institution that examines the program publicly. SSAAT is a registered independent society with a governing board; the chief minister of the state is the nominal head. It is funded by the state and its members

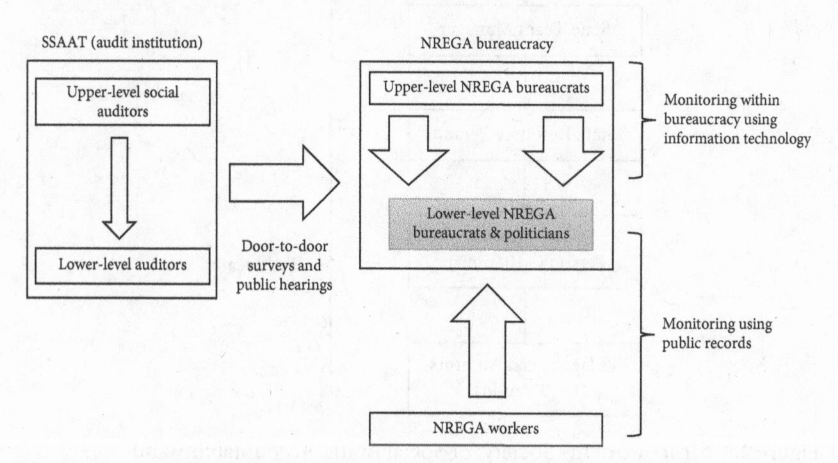

Figure 2.2 Andhra Pradesh model of dual-process last-mile governance.

are recruited from nongovernmental organizations (NGOs). The audit unit consists of a core team that travels around the region and local contingents from the villages. This team is supplemented at the local level by village auditors; typically, the literate children of NREGA workers. These local auditors are hired and trained on a per-audit basis. The team is split into the administrative staff, which is located in an office in the state capital of Hyderabad, and the auditors at large, who assemble at villages for audits. The audit team for the state of Andhra Pradesh has around 1,000 members. The field-level staff are distributed in a hierarchy that has four levels: state team monitors, state resource persons, district resource persons, and village social auditors. This hierarchy shown in Figure 2.3, is distinct from the hierarchy of the NREGA bureaucracy. To ensure compliance with the law, the audits are supposed to be conducted by villagers facilitated by the leaders of the Gram Panchayat; thus, the only level of employees with the word *auditor* in their titles are the village social auditors. Other members of the audit team are facilitators and have titles such as monitor and resource person.

The social audit is conducted in three stages. First, social auditors open up everyday government documents not previously made public, such as muster rolls and the measurement books that contain the locations and dimensions of

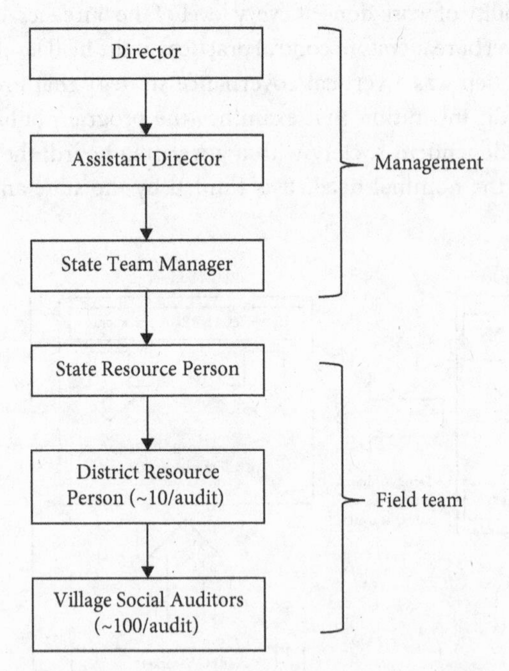

Figure 2.3 Structure of the Society for Social Audit, Accountability and Transparency.

NREGA projects. Auditors also measure worksites to make sure that they match the dimensions in the records, read muster rolls aloud to verify that the details in these documents match what the workers recall, and record all discrepancies between the official records and what they learn in the course of the audit.

In the second stage, workers produce written testimonies that support or counter NREGA records. The audit team conducts household surveys door to door, a practice that creates space for private discussions in which workers can air their grievances. When the workers are willing, these private discussions are recorded in an audit document that includes the workers' signature or thumbprint. In the third stage of the audit, all the audit documents are examined in a public hearing. At this hearing, in which workers, activists, government officials, and NREGA bureaucrats attend, the audit team presents the government records and the audit report to the public. The audit report is read out loud, after which the public is offered a chance to speak. A government officer presides over this meeting and levies penalties in the form of fines, suspensions, or termination to bureaucrats who are found to be corrupt. In some cases, representatives from the media also attend. In troubled regions, the police also attend. The audit documents are publicly presented first at the village level (in the *gram sabha* meetings) and then at the mandal (subdistrict unit), or regional administrative hub, in a meeting that district-level bureaucrats preside over. These mandal public hearings offer new opportunities for citizens to critique the state. But as we will see in the coming chapters, very few travel willingly to the mandal to testify. Those who do are typically mobilized by the local power system and more often than not testify to support local elites.

Payment Infrastructure in Andhra Pradesh

The NREGA records the work done by a worker in a muster roll (attendance register) that captures attendance at the worksite. The payment is based on measurement of work at the worksite, typically two weeks after the start of work. The payment system has gone through many experimentations to ensure that workers get paid in time. For every NREGA worker, there has been an account created with the postal office or a bank. Once the measurements and attendance are gathered, the average wage per day for each worker is calculated and the payment is initiated with a pay order by the mandal. The pay order is processed by higher levels of the government before cash is transferred to the account of the worker in a bank or a post office.[32] In regions with low banking density, the state has appointed a system of intermediaries between workers and the bank so that workers are able to avail their payments closer to home.[33]Workers are expected to be paid within two weeks of their work in cash in their own village. But how do these provisions are governed in practice is what we will turn to in the next chapters.

Conclusion

In this chapter, I have discussed the legislative context and establishment of NREGA, which is essential to its functioning. In tracing the historical circumstances that led to the creation of NREGA and its particular implementation in Andhra Pradesh, three factors were crucial. First, national legislation was passed thanks to mobilization from networked civil society actors, and electoral competition produced a coalition government which made it politically feasible. Second, the political competition essential for the effective establishment, design, and implementation of NREGA in Andhra Pradesh was present and assertive. The late chief minister, Y. S. Rajasekhar Reddy, gave complete autonomy to the bureaucrats to control NREGA funds, rather than routing through local panchayats.[34] Third, this system also required the support of willing and capable upper-level bureaucrats, who designed programs that countered any resistance to their power at the last mile of the implementation. Fourth, and most crucially, the historical mobilization by Dalits through struggles for equality and justice politicized and empowered them to be receptive to change from the top.

Most accounts of NREGA stop here. They tell a straightforward story about how social movements and/or decentralized collective action generate political support that empowers bureaucrats and gives them autonomy. The theory is that states with bureaucratic capacity will get institutions right and successfully implement government schemes. But that narrative is too simple. As Witsoe aptly summarized, there are three distinct NREGAs: the NREGA that was enacted through legislation, the NREGA the bureaucracy perceives, and the NREGA that is practiced in villages (Witsoe 2014, quoted in Sukhtankar 2016). As we will see in the coming chapters, resolving the first-mile problems is a necessary but not a sufficient condition for addressing the last-mile problems.

3
Patching Technologies of Control

This chapter examines how digital technology became a central instrument in a struggle for control of administrative processes between upper-level and lower-level NREGA bureaucrats in Andhra Pradesh. The features of technology influence interactions, in this case, interactions between employees of a government bureaucracy (Srinivasan 2011; Fung et al. 2007; Masiero 2015; Madon 2005). However, by focusing only on the technical specifications of a system or the overarching policy decisions, one misses the critical way in which these two dimensions interact (Benjamin et al. 2007; Heeks and Bailur 2007). As I illustrate, while upper-level bureaucrats' use of technology amplified their ability to render transparent the actions of the bureaucrats they supervised, lower-level bureaucrats and local politicians found creative ways to thwart these efforts (Toyama 2015). In response, upper-level bureaucrats sought to regain control through patching NREGA's socio-technical system.

In my fieldwork and research, I came to understand not only that small details mattered, but also that these seemingly inconsequential changes in software were central to fixing the problems of NREGA's last-mile governance and consequential to the implementation. Lawrence Lessig, a lawyer, originally coined the phrase "code is law" to describe a form of regulation in which private companies use software code to regulate our actions in lieu of laws (Lessig 1999). His insight echoed Science and Technology Studies scholar Langdon Winner's proposition that technology artifacts embody politics (Winner 1980; Flanagin et al. 2009). Following Lessig, in Andhra Pradesh we could say code is policy.

Like the welfare program itself—and the people who deployed technology to gain specific ends—the digital applications embedded in NREGA had politics. In the analysis that follows, I ask: How and why did upper-level bureaucrats make changes in the technology the program uses? How did the affordances of these technologies affect both specific outcomes and the ultimate possibilities for NREGA's success? How did these changes affect the discretion of the lower-level bureaucrats?[1] And how did they shape the ability of the upper-level bureaucrats to retain control of the implementation of NREGA at the last mile?

In software development, patching refers to correcting problems in software; it is how companies maintain software systems over time. Patches are bits of software code targeted to amend the specific parts of a larger software system that are not functioning as originally intended. They are incremental; patches don't eliminate problems in one shot because the full scope of the issue is often not fully known at first. This is especially true when code patches aim to resolve bugs not in the software systems, but in systems of governance.

We need a process-based understanding of how technology interventions work and what lessons can be learned. This is important because the designs of technology, as I will show, are made in response to reactions by local bureaucrats and are shaped by particular politics (Chadwick 2003). Impact assessments don't tell the whole story. For example, a study of one aspect of technology use in NREGA in Andhra Pradesh, the digital payments platform, found that it resulted in a significant reduction in corruption (Muralidharan et al. 2014b). However, this finding alone doesn't explain the myriad ways in which digital technology was successfully employed in Andhra Pradesh. Likewise, while the political incentives of the bureaucrats in Andhra Pradesh may explain their use of technology, it does not help us understand how that technology was used, to what ends, and what problems at the last mile it helped overcome.[2]

In what follows, I look at three cases which illustrate (1) how supervisors develop patches for problems within NREGA, (2) who develops them, (3) how lower-level bureaucrats have sometimes thwarted the attempts of their supervisors to acquire greater control over their work processes, and (4) how upper-level bureaucrats, attentive to such resistance, act to release new governance patches to deal with it.

Legibility within the State

From the outset, two principles guided how NREGA administrators used digital technology: it should increase the visibility of work done at every level of the bureaucracy, and it should enable upper-level bureaucrats to determine how people do their jobs at the field level. One of the first steps they took was introducing a public server to make raw data from the field available and to store reports. Upper-level bureaucrats envisioned that the digital system would both centralize power in their hands and make it easier for lower-level bureaucrats to meet the increased reporting demands of NREGA's new transparency requirements.[3] Also, they realized that once the reporting system came online, they could generate field-level reports at any level of granularity whenever they wished.

A useful starting point for understanding the actions of the upper-level bureaucrats in Andhra Pradesh is James Scott's analysis of the concept of legibility in his book *Seeing like a State*:

> Legibility is a condition of manipulation. Any substantial state intervention in society—to vaccinate a population, produce goods, mobilize labor, tax people

> and their property, conduct literacy campaigns, conscript soldiers, enforce sanitation standards, catch criminals, start universal schooling—requires the invention of units that are visible. The units in question might be citizens, villages, trees, fields, houses, or people grouped according to age, depending on the type of intervention. Whatever the units being manipulated, they must be organized in a manner that permits them to be identified, observed, recorded, counted, aggregated, and monitored. The degree of knowledge required would have to be roughly commensurate with the depth of the intervention. In other words, one might say that the greater the manipulation envisaged, the greater the legibility required to effect it. (Scott 1998, 183)

Legibility is thus a "central problem in statecraft" through which states "arrange the population in ways that simplify their classic functions" (Scott 1998, 2). Moreover, it provides the state with a "schematic view to amplify its capacity for discriminating intervention" (78–79). States obtain legibility through what Scott calls "state simplifications" (Scott 1996, 43), a narrowing of vision that brings limited aspects into focus—"only that slice of it that interest[s] the official observer" (Scott 1998, 3).

Scott's view was defined through the lens of states seeking to control society through making it readable, i.e., legible. For Scott, then, seeing has a purpose: state control of the population. Legibility was attempted by the state. As a foil to state-controlled legibility, Scott also introduces the concept of "metis" (practical knowledge) that is the province of citizens. For his empirical analysis, he chose large-scale state actions that had the goal of restructuring society. In Scott's analysis, these projects often failed because those at the top levels of state governance could not "see" what was really happening on the ground. As he notes, it is often not possible for upper-level bureaucrats to ensure that the policies they institute will be implemented at the local level. Efforts to bring about large-scale change often fail because reality is complex, and plans to increase legibility are often static and not flexible enough.

The implementation of NREGA in Andhra Pradesh demonstrates dynamics of legibility that go beyond Scott's state versus society dichotomy. Here, upper-level NREGA bureaucrats worked to render the actions of lower-level bureaucrats at the last mile visible. In other words, bureaucratic documents of NREGA were not only a tool that the state uses to control its citizens; they can also be used within the bureaucracy for upper-level bureaucrats to control lower-level bureaucrats, and can be made accessible to citizens in order to monitor the state. The politics and mechanisms of legibility depend both on the direction of legibility and the local context into which it is implemented.[4] Because Principal Secretary of Rural Development Raju had had years of experience in the Indian bureaucracy, he knew that efforts to centralize power within NREGA were likely to fail because of political interference at the local level. He wanted to find a way to overcome this resistance by changing how upper-level bureaucrats gained access to legibility. Raju and other bureaucrats used governance by patching to increase their access to information on the ground. As the chapter details, this was not a one-time secure accomplishment, but rather one that was constantly ongoing to deal with resistance at the last mile from local politicians and bureaucrats.

The study of the Food for Work Program in Andhra Pradesh corroborated Raju's analysis: it found enormous misappropriation of that program's funds at the last mile, mainly by contractors, engineers, and politicians (Deshingkar et al. 2005). Further, Deshingkar and colleagues note that, in that program, upper-level bureaucrats were better monitored and rewarded than lower-level bureaucrats. They write that "the Indian system of public administration" is "relatively weakly" monitored "among the frontline officials whose actions and incentives are arguably most crucial to the livelihoods of very poor people" (Deshingkar et al. 2005, 599).

During my fieldwork, I observed that the pressures from local politicians on lower-level bureaucrats were immense. The bureaucrats told me that it was often hard to get a government job without the support of the local politician (a sarpanch, or member of legislative assembly, MLA). As social scientist Vivek Srinivasan notes, politicians spend a lot of money to win local elections. "This involves campaign expenditure as well as money spent in distributing gifts to secure votes. It is commonly understood that presidents [sarpanches and elected officials] considered this money as 'investment' that has to be recovered from various schemes when they hold political office. . . . These[,] put together, created a strong incentive for Panchayat presidents to indulge in corruption in NREGA and other programs" (Srinivasan 2010, 132). I heard local politicians talk about their need to spend money to bribe local citizens for votes. Thus, it is not surprising that local politicians often try to control lower-level bureaucrats to redirect development funds intended for public works toward their private ends. As Raju described earlier, this often happened through the support of local contractors who were often charged with implementing government programs.

The designers of NREGA were acutely aware of this problem and sought to ban contractors from becoming NREGA employees. Yet in practice, enforcing this part of the law required tremendous efforts by NREGA senior administrators. It should be noted that when I refer to the actors at the last mile, this includes all the stakeholders that interact around NREGA implementation: lower-level bureaucrats, contractors, politicians, and workers. When I discuss the *contest* between the upper-level bureaucrats and the lower-level bureaucrats, it should also be borne in mind that local politicians often colluded with the lower-level bureaucrats and that the designers of NREGA imposed multiple transparency requirements specifically to prevent such collusion.

In her book *Paper Tiger*, anthropologist Nayanika Mathur documents the effects that transparency requirements had in the functioning of NREGA in Uttarakhand (Mathur 2015). Mathur argued that the focus on transparency generated increased paperwork for lower-level bureaucrats to the degree that the upper-level bureaucrats' obsession with documentation led to NREGA, for all intents and purposes, being "unimplementable." She writes, "in its quest to make things auditable, NREGA has converted easily-executed—at least on paper—public works schemes into unimplementable ones *even on paper*" (Mathur 2015, 95). This was because she argues, the lower-level bureaucrats were overburdened with creating the copious paper documents—muster roll, job cards, measurement books—that were demanded of them.[5] She argues that while corruption did decline because of the extra scrutiny of their actions, the lower-level bureaucrats spent their time filling out forms, rather than doing what was necessary to implement NREGA in the villages by timely requesting funds and opening up documents for NREGA workers. Not wanting to take on the additional burden of even more paperwork that the new transparency requirements put on them, the lower-level bureaucrats chose to not implement NREGA and thus, she argues, the transparency requirement made NREGA "unimplementable."

Raju attempted to preempt the problem described by Mathur as the need to avoid burdening the lower-level bureaucrats with extra work. He said:[6]

> The entire bureaucracy was top-down; half the time goes in preparing reports and reports and reports. Because of this, whichever functionary I asked, "What is the single most irritating thing?" they told me it is the need to fill out so many forms and send so many reports. I thought, "I must have a system where I should not ask anybody for any report."

Instead of burdening the lower-level bureaucrats with additional transparency requirements, Raju sought to digitize the implementation. As we will see, digitization did not eliminate the problems and created new problems, but one that was attended to. However, the contestation shifted to the digital realm. Technology, then, was contested and political from the outset.[7] Upper-level bureaucrats like Raju responded to reforms needed further interventions to make it work. Therefore, the effect it had must be studied to ascertain how local conditions necessitated the evolution of technology systems.

Using Technology to Increase Legibility

Raju's solution to the last-mile problem was to take power away from implementing bodies at the local level so that the everyday governance of NREGA could be centrally controlled. He sought to create a digital system that would give him access to information about the daily practices of lower-level bureaucrats, and to this end he hired a private software company, Tata Consultancy Services (TCS), to build a software system customized for NREGA. This software controlled every aspect of NREGA's work processes. It maintained information about everything, from the list of projects that were allowed to a database of workers' names, to a tracking system for payments, to the performance of lower-level bureaucrats. In the words of an upper-level bureaucrat, the goal was an "end-to-end transactional system" that would allow Raju and his colleagues to follow the entire project pipeline, including the issuing of work permits, entering data on workers' time sheets, tabulating the amount of work done, determining the total cost of work, and tracking when workers got paid. The system was extremely sophisticated, with a suite of technologies that included computerized databases, text messages, mobile phones, and geotracking to monitor the work practices of lower-level bureaucrats. Upper-level bureaucrats worked closely with TCS to maintain total control of changes that were made to the software. Today, every NREGA mandal office has computers and one or two computer operators who use the NREGA software system.

Using computer technology to increase the ability of NREGA supervisors to "read" what happens on the ground in Andhra Pradesh was not a one-time, static event. Because the goals of bureaucrats who used the software system changed over time, it was necessary to develop a mechanism for updating their rules and plans. Traditionally, upper-level bureaucrats who administer any complex development program have relied upon paper circulars and government orders to communicate these updates, with rule changes typically emanating from the offices of state-level bureaucrats who design these programs. In India, government circulars and government orders are very detailed documents that control program practices at the microlevel. At first, the Andhra Pradesh bureaucrats administering NREGA continued issuing circulars and government orders concerning wage rates for workers, the type of work that workers were allowed to do, the deadlines for completion of projects, changes in the payment scheme, hiring procedures, and changes in the formats to use for documentation.

My conversations with upper-level bureaucrats revealed that, historically, a number of problems were associated with paper circulars. Lower-level bureaucrats could deny they had received a circular or could misinterpret it. Communication could be delayed as circulars traveled through the postal system and down the bureaucratic hierarchy. The information in the circulars was sometimes not fine-grained enough to respond to local contexts. In addition, the policies mandated were effective only to the degree that local bureaucrats were willing to implement them. The upper-level NREGA bureaucrats sought to address each of these problems with digital solutions.

The software system that upper-level bureaucrats used to implement the program made it easy for them to modify circulars through software updates. Software patches perform the same function as paper circulars: they announce updates to a particular policy that are designed to address a problem or improve practices in the field.[8] Given this similarity, the transition from paper to software patches should have been feasible, especially since a software patch has a far greater likelihood of being effective; no one can pretend that they have not received it.

Controlling Which Projects Are Done

To see how a software patch works, consider the case of a popular type of project undertaken through the NREGA: maintenance of irrigation canals. Heavy rains made it impossible for upper-level bureaucrats to audit a certain type of canal repair work because water covers up any evidence of repairs. Yet, local bureaucrats often chose canal repair as the type of work to be undertaken during the rainy season. In pre-digital days, upper-level bureaucrats would issue circulars disallowing canal work during a particular season in a particular district. But there was no way to ensure that these circulars were followed in the field. Today, a software patch deletes canal work from the list of approved projects in a particular region (typically a mandal) during the rainy season, providing upper-level bureaucrats with the ability to fine-tune the system on an ongoing basis and to control the type of NREGA work to be performed based on the season and local conditions.

The centralized power that upper-level bureaucrats gained on work allocation also had another benefit: it enabled lower-level bureaucrats to cope with local pressure from politicians to implement their favorite projects. Because politicians were accustomed to using public funds to implement their pet projects, this was a significant source of corruption at the last mile. Once projects became digitally controlled, lower-level bureaucrats could simply refuse to accommodate such requests by saying they no longer had the authority to select or approve projects locally. Making changes in the software to create a new type of project in the system requires approval from upper-level bureaucrats. While some lower-level bureaucrats complained to me about their inability to make such decisions, they also noted the benefits of not having to face pressure from local politicians. Lower-level bureaucrats often use the same excuse to NREGA workers, and *effectively hide behind the computer*, making it hard for workers to request changes. However, I also found cases where lower-level bureaucrats did not install the new patches. This in turn highlighted a technical issue related to how these patches were updated.

Rapid and Documented Delivery of Circulars

Initially, software patches commonly arrived at mandal computer centers on CDs or as e-mail attachments. The first iteration of patches thus was similar to circulars in that human intervention was required to implement them. Computer operators in the field could choose which software updates to install. One computer operator told me that when he received an update he would look at the list of changes in the metadata file accompanying the update and would delay installation if he found something he considered to be undesirable. The metadata file is a text document that is typically sent with the software update to inform users about the changes the software will make. This was also confirmed to me by an upper-level bureaucrat who had detected this behavior across the state.

Once upper-level bureaucrats were aware of what was happening, they made changes that bypassed the need for human intervention. In the new system, updates take place automatically when the system detects an internet connection. Transferring software patches to the internet eliminated delays and the manual process of installing CDs. But the offline world still had to be integrated with the online one, and the separation between these two worlds caused multiple problems for upper-level bureaucrats and opportunities for lower-level bureaucrats. At this stage, NREGA software did not require network connection to function; the software worked well offline and just needed to be synced up with the network once the connection was back on. Network access in rural Andhra Pradesh was intermittent due to frequent power cuts and other infrastructure problems, so it made sense to design software to work offline. But this also gave the computer operators opportunities to exploit the offline feature. One computer operator told me he would disconnect his office's computers from the internet and then call and complain that he wasn't able to connect and was therefore working with the offline version. For example, if he learned that a certain work was going to be banned, he would disconnect the computer from the network and use the extra time to initiate new projects in the banned work categories before he updated the system to the latest version. Eventually, upper-level bureaucrats discovered this behavior as well and eliminated the software's offline functionality. Now, operators must be connected to the internet before they can enter any data.

In the paper era, learning what happened on the ground was costly and impractical. The shift to computer updates was not merely a shift from paper to software; it created a fundamental change in the degree to which upper-level bureaucrats can monitor the practices of lower-level bureaucrats. The shift to software did not automatically present them with greater control, as some changes were resisted, but the software created more possibilities for upper-level bureaucrats to issue patches.

The digitization of Andhra Pradesh's NREGA program underwent several iterations. In what follows, I focus on three iterations related to the muster roll. The first was the move to digitize the muster roll. The second focused on controlling elements of the muster roll by generating it remotely at the state level. The third focused on the speed at which the data were collected by introducing mobile phones to transmit data. In every instance, upper-level bureaucrats initiated the changes in an effort to tighten their control of the implementation of their policies and in response to contrary actions by lower-level bureaucrats.

Preventing the Forging of Documents

The muster roll is a paper register that records workers' attendance at a field site. Typically, it documents work for a two-week period for twenty workers at one NREGA project site, along with their signatures or thumb impressions. Muster rolls record who worked, how much they worked, where they worked, and what they worked on. Muster rolls are usually stored at the local mandal government office. Every two weeks, lower-level bureaucrats aggregate the data from the muster rolls and pay workers based on the amount of work their group has completed, using a piece-rate system based on the minimum wage. Because payment is tied to this document, records of every work session in the muster roll must be signed by the workers, the field assistant, and the local mandal program officer in order to be valid.

In Andhra Pradesh, the muster rolls did not just record work that had been done; they also captured trails of misappropriation. Studies examining the performance of development programs in Andhra Pradesh frequently report that lower-level bureaucrats pad muster rolls by using fake names, recording the same name at multiple sites at the same time, exaggerating the number of days that people work so they can pocket the difference in wages, underpaying workers, executing public works of substandard quality, or claiming funds for old work that has already been completed under another program (Deshingkar et al. 2005; 2007).

The actions of lower-level bureaucrats in this regard were often not legible to their supervisors. One of the upper-level bureaucrats in Andhra Pradesh opined in a report that "while information sent by field functionaries was always under scrutiny, program documents often were not made available until after a few years, undermining real-time checks and balances" (Murali 2013, 234). Upper-level NREGA bureaucrats quickly realized the problem was that paper-based documents did not allow for real-time checks. Their solution was to install patches to NREGA's digital system to enable it to monitor all program activities in real time (Murali 2013).[9] But, like all patch updates, this was a stepwise process.

The first step was to digitize muster rolls. Most states used the services of the central government's software arm, the National Informatics Center (NIC), to accomplish this. However, as stated earlier, Andhra Pradesh bypassed NIC and hired a private software company, TCS, to install TCS-operated computer centers in every mandal of the state. This decision gave Andhra Pradesh bureaucrats greater authority over implementation of the new software system (Kuriyan and Ray 2009a). Additionally, while the NIC software was built in Delhi, the offices of TCS were in Hyderabad, a physical location that was more convenient for upper-level bureaucrats in Andhra Pradesh because they could communicate with the TCS team in person as often as they wished.

NREGA bureaucrats in Andhra Pradesh were totally dependent on the software system that TCS built to control the everyday functioning of the program. TCS representatives visited the Office of the Principal Secretary daily to discuss recent updates to the software. While most visitors to the Office of the State's Rural Development (even visitors from other state departments) had to wait in line to meet with the principal secretary (i.e., the director) of the bureaucracy that managed the program, software representatives from TCS enjoyed easy access without prior permission or authorization.

The digital system helped upper-level bureaucrats remotely track work done under the auspices of NREGA. For example, they could see how many NREGA workers showed up at a worksite on a particular day. They could also monitor the time it took lower-level bureaucrats to complete individual tasks. The software automatically gathered metadata showing when information regarding individual tasks was updated. Access to detailed statistics about, say, the attendance of NREGA workers enabled upper-level bureaucrats to compare the performance of different mandals. This in turn gave them leverage to pressure the bureaucrats of mandals that were underperforming. Senior bureaucrats organized frequent videoconferences in which the performance of individual mandals and districts were often the subject of discussion. They also held monthly review meetings at the district level to further analyze performance. The pressure trickled down: mandal bureaucrats held weekly meetings to pepper individual field assistants with questions about why there were fewer workers in a particular week compared to prior weeks and compared to the number of workers in other villages.

Digitization also made it possible to create software tools that checked for inconsistencies in the data that had been entered. Prior to digitization, the veracity of these documents could not be confirmed automatically. The monitoring was accomplished by a form of software triangulation. For example, upper-level bureaucrats could run a software query to discover when the same workers were recorded as working on multiple sites on the same day. If there were any transgressions, the offending mandal and district officers were issued "show cause" notices and were subjected to disciplinary actions.

In one public meeting of a social audit I attended, the entire team of lower-level bureaucrats from a nearby mandal were present. They had no official reason to be there, as it was not their audit. When I asked them why they had elected to come, they said they wanted to learn about the types of issues that were being raised at the audit to ascertain the current priorities of the social auditors. During these audits, social auditors had started using sophisticated software queries to look for patterns. The lower-level bureaucrats did not have access to the software code, but just by attending the social audit meetings, they were reverse engineering the type of queries the auditors had used to identify misappropriations. The lower-level bureaucrats then used that information to develop strategies in the field for avoiding the disciplinary actions that were being imposed on their counterparts in the neighboring mandal.

One of the potential responses of learning the priorities of upper-level bureaucrats is greater adherence to the rules. But the lower-level bureaucrats attending this meeting were also looking to discover which rules to follow and which they could ignore—evidence that as social auditors focused on a particular type of transgression, lower-level bureaucrats sought to escape that gaze by learning which patterns their employers were identifying.

Lower-level NREGA bureaucrats also shared information through organized channels. Those who were temporary workers had a union that concentrated on salary and benefit demands. However, the workers had also set up informal communication channels among themselves. The field assistants were connected to each other via mobile phones that supervisors had given them to track their work. I witnessed them constantly using group text messages to exchange information and build solidarity. While I was not privy to the content of the internal communication among these teams, I got a sense of the conversations with the leaders of the union. In one such discussion, a district field assistant who was a union leader told me there had been a conscious shift in the type of actions some lower-level bureaucrats were engaging in. Previously, their transgressions had consisted of cheating workers out of their wages by altering the muster roll, but over time field assistants had turned to making money on materials.[10]

Clearly, the digital system that was used by the upper-level bureaucrats did not monitor every issue. For one thing, it didn't scrutinize the actions of upper-level bureaucrats. In addition, not all NREGA documents were digitized. What gets digitized (and thereby has the potential of scrutiny) is solely decided by upper-level bureaucrats constrained by demands from politicians (Masiero and Maiorano 2018; Bussell 2012; Heeks 1999). They chose to digitize muster rolls but not all the details of payments for materials. When I raised this issue, one upper-level bureaucrat said it was too onerous to digitize every single document, that doing so would entail a significant increase in the number of data-entry personnel. It was perhaps a conscious political choice by the upper-level bureaucrats to not digitize, as there is a strong local lobby that benefits from keeping procurement details close at hand. Digitizing payments for work materials would require scrutiny of these documents, and this would pit upper-level bureaucrats against material suppliers who enjoy the strong backing of the local political party (Bussell 2012). In other words, there were limits to the lengths upper-level bureaucrats were willing and able to go to stamp out misappropriations. As one social auditor pointed out to me, upper-level bureaucrats are not opening up processes for audits that might directly expose them. For example, documents on NREGA budgets, records of decisions upper-level bureaucrats make during social audits, and data relating to the process of deciding the proportion of the budget to allocate to labor and the proportion to allocate to materials in each mandal, are not part of the audit process. Moreover, not all upper-level bureaucrats agreed about which documents to digitize and which to exclude. Reflecting on the digitization that had occurred in her division, one senior bureaucrat told me, "The only documents that seem to matter are the ones that are getting digitized, and the rest of the documents are gathering dust in the offices with no effort to maintain them anymore." She was trying to make a case for ensuring that all documents were properly preserved, but that was not happening. Indeed, even the decisions upper-level bureaucrats make about which forms get digitized and where to focus their attention are governed by political considerations.

Wresting Control from Local Bureaucrats

The second means by which upper-level bureaucrats attempted to increase their control of muster rolls was to alter how they are produced. Previously, muster rolls were paper-only documents filled in locally at the mandal. With this patch, the upper-level bureaucrats generated a pre-filled paper muster roll with the names of workers who were allowed to work at a particular project site. This meant the list of workers on any given job was determined in Hyderabad, rather than allowing subordinates to create such lists at the mandal or district level. Each prospective NREGA worker had to first register with the state and acquire an NREGA job card. The worker was then assigned to a specific group. All workers in a particular work group were to be paid the same wage based on the total amount of work the group does. In the early years of NREGA, lower-level bureaucrats at the mandal office determined the membership of work groups. Sometimes workers in a neighborhood formed their own group. Now that the muster rolls have been digitized, the state database records information about each worker's village, caste, and gender, and upper-level bureaucrats are in charge of group assignments. When the computer operators upload the muster roll to the software system, they can't modify the workers' names, as they have already been filled in. The only new data able to be entered in the computer are the number of hours worked by each worker.[11]

Centralized generation of muster rolls accomplished two things: it eliminated the power of local bureaucrats and workers to form groups, and it assigned each group to a particular worksite using a randomized algorithm. Upper-level bureaucrats reasoned that randomization would prevent transgressions on the part of lower-level bureaucrats, such as reporting that individual workers had worked at multiple sites in the same day.

Another tool instigated by upper-level bureaucrats to avoid entries claiming the same worker had been at multiple worksites was to limit how often workers can change groups. Once a worker joins a group, he or she must remain in that group for a year. This restriction is intended to prevent field assistants from falsifying reports by moving a worker to multiple groups. The new state-issued muster rolls were pre-filled with both the group and the worksite assignments for each worker. Upper-level bureaucrats have focused on such granular details of the muster roll because they understand the politics of implementation at the last mile. This is not a case of Scott's "high modernist" state that is not able to understand the local; rather, this is case where state officials understand only too well the practices by which programs are often derailed and seek to eliminate them with the enhanced supervision and surveillance that digital technology makes possible (Lyon 1994).

Instant Legibility

A third way upper-level bureaucrats achieved control over the muster roll was by speeding up the reporting of attendance data. Under NREGA, each field assistant takes attendance at the worksite daily and obtains the thumb impression and/or signature of each worker. Previously, at the end of a two-week period, computer operators at the mandal office would digitize the paper muster rolls. Once that was complete, the records were available to all NREGA bureaucrats, including those at the state level. Upper-level bureaucrats wanted to speed up this process—as well as add another layer of oversight—by requiring field assistants to record attendance data in real time at the worksite, using mobile phones, every day.

Field assistants are now equipped with mobile phones loaded with an application called eMuster that enables them to record attendance directly onto the phone in addition to capturing the data on paper. The application already has the workers' names pre-loaded in a form; all the field assistant has to do is record who is present on the form. Once that is entered on the phone, it is transmitted electronically to the server and is accessible to upper-level bureaucrats.

These digital muster rolls do not eliminate the need for paper muster rolls. Computer operators at the mandal office and social auditors cross-check the hard-copy attendance sheet and the digital muster rolls for accuracy. I was told that this additional step was put in place after social auditors insisted they be allowed to manually verify the paper muster roll. The computer operator and the field assistants had to ensure that there were no discrepancies between what was reported from the mobile phone and what was later entered at the computer. This extra attention has acted as a deterrent against inaccurate reporting on the part of computer operators and field assistants. Thus, the work process patched in by upper-level bureaucrats disciplines lower-level bureaucrats. The social audit process is the reason why upper-level bureaucrats have insisted on a dual process of data collection. That level of legibility is necessary if the NREGA unit is to avoid public criticism in the village audit meeting.

The data from the electronic muster roll are immediately uploaded to central servers that upper-level bureaucrats can access. This took legibility to a new level; upper-level bureaucrats are able to see the number of workers at any worksite instantly. A company report from the developer of the software that generates the mobile phone–based muster roll explained the rationale for the transition:

> The objective is to achieve complete transparency in NREGA by transferring live data from the worksite to the website on a daily basis. It is designed to arrest distortions in the program like muster fudging [forging], delays in payments, benami [fictitious] wage seekers, fake measurement, and work duplication.[12]

The immediacy of the data-collection process using mobile phones put pressure on field assistants to report attendance data daily. The availability of real-time data made it possible to create additional oversights. However, upper-level bureaucrats were not technology determinists, that is to say, they did not rely solely on technology to determine outcomes. They realized that mobile phone data also needed to be verified. Consequently, they found a way to audit instant attendance updates: by requiring supervisors to visit worksites and verify official reports. These supervisors are government employees who often work in a different department and are not from the local area. Field assistants must take attendance in the morning by a certain time, and randomly assigned supervisors then audit the worksite the same day. Each supervisor gets a message that tells him or her which worksite location to visit and which attendance report to audit. Upper-level bureaucrats know that if muster rolls existed only on paper, it would be possible for field assistants to add fictitious names at the end of the day. The combination of instant uploads of digital attendance data and the ability of a supervisor to crosscheck these data on the same day they are created makes this particular type of fraud extremely risky. This is another example of how upper-level bureaucrats were able to go beyond relying purely on technical controls by also instituting processes that involved human beings in the monitoring loop to ensure accountability (Gigler and Bailur 2014; Kuriyan et al. 2011).

But, as is indicative both of patching and of programs in the process of being newly implemented, this new system created a new problem: upper-level bureaucrats had to address the potential issue of collusion between lower-level bureaucrats and visiting supervisors. Even with random assignment, it was possible for the supervisors sent to the worksite to verify attendance records to collude with field assistants in fraudulent behavior. They could also simply refuse to go to the worksite to avoid the extra work. Because of this issue, upper-level bureaucrats created a central survey team that located each NREGA worksite in the state and tagged its GPS location. In addition, the mobile phones that supervisors use were outfitted with GPS tracking. Supervisors must send the attendance verification from the field site so that their location travels as metadata, along with the attendance data. A location-based deviation report shows the supervisor's exact location on a map and his or her distance from the field site. This report is automatically generated and produced for the district program director. Upper-level bureaucrats believed that their access to information about supervisors' visits would motivate them to actually visit worksites and that their presence on the ground would deter field assistants from tampering with muster rolls.

Upper-level bureaucrats recruited supervisors from other rural development departments to take on the responsibility of inspecting worksites, as there were many worksites and the NREGA bureaucracy did not employ enough staff. Not all supervisors were excited about this extra work, as they felt they had nothing to do with NREGA. A few of them also resented the location-based monitoring of their work and took actions to undermine it. For example, location-based deviation reports showed that supervisors chose to update attendance reports from their offices, which were several kilometers away from the field location. The representatives of the software company that built the system told me some supervisors were reluctant to even use the system, but that upper-level bureaucrats forced them to do so. When a report showed deviation, supervisors typically blamed spotty network connectivity in rural areas for preventing them from sending updates directly from the field site. They also complained about the process used to tag worksites, claiming the locations had not been properly recorded and that the entire exercise was pointless since the deviation reports could not be trusted.

Upper-level bureaucrats responded to these complaints in two ways. First, they paid to have the central survey team revisit the worksites to tag them again.

Second, they implemented a software fix that made it possible for supervisors to cache worksite GPS locations on their phones and upload them when network connectivity became available. This caching feature enables supervisors to record the location of the field site even when a worksite does not have network service. The software on the phone automatically sends attendance data paired with the GPS location whenever the phone detects the network.

Compromises in Algorithmic Hiring

Upper-level bureaucrats also had to contend with pressures from local politicians who resented NREGA's diminishment of their power. The appointment of village-level field assistants is one of the key ways to control what happens at the last mile in the NREGA program. Because of this, upper-level bureaucrats took control of the hiring of employees who reported to them. To the extent possible, they hired temporary employees to run the program. Lower-level employees such as technical assistants, engineering consultants, and computer operators all had to appear at the state headquarters in Hyderabad for job interviews. Two positions were excluded from this requirement: mandal program development officer (the senior bureaucrat at the mandal level) and field assistant. The former is a permanent employee who is part of the regular bureaucracy that the state loans to the NREGA for a period of time. Field assistant is a village-level position.

In the past, the appointment of field-level functionaries in development programs had been left to locally elected political representatives. To gain control of the hiring of field assistants, upper-level bureaucrats created a computer algorithm to select these employees. The algorithm restricts who can be appointed to those in the top bracket of the number of days worked for NREGA during the previous year.

I relied on conversations with district-level officials to see how this worked and to understand whether they found the automatic system of algorithmic hiring to be a hindrance or a help. Their responses varied, depending on the place and the local political situation. In one case, the program director at the district level told me the software was a boon because he could hide behind the algorithm when a local politician insisted that he appoint a person the politician favored.[13] He could now tell the politician to appeal to upper-level bureaucrats since the computer program excluded him from hiring decisions and there was no way to override the program locally.[14] The digital system is thus facilitating and blocking transparency at the same time, a finding that resonates widely in the literature (Chaudhuri 2021; Furlong 2014; Hetherington 2011; Masiero 2015).

In some districts, however, when a politician's choices have not been honored, the politician blocks the appointment of field assistants and often refuses to sign off on the selection. Such resistance has meant that field-assistant positions have not been filled in many places where the local political power is too strong (Mukhopadhyay et al. 2013). Not being able to hire local field assistants effectively shuts down NREGA functioning in that village. Ultimately, upper-level bureaucrats were forced to settle on a compromise whereby the algorithm would pick the top three field-assistant candidates and allow local politicians to select among them.

Forcing Upper-Caste Workers to Work on Dalit Lands

Upper-level bureaucrats also attempted some social engineering. NREGA workers were poor but came from different castes. This sometimes meant that upper-caste workers were slotted to work alongside Dalit workers. In addition, upper-caste workers were made to work on lands in the village that lower-caste people owned. Historically, Dalits were the workers employed on lands that upper-caste people owned, but when upper-level bureaucrats centralized the creation of work groups, that process ignored identity in work assignments. Upper-caste workers complained and said they wanted to choose where they worked. Work had to be halted temporarily because of tensions between caste groups that had a history of conflict. In a few cases, workers withdrew from NREGA work because the work-group assignments disregarded prevailing social and cultural norms.

But such complaints were not typical. I asked one group of upper-caste men whether they would feel comfortable working on Dalit lands. One of them replied that they didn't have a problem working on any lands, as they needed the money. The rest nodded in agreement. When I asked how it was that there were no caste issues, he said, "It is not SC [scheduled caste; i.e., Dalit] land, it is government land." He said, "Therefore we don't have any SC feeling. We have government feeling." I pointed out that really Dalits owned the land because the government had recently given it to them. He replied that those lands were actually owned by upper-caste people who had given it to the government many years ago. He repeated that they would gladly go to the site and work because it was on government land. He also said that they got their wages directly from the state and not from Dalits. I asked, "What if the field assistant was not one of yours, a Kapu [upper caste], but an SC, would you go and work on Dalit lands?" He said, speaking on everybody's behalf, that they wouldn't see caste in the government worker; he was a government worker and they would go to work.

One of them added, "If we had to go work in Dalit-owned lands and [the job was] not part of the NREGA, then we would not go." I asked them why they would not go. They said, without any reluctance, that it would hurt their "feelings." Although the body language of everyone present indicated discomfort with this line of questioning, I persisted and asked "Why is that so?" One of them looked at me and said:

> See, imagine we are working on a Dalit land, it is hot out there and we take a break for a second, then the Dalit owner of the land would drive us to work and say something like. . . . "Hey you, go and do this work! Get up!" We don't want to hear those words! So that's why we wouldn't go.

Yes, the senior mate echoed, they didn't want to hear those words from Dalits. They were scared of those words. Perhaps they remember that they had done this to Dalit workers in the past and did not want the same treatment in revenge. Such rationalizations are a reflection of the social context of Andhra Pradesh. It is not conceivable that forcing upper-caste workers to work on Dalit lands would have resulted in such outcomes in a state like Bihar, where members of the upper castes would never consent to such an assignment. Technology makes certain changes possible but has to be responsive to what is politically feasible.

While it is clear that the caste engineering that upper-level bureaucrats have attempted does not extend beyond the NREGA, it forced upper-caste men and women to work on Dalit lands. An upper-level bureaucrat who is a Dalit himself said, "This is revolution. This is the first time we have higher-caste people working on Dalit lands."

As in so many decisions regarding NREGA, the practice of ignoring caste in work assignments did have unintended consequences. Lower-caste workers felt burdened because the centralized algorithm for forming groups did not allow for strategies to avoid local conflicts.[15] In response, upper-level bureaucrats issued a number of patches implementing a more flexible enforcement of rules. They changed the period of time when the composition of work groups was frozen from one year to six months. They also began allowing workers to change groups more frequently than six months if they registered a complaint.

Conclusion

In this chapter, I have illustrated how digital technology has become a central instrument in how NREGA is governed in Andhra Pradesh. Upper-level NREGA bureaucrats used technology to make transparent to them local bureaucratic records previously available only at the lower level. When lower-level bureaucrats attempted to avoid this gaze, their supervisors in Andhra Pradesh refined their control of and access to data by developing increasingly sophisticated automated tools.

They rely on a number of different ways to understand what is happening in the field. In addition to the digital data they receive, upper-level bureaucrats employ supervisors who randomly visit NREGA worksites to understand how NREGA works on the ground. Audits also reveal the latest ways that lower-level bureaucrats are subverting the system by educating themselves about how to avoid digitized scrutiny. Upper-level bureaucrats spend a great deal of time modifying the technology to cope with the actions of the lower-level bureaucrats. While a digital system makes it easy for upper-level bureaucrats to control those at lower levels, the latter continue to subvert technical fixes. In the final analysis, though, upper-level bureaucrats in Andhra Pradesh have used technology systems effectively to implement NREGA. The outcomes of these interventions will be discussed in later chapters.

The deployment of technology was inherently political and aimed to eliminate interference by politicians and lower-level bureaucrats at the last mile. By asking why and how technology actually changes over time, we can take into account the effects that technology causes. The conflict between upper-level bureaucrats and lower-level bureaucrats in NREGA happens in the realm of technology. The shift from paper to digital governance makes fraudulent behavior more visible but does not necessarily curtail it completely. The choice of technology at each stage has unanticipated outcomes that are caused by the technology itself.

I encountered two different kinds of stories about what motivated lower-level bureaucrats to circumvent transparency requirements. According to one kind of account, they engaged in hacks because they were simply corrupt and wanted to avoid the gaze of their supervisors. But from a different and more nuanced view, they were caught between the centralizing tendencies of upper-level bureaucrats and the demands of corrupt local politicians. Thus, sometimes they benefited from the patches because they enabled them to withstand local political pressures. The fact that upper-level bureaucrats selectively chose what needed to be digitized indicated that, at some level, they too were constrained by political concerns.

Because technology can be resisted and repurposed to unanticipated political ends by different actors, attention must be paid to changes in technology over time if we are to understand how they affect political realities on the ground. By foregrounding these design changes, we move from thinking about the need for these technology changes as a failure to plan to an approach that considers patching as part of the design process.

The story of technology within the bureaucracy was only part of the Andhra model of controlling the last-mile problem. The documents that were legible to upper-level bureaucrats were made transparent to NREGA workers and social auditors. This raises the question: How can a social audit institution that conducts such audits in scale across all the villages in Andhra Pradesh be created? This is the topic that I examine in the next chapter.

4
Patching Institutions

> Imagine an information department with the commitment of a [*sic*] NGO and the knowledge of a tout [broker] and his enthusiasm. We can go far in reworking the state.
>
> —Visvanathan (2008)

In Chapter 1, I discussed a confrontational public hearing that took place in Bihar in 2010. The Jan Jagaran Shakti Sanghatan (JJSS), a workers' union in Bihar, had organized the hearing to audit NREGA accounts. JJSS made use of these public hearings to expose corruption in NREGA. The meeting was intended to raise worker consciousness and to encourage public confrontation with local political leaders and bureaucrats in order to bring them to account. The raucous meeting ended with workers feeling good about their collective challenge to powerful village elites in a public forum, an event that one of them noted was rare in the remembered history of that village.

The vignette illustrates how social movements help strengthen and collectivize resistances from marginalized people, who otherwise must resort to spontaneous actions or private expressions of resistance that Scott memorably called the "weapons of the weak" (Scott 1985). Social movements offer a countervailing power to keep actions of state bureaucrats in check (Piven and Cloward 1978). In particular, the social audits organized by JJSS in Bihar and MKSS (Mazdoor Kisan Shakti Sangathan) in Rajasthan were an exercise in democratizing access to formerly closed government records and helping citizens "see the state" (Corbridge et al. 2005). Social movement–initiated audits rely on activists to politicize information in order to mobilize citizens, who in return make the state accountable.

Recall also from Chapter 1 the account of being accosted after the social audit meeting by an angry local contractor who had been exposed as having swindled public money. In no uncertain terms, he reminded us that while we would soon be gone from the village, he would remain, and so, by implication, would his corruption. After a few such encounters while conducting audits in different villages in Bihar, JJSS leaders became wary of continuing social audits without guarantees that the state would take action in response to the group's findings. JJSS worried that if it could not guarantee outcomes that would materially improve workers' situations, workers would not participate. In addition, while these public protests offered a forum for exercising the power to collectively express grievances, participating in such actions could also make the material situation of workers worse because of backlash from the local power system. In order to sustain the long-term institutional change necessary to bring corrupt officials to account, state support, JJSS realized, was crucial.

This chapter explores the remarkable evolutionary process by which upper-level bureaucrats in Andhra Pradesh with links to social movements created a social audit institution that met the requirements of both worker participation and state accountability. I explain how the state government in Andhra Pradesh collaborated with civil society activists to create a "participatory bureaucratic" audit institution that had autonomy (Aakella and Kidambi 2007a; Moffitt 2014).[1] How did bureaucrats and activists work together to resolve their myriad differences between mobilization and institutionalization? The official name for the institution is the Society for Social Audit, Accountability and Transparency (SSAAT). The process is colloquially referred to as "social audits," to differentiate it from financial audits and also to indicate that the audit process is not a closed-door process, but, rather, a *social* process that involves participation from the broader society.

I describe how the participatory bureaucratic audit institution came to be as a result of *patching* that focused on three distinct goals: recruiting activist auditors who had a commitment to marginalized residents of the state, gaining the trust of workers, and operating within the boundaries of what was politically feasible. While patching was initiated by a leadership team that consisted of upper-level bureaucrats, MKSS activists, and a few representatives from NGOs in Andhra Pradesh, the upper-level bureaucrats played the significant role in making the ultimate decision about the institutional form that social audits would take in Andhra Pradesh.

What form should such an institution take to deal with local power system? The three goals of recruitment of marginalized citizens, gaining trust, and operating within political constraints immediately raised the question of who should run social audits in Andhra Pradesh—the state or members of civil society? If the state needed to play a role, what exactly should that role be? Alternatively, should the audits be completely outsourced to civil society groups? The scale of the audits was also an important issue: Should each social audit cover entire districts at one time, or should it be conducted at the village level? The institution had to be iterated upon—patched—to deal with these challenges, which often involved focusing on very small details to change how it operated. The details ranged from who should be hired as an auditor, to what clothing the auditor should wear, to whether what they were allowed to eat mattered. All the three elements of patching—top-down, focused on small details, and iteration—were central to the evolving formation of the social audit institution in Andhra Pradesh.

Scholarship on social movements is highly suspicious of such state-driven collaborations with civil society. The classic position of these scholars is that when social movement demands become institutionalized, the state co-opts the movement (Piven and Cloward 1978; Meyer and Tarrow 1997). Heller argues that there is a tension between mobilization and institutionalization in efforts that brings social movement activists to work with the state. He asks, how do you retain the mobilization aspect of the movement yet institutionalize to attain scale? (Heller 2013). It is widely held that movements which become institutionalized will change course and become conservative, and then will be co-opted by the state. The implication is that it is better for these groups to operate from the outside and remain contentious (Piven and Cloward 1978).

On the other hand, there is support for coalitions in which the state and civil society actors are equal partners (Fox 1993; Heller 2000; Evans 1996; Ostrom 1990; Fung and Wright 2001; Baiocchi 2005). One such possibility is what Fox calls the "sandwich" strategy. He imagines a countervailing power from the grassroots ("below") that takes advantage of "openings from . . . reformist state bureaucrats" ("above"). Fox writes, "The term 'sandwich strategy' is shorthand for these coordinated coalitions among pro-accountability actors embedded in both state and society" (Fox 2015, 356; also see Fox 1993).

Sandwich strategies assume that civil society and the subnational state can come together when civil society has mobilized citizens. A recent example is Movimento dos Trabalhadores Sem Terra (MST), a social movement in Brazil where MST activists have assumed control of overseeing schools (Tarlau 2019). Tarlau finds that these partnerships are crucial for improving both state capacity and social movement capacity. But, ultimately, state-society partnerships of the MST kind that Tarlau writes about rest on the ability of social movement actors to penetrate the state to take control of state bureaucracies, a revolutionary possibility that is not common.

The audit structure that developed in Andhra Pradesh was different. Instead of seeing activists as operating fundamentally outside the state, I emphasize the possibilities that develop when activist bureaucrats actually create institutions that generate space for civil society actors to have a lasting influence. To recall, the mandate for social audits came from the NREGA legislation was originally placed there by activists and movements but, nevertheless, was still a top-down mandate that did not have the "joint intentionality" of state and society coming together.[2] That is, it was not the result of a social process from the civil society in Andhra Pradesh that found support in the bureaucracy; instead, it was an initiative by reformist bureaucrats in the state with strong leadership from key activists from MKSS, who had the networks in a few districts in Rajasthan but not in Andhra Pradesh.[3]

I call the audit institution a "participatory bureaucratic" institution to indicate that it is a bureaucracy in the Weberian sense, with norms, rules, office, documents, and paid officers (Moffitt 2014). It is "participatory" in that it involves NREGA workers, civil society members, recruits from the village to do the audits, outside activists, retired government and civil society members, and bureaucrats. It is, in other words, an institution designed for day-to-day oversight.

One of the strengths of the institution is its ambiguity; it is seen differently by different actors. Rather than viewing the audit institution through the lens of a fixed identity—a state institution, or a civil society institution, or simply to celebrate the extent to which social movements have penetrated the state institution (Tarlau 2019)—I argue that the position of ambiguity which the social audit institution in Andhra Pradesh managed to accomplish, i.e., being perceived differently by different actors, was integral to the legitimacy of the process and, ultimately, its autonomy.

In fact, the institution was not intended to be ambiguous. Its lack of precise definition emerged as an outcome of a power struggle at all levels, which, in the end, helped maintain the autonomy and objectivity of the audit process. The ambiguity also allows the structure itself to not ossify, and hence resist strategies for cooptation. At the leadership level, the director's role as an activist bureaucrat recruited from civil society was key to warding off pressures to make the audit unit completely autonomous. The recruitment process of the field-level auditors who conduct the audits are similarly seen to be different, with differing advantages. The lower-level bureaucrat views them as not part of the state and hence not easily captured. Workers see the auditors as an arm of the state, but one that is independent from the implementation unit, which gives the operation legitimacy. Thus, the process of maintaining such ambiguity is often resisted by different actors, for different reasons. However, the social audit institution did not have sanctioning powers over its findings. That power was entrusted in a separate vigilance department, which was controlled by the rural development department administering NREGA, an inherent limitation to the process.

In what follows, I identify three stages in the process of patching that resulted in the social audit institution achieving its current form. First, the upper-level bureaucrats in Andhra Pradesh imported a direct, MKSS-style audit at the village level that was run by members of civil society. One of the outcomes of that audit was the realization by the audit leadership that it was necessary to have bureaucrats attend the audit meeting so they could follow up on audit findings. The second major phase of patching was an audit in Anantapur that also replicated the social audit format MKSS had developed. This audit covered a large area and had support from both state bureaucrats and NGOs. The audit revealed multiple discrepancies that showed the political party in an unflattering light. This triggered a significant backlash from local politicians. They realized they had to gain better control of how the audit process was run, rather than yielding control to civil society groups, whom they could not keep in check. The outcome was that social audits in Andhra Pradesh are no longer conducted by civil society activists. The third stage of patching the social audit institution, its current form, differs from the first two in that audits in Andhra Pradesh are funded by the state but are conducted by auditors who contract with the state for the duration of the audit and do not enjoy permanent status.[4] Additionally, upper-level bureaucrats attend audit meetings and are empowered to impose fines on corrupt officials on the spot. Upper-level bureaucrats, who have retained control of the process, are strictly focused on the last mile, i.e., problems and irregularities of NREGA implementation as they pertain to the subdistrict (mandal) and below. This process brought upper-level bureaucrats back into the loop so they can take action in response to audit findings. Upper-level bureaucrats became the sole arbiter of the post-audit process, and their process of meting out fines is a closed-door process that they control. Tracing the patching processes revealed that while upper-level bureaucrats were initially very open to yielding control of the audit process to civil society, their experiences in the field changed that. The final result was a participatory bureaucratic setup in which upper-level bureaucrats retain control of the post-audit institution, and a social audit process is independently run by an autonomous institution. I have tried to reconstruct the events that led to the creation and maintenance of the audit institution based on interviews and informal conversations with senior activist auditors, upper-level bureaucrats, and members of civil society in Andhra Pradesh. The journey shows that patching was a necessity—conceptually and in practice—to sustain institutions that were responsive to problems and conflicts at each stage of the pilot process.

Piloting Social Audits in the Food for Work Program

The chief bureaucrat in Andhra Pradesh's Rural Development Department, Koppula Raju, is the progenitor of the social audit process in that state.[5] His department administers many of the development schemes in the state, including NREGA. During our interview,[6] he recalled how he and several others in senior bureaucratic circles had heard about the innovations of the MKSS in Rajasthan, a state in northern India.[7] The first thing Raju did when the Andhra government decided to implement social audits was to go to Rajasthan and witness the audits of MKSS firsthand.[8] The institutional mechanism and initial funding for this audit initiative derived from the United Kingdom's Department for International

Development. That department had been involved with the government of Andhra Pradesh for more than a decade, helping to modernize the state by creating strategic planning and innovation units in health, rural development, and education. To pilot the audits, Raju turned to the strategic planning and innovation unit in rural development. That unit contacted ActionAid International, an international NGO that had been involved in several grassroots projects and had a prominent presence in India. ActionAid in turn looked to MKSS for help and asked them to conduct a workshop.[9] The story that follows shows how MKSS began exerting its influence from the earliest days of the audit process in Andhra Pradesh.

MKSS activist Sowmya Kidambi, who now runs the social audit unit in Andhra Pradesh, is what I call a bureaucratic activist. Her first step after being contacted by Action Aid was to reject the state's initial request to run a workshop. Believing workshops to be essentially useless, she maintained that if state officials were really interested in learning about social audits, they should instead audit a real-world case. After she refused their request, state officials took a few months to get back to her, but eventually they came around and asked MKSS to train lower-level bureaucrats to do the audits. She responded, "We don't want to train the government people to do social audits. Why would I train a BDO [Block Development Officer] in conducting a social audit? Pointless, no? It is like teaching a thief how to catch thieves."[10] In fact, Sowmya Kidambi's pessimistic view of corrupt lower-level bureaucrats mirrored the way some upper-level bureaucrats also saw the problem, and she was easily able to convince them to involve NGOs as neutral third parties who would train state officials to conduct social audits. At this point, an ad hoc audit leadership team emerged, consisting of representatives from MKSS, ActionAid, and upper-level NREGA bureaucrats.

The audit leadership decided to conduct their first audit of the National Food for Work Programme, a central government public works program initiated in 2004 that provided food grains to the rural poor in exchange for manual work in the villages. One study had already analyzed the program and declared it to be a waste. Its authors concluded, "One of the most disturbing findings that emerges from this research is that almost everywhere we studied, panchayat officials and sarpanches were instrumental in the corruption of 'food for work'" (Deshingkar et al. 2005). Several newspaper reports suggested that local officials embezzled funds by fudging muster rolls, paying lower daily wages than the prescribed minimum wage, and taking bribes to allot work (Maiorano 2014). It is not surprising that the audit leadership chose to audit the Food for Work Programme, as they knew that it was corrupt and would reveal numerous discrepancies from the official records.[11] The audit team identified three villages to audit that were located close enough to Hyderabad to make it easy for upper-level bureaucrats to visit them. Instead of inviting lower-level bureaucrats to be trained for the Food for

Work audit, ActionAid asked each NGO in its network to send one person to be trained to do audits. The idea was to avoid any state interference in the audits and to build local capacity in civil society. The training was held in Hyderabad. Staff from thirty-two other NGOs from all over Andhra Pradesh attended the meeting. This was their first encounter with social audits.

An NGO worker and a senior auditor I interviewed who had attended this pilot audit of Food for Work recalled the training as hugely beneficial and worthwhile.[12] As she described the details of this 2006 pilot audit, I realized that the training template had not changed over the years; what she described was the same pattern I had encountered in NREGA audits during my fieldwork. The training process takes two days and is divided into two distinct parts. The first part, often half a day, is a lecture on the various elements of the RTI Act, followed by a series of speakers emphasizing the power of social audits. The second part involves learning by doing: the auditors are taught how to accurately examine audit reports, check for inconsistencies, cross-check reports against supporting documents, and verify official signatures (Brown and Duguid 1991).

In the early days of social audits, the work was much more laborious than it is now. During the 2006 pilot, records in Andhra Pradesh had not yet been computerized and auditors had to manually check Food for Work reports against data collected during audits. The NGO worker I spoke with remarked, "Nowadays it is as easy as removing a banana peel. All this [digital records] was not there then. It was done manually."[13]

I had firsthand experience of this in Bihar, where preparing documents for the audit was still a manual process in the summer of 2010. The documents had to be arranged and indexed to make it easy for auditors to cross-check information. The manual process was tedious and time-consuming; it often took several days to compile all the records. This part of the audit resembles a typical financial audit that accompanies most government processes.

The auditing process revealed many problems with the Food for Work documents, in particular the attendance register, commonly referred to as the muster roll. The auditor I interviewed recalled, "These documents were a dead giveaway that something was wrong. The muster rolls were neat, clean; everybody gets . . . so much grain. They were freshly written and given to us when we applied to get the document."[14] The immaculate physical condition of documents like the muster roll made it apparent to the auditors that they had been created just before the audit. The materiality of documents had a "social life" that often revealed the politics, in this case the corruption behind them (Brown and Duguid 2017; Hull 2012b; Finn et al. 2014). The fact that the documents were fake became even more apparent when the auditors talked to workers in the program.

While the auditing of records by laypeople is in itself a big step in democratizing the audit process and bringing to light obvious fabrications, the major innovation of social audits is that they extend the verification process to the field. Sowmya Kidambi, the senior auditor, explained the "go to the field stage" aspect of the MKSS audit:

> Whether you do it in Bihar, Jharkhand, Andhra Pradesh, Rajasthan, anywhere else, it is the same technique. . . . The technique is you take the record and go and ask the worker: Rajesh, the record says this much money and this much grain, did you get this or not?[15]

Sowmya was outlining the key difference between financial audits and social audits: talking to real people about the documents. The auditors took documents such as the muster roll and interviewed village residents in their homes. This process showed the differences between what was in the documents and what had actually transpired, at least according to the workers who were interviewed.

The next stage in the audit is the open public hearing, where auditors put forth their findings openly in the presence of workers, politicians, bureaucrats, and others in the village. But, as I discuss in Chapter 7, the negotiations that happen outside these formal meetings are equally important. The auditor I spoke with recalled that the night before the first public hearing in Andhra Pradesh, a small group approached the building where the auditors were staying.[16] The group showed the auditors a tattered document the laborers who had worked on the project had signed. It turned out they had been hired from outside the village and that machinery had been used to do much of the work. (The Food for Work Programme banned the use of machines that would displace workers; Deshingkar et al. 2005.) The information in the tattered notebook, which showed what had actually occurred, contradicted official records. The audit team used this notebook as evidence when they prepared their report and were ready to present it the next day. What happened next, and the role the MKSS activists played, shaped how audits in Andhra Pradesh are done today and is an example of the efficacy of patching as a response mechanism and corrective tool.

Approximately 250 people showed up for that meeting.[17] This was a large turnout compared to what I witnessed in later audits. The presentation started with the summary statistics recorded in the Food for Work Programme's official documents, including the total amount of money spent, the list of program-approved public works in the village, and the number of workers who had participated. Following that, the auditors presented their report, which revealed findings that differed from the official Food for Work Programme documents. At this point, the auditors seemed to be focused exclusively on numbers and there was no response from the people present.

Then, one senior MKSS activist who had come from Delhi to attend the audit meeting stood up and said: "I have come from Delhi. I am going back to Delhi and will tell people that all is well in Andhra Pradesh and it was a good experience for me to participate in."[18] This provocation worked. The villagers suddenly realized that the meeting was nearly over. Until that point they had sat silently through the reports of corrupt acts. However, when they realized the meeting was drawing to a close, they started making noise. A group of workers confronted the three sarpanches who were present. After the auditors' revelations, they knew who to blame for misappropriation of food grains. As the meeting tilted toward chaos, the local ActionAid organizers looked to MKSS activists for support. The activists seized the moment and directed the pressure toward the senior Food for Work Programme bureaucrat from the Rural Development Department who had come to address the meeting. This bureaucrat stood up and promised action. Soon after that, the workers returned to their seats. Although no framework yet existed for follow-up, a state bureaucrat had been forced to publicly state that future action would be taken. It was a crucial step in the recognition that it was necessary for upper-level bureaucrats to participate in audits to ensure that audit findings would be officially recorded. The Bihar experience also showed that workers would not continue to participate in audits if there was no accountability. It was clear that the presence of upper-level bureaucrats could legitimize these audits and ensure that the proceedings enter the official government record, the first step to taking action on these findings. Economist Biju Rao and sociologist Paromita Sanyal find statistical evidence supporting the claim that "lower" caste citizens talk when state officials are present at gram sabhas (Sanyal and Rao 2018). In their expansive study, which covered all four southern states in India, they found "the best functioning gram sabhas show that power inversion between citizens and the state can be socially engineered by the state [. . .] a critical role when it temporarily neutralizes power disparities among citizens by giving everyone the time and space in which to speak" (Sanyal and Rao 2018, 185).

After the public meeting of the Food for Work pilot audit in Andhra Pradesh, the top bureaucrat, Raju, held a debriefing session with all the auditors to discuss future strategy of audits for NREGA. He deemed the pilot audit a success. Raju was convinced that social audits would be an effective way to understand field realities, and he made the decision to conduct more pilot audits.[19] The upper-level Andhra Pradesh NREGA bureaucrats at the debriefing session were convinced that such blatant corruption was not occurring in NREGA and were keen to show off their ability to manage the program. There was discussion about where to conduct the next audit. The audit leadership quickly realized that if they did audits in each village, it would take ten years to audit the entire state. They began looking for ways to speed up audits in Andhra Pradesh.

Because MKSS had experimented with a massive social audit to cover an entire district in Rajasthan, upper-level NREGA bureaucrats in Andhra Pradesh, once again applying the concept of patching to change course, decided that the state should also experiment with mass social audits.[20] This is what they set out to replicate in Anantapur, a drought-prone district in Andhra Pradesh where YSR had first launched NREGA and where he came from.

Social Audits in Anantapur: High Expectations and Ruffled Feathers

Upper-level NREGA bureaucrats in Andhra Pradesh chose the district of Anantapur for the first official audit of NREGA in part because of YSR's history. In addition, a large number of NGOs were active in Anantapur and their members could be mobilized for audits. More than 1,500 volunteers from various parts of Anantapur, as well as the principal secretary of Andhra Pradesh's Rural Development Department, officials of the district's administration, representatives of voluntary organizations, elected representatives of the district, and representatives of MKSS took an oath to work together to encourage people to participate in the audit and exercise control over programs such as NREGA.[21] These vows were enshrined in a 2006 declaration called the "Anantapur Mass Social Audit Padayatra," which clearly enunciated the lofty goals of the audit:[22]

> The social audit helps bring out the strengths and the weaknesses in the implementation of the APREGS [NREGA] to ensure that the strengths are replicated and corrective action is taken where there are loopholes. The padayatra [audit] aims to create a strong alliance of those vested with administering the NREGA with those outside of it who genuinely wish to work together to achieve the principles and goals of the right to employment and minimum wage. This padayatra is a step to ensure that the entitlements under this law reach the people by creating the conditions for the proper implementation of the Act and scheme in its letter and spirit. It hopes to bring about awareness in the people about NREGA and to ensure that the non-negotiable facts in the NREGA would be met and to show solidarity with the wage seekers. The people from government, non-government, academicians, and intellectuals would work together to ensure that every wage seeker could seek labor with dignity.

The declaration was meant to engender the best possible level of cooperation between the various actors. It stated that all the stakeholders were united in the goal of ensuring that workers received the benefits[23] they were promised. While the rhetoric was idealistic, it also, shrewdly, focused attention on the last mile of delivery of NREGA wages. As mentioned earlier, the audit was not a result of grassroots mobilization by civil society groups in Andhra Pradesh seeking support from the state. Rather, it was a top-down process initiated by upper-level bureaucrats. However, it established a clear division of labor from the outset, a process of creating autonomy for the audit institution.

In the first NREGA audit in Anantapur, upper-level bureaucrats handed NREGA records over to NGOs with the promise that they would have full autonomy in administering the audits. Additionally, the state government sent instructions in a letter to district and mandal bureaucrats:[24]

> Since the Government is also a partner in the padayatra and is interested in ensuring that the whole exercise of APREGS [NREGA] is implemented well, I request you to pay personal attention to the following items of work. Further, the participants of the padayatra would be applying under the relevant sections of the Right to Information Act and NREGA for the above information. I request that this information may be made available immediately and without any negligence.

It was clear that despite (or in addition to) the auditors' invocation of the RTI Act, an internal government circular was also needed to legitimize their request and ensure that NREGA employees would honor it without creating delays. At every step of the way, the Andhra model of social audits relied on the support of the state. The letter demonstrates the state's desire to use the audit to showcase the success of NREGA:[25]

> Since honorable state and union ministers, several national and state government and non-government functionaries, academicians, and members of the media will also be present and this is the first of its kind event, I would like to showcase our administration as an efficient and responsive one. Hence I request you to kindly spare no efforts in making the padayatra a success.

One ActionAid activist who was a coordinator of the first mass audit told me that many of the bureaucrats expected that no serious violations would be found in NREGA. Thus, a lot was at stake and expectations were high.

This was the first time a state government program in India had allowed a public audit of its workings by civil-society actors on such a massive scale. In the inaugural address that launched the social audit process in Anantapur, one of the upper-level bureaucrats compared the padayatra to Mahatma Gandhi's march: "This social audit process is like the Dandi March of Mahatma Gandhi, which got us the freedom from the British. Freedom is our right, and we need to instill enthusiasm in the people in the villages."[26]

Again, one reason for upper-level bureaucrats' optimistic support for the audits was the assumption that the audits would show them in a good light.

They believed the implementation was perfect and that the auditors would not find anything amiss. That did not happen. The audits showed there was corruption in NREGA. One activist who attended the audits told me, "the results were shocking to the bureaucrats; against the initial expectation of no corruption, [we found that] there was a lot of corruption in NREGA."[27] Additionally, the audit process created a tense atmosphere in the villages, particularly with the lower-level bureaucrats who encountered it first. These bureaucrats felt that the whole audit process was aimed negatively at them. The official report of the audit noted that "more than social auditing it was *policing* [of the lower-level bureaucrats] that led to confrontation" [my emphasis].[28] Lower-level bureaucrats began threatening the auditors, ratcheting up the tension in the villages to even higher levels.

Without knowing the results of the audit, and thus still confident about the absence of corruption, the upper-level bureaucrats invited the media to attend the public hearing portion of the audit. Local members of political parties also showed up, in particular, members of the Indian National Congress. While state officials had promised that the auditors would conduct the hearing, upper-level NREGA bureaucrats ended up taking charge. They determined which parts of the audit team's findings were read aloud. One of the important parts of this meeting was to be an open discussion of the auditors' findings, but the upper-level bureaucrats did not permit that to happen, presumably because of the corruption that an open discussion would reveal.

Despite the best efforts of the upper-level bureaucrats to control the narrative and prevent negative information from being made public, the audit process still managed to ruffle a lot of feathers among members of the Indian National Congress and NREGA bureaucrats. Some members of civil society were upset that they had not received a fair hearing. Everyone walked away dissatisfied. In fact, the backlash from the local political party was so strong that no audit was allowed in the Anantapur district for two full years, even when other districts started to carry out smaller audits.

The shortcomings of the Anantapur experience set social audits in Andhra Pradesh on a new trajectory. There were diverging opinions about the reasons for its failure. The current director[29] of SSAAT felt in hindsight that district-wide audits were a mistake and should not have been attempted. According to her, the reason for the strong backlash from the political parties was because the audit covered the entire district, which raised too much attention. She felt if audits were restricted in scope, they could handle resistance locally. But the NGO members who served as auditors in Anantapur were disappointed that the government had not taken their opinions seriously. Some decided not to participate in future audits, while some waited to be called again.

Struggle for Control of the Social Audit Process

After the Anantapur audit, Raju organized a meeting of the ad hoc audit leadership team, whose members consisted of upper-level bureaucrats, activists from MKSS, and representatives of a few other NGOs. This group drafted new rules for mass audits. Once the rules were drafted, there was a wider consultation with civil society groups in Andhra Pradesh. The consultative process turned out to be a power struggle pitting the ad hoc audit leadership team and upper-level NREGA bureaucrats against key civil society groups. What was at stake was who should control the audit process and how it should be run.

One prominent NGO, a critic of the audit institution, accused the audit leadership of keeping the NGOs out. I asked Sowmya Kidambi about this criticism and she agreed that she was one of the persons who fought against having NGOs control the audit.

She said, "You cannot have, in terms of scale, 500 organisations doing 500 different kinds of social audits, with 500 different kinds of quality, 500 different kinds of norms, 500 different kinds of style. Not practical, it doesn't work."[30] She added that she was from the civil society and knew the NGOs intimately, better than the state bureaucrats. While her other bureaucrat colleagues viewed NGOs as a uniform entity, she had learned through implementing the pilot audits that NGOs rarely agreed with each other and fought among themselves about who should have access to doing the audits. She worried that paying NGOs to do social audits would lead to local capture of the auditors and would corrupt the audit process. She emphasized that the NGOs would never be able to prioritize audits and also implied they could not withstand pressures from the local power system. Another senior bureaucrat whom I interviewed allowed that "not all NGOs are equal."[31] He added that many of them had local political party connections that propped up NGOs to do their bidding.

Ultimately, the differences came down to control. Sowmya added, "See, it's so much easier for us to call our DRPs and SRPs [auditors] and have the schedules worked up. Look, the social audit is not a joke, you bloody have to go through one million things before you even have a single social audit to take place. [. . .] I can dictate through the social audit team, I can't dictate to an NGO."[32] She presented a hypothetical situation, "Let us say a particular NGO has a donor visiting. That fellow calls and says, "I can't start the audit tomorrow, my entire team is busy with this World Bank visit, we will do the audit after two weeks."[33] To me, that implied working with NGOs was not acceptable. She wasn't biased against any particular NGO, she insisted; even if MKSS decided to run the audits, she would be opposed. In her view, the role of the NGOs should be to not accept state money but to remain outside the state, come to the audits and monitor the proceedings and raise critical questions about the audit process. Ultimately, her vision prevailed.

These deliberations were internal, with a very small set of actors involved along with the highest-level bureaucrats. The NGOs were not included.

As a result of these restricted deliberations, the upper-level bureaucrats who had originally consented to the NGO demands that anyone be able to conduct the audits changed their position. They decided to build an audit institution funded by the state. They also decided that the findings of that audit group would be considered official. One NGO representative who was part of the consultative process was critical of this move:[34]

> The draft rules [of social audits in Andhra Pradesh] specified that the government need not do the social audit. Anybody can do social audits, and the government will fund. The findings will have the same bearing, and it would not matter who conducted the social audits. They [upper-level bureaucrats and members of the ad hoc audit leadership team] removed all that in the final draft. They defined the social audit finding: one that was done by the state. The draft rules created an opening for civil society to be part of the audit process, but the final audit resolution closed that opening.

Several members of the present-day audit team in Andhra Pradesh (the SSAAT) challenged this view. One of them asked me,[35] "Where are the NGOs today? Who is stopping them from using the Right to Information Act and doing a counter social audit on their own and contesting our audits? If they feel that the state audit team is captured [co-opted], let the NGOs do them and submit reports." The SSAAT activist auditors also felt that there was nothing to stop independent NGOs from conducting social audits. On the other hand, some NGOs who were involved in the first pilot felt that they were deliberately kept out of audits after the political backlash from the Anantapur audit. These groups wanted a formal relationship with the state in which the state would provide funds to run audits and their findings would be seen as official. As one activist summed it up:[36] "There were no active efforts from the state to include civil society actors. [. . .] If civil society actors are really serious, they can push it, they can make a hullabaloo and make their voices heard. But from both sides there was no active interest."

However, activists raised serious questions about whether the state should continue to control social audits. One activist asked rhetorically:[37]

> Who defines that social audit should mean [what is currently practiced]? It has become like a dictionary definition. No one should appropriate the word. Social audit is not trademarked. . . . There are ideological issues. . . . I am not trying to portray that civil society is an ideal thing. . . . There should not be any extra credit given to civil society. It is just an actor. The variability is what is interesting.

This activist was making a case for having many different types of social audits. He was arguing that the current form of social audits in Andhra Pradesh should not be the only type of audit, with the implication that some audits should not be part of an institutional process. What was at stake was who, if anyone, has the authority to conduct audits that are not run by state-sanctioned auditors but are still considered legitimate. Some NGO leaders felt that if they conducted audits, their results would not be considered official. Sowmya Kidambi disagreed fundamentally with the NGOs' demands to be insiders. She felt NGOs should come to the audit meeting as outsiders and raise critical questions. She feared "outsourcing" social audits to NGOs would lead to capture.

Ultimately this was a struggle about what information the state considers to be legitimate. NGO leaders wanted guarantees that state bureaucrats would act upon their audit findings. In software parlance, the NGO leaders wanted "write access" to the state; that is, they wanted to be able to write documents that the state would regard as official. NGOs did not want their audits to produce documents that were not considered proper evidence. They knew that if that were the case, workers would not participate in audits that did not lead to action against corrupt administrators. While the audit processes approved by the state had solved the legitimacy problem, the concern was that the findings of an independent audit run completely by an NGO would not be taken seriously.

One significant difference between social audits in Andhra Pradesh and those in other states is that in Andhra Pradesh state bureaucrats attend the public meetings associated with audits. During the MKSS audits in Rajasthan and the JJSS-organized audits I witnessed in Bihar, no state representatives were present to even acknowledge the findings of the audit in a public setting. In Bihar, as we saw in the opening vignette, although the local sarpanch admitted his guilt publicly, no accountability mechanisms were in place to force him to take corrective actions in response to the information the audits revealed. If upper-level state officials had been present at that meeting, they might have taken steps to ensure that workers received the money they were owed.

Ultimately, upper-level bureaucrats and the ad hoc audit leadership team decided to look inward and build their own audit institution, hiring individual NGO workers as senior auditors. The next section describes the institutional structure of what I refer to as the participatory bureaucratic audit.

Creation of SSAAT

In 2009, after these different experiments with audit structures, the upper-level bureaucrats created formally the Society for Social Audit, Accountability and Transparency (SSAAT).[38] This audit institution was funded by the state but was given independent status. Because upper-level bureaucrats viewed it as representative of civil society, they registered it as a "society." A government circular declared the SSAAT independent from the state in order to retain its "cutting edge machinery."[39] The principal secretary of rural development in Andhra Pradesh maintained that if the social audit process could be divided into three phases—pre-audit, audit, and post-audit—the audit phase could be largely left to the SSAAT. The most active role of the state (i.e., upper-level bureaucrats), he determined, should occur in the post-audit phase, when it would act on the findings. Its only role in the pre-audit phase should be to hand over the requested documents to the audit team.

The reasoning behind allowing separate entities to control different phases of the audit process was that upper-level NREGA bureaucrats wanted to go outside the traditional bureaucratic chain of command and mobilize non-state actors (in this case, the auditors) to oversee lower-level bureaucrats. Upper-level bureaucrats blamed lower-level bureaucrats and local political party members for the problem at the last mile. Their solution was to use the testimonies auditors obtained from workers as a check on the behavior of lower-level bureaucrats. The state did not rely on an organized civil society group in Andhra Pradesh; instead, it built a parallel institutional structure that included members of civil society to build SSAAT.[40]

In an interview, one upper-level bureaucrat pointed out to me that in Andhra Pradesh, the social audit unit director is not hired from the permanent government bureaucracy: the state has recruited an MKSS activist for that job.[41] It was an interesting observation in that while NREGA bureaucrats at every level think of the members of SSAAT as NGO people, NREGA workers and other villagers think of the audit team as representing the state. Lower-level bureaucrats regard SSAAT as a powerful actor that exerts authority without deserving its power. The audit management seems to enjoy this ambiguous position, but the field-level auditors do not appreciate the ambiguity. They do not like the fact that they work on contract and would prefer to see themselves as more definitively part of the state. They want permanent jobs.

A senior activist auditor of SSAAT told me that the audit unit is maintained in this way intentionally, so that auditors will not become part of the permanent bureaucracy. It was important for the audit leadership of SSAAT to be able to signal to NREGA workers that the auditors are not from the state, so they can win their trust. One way to do that is to ensure that the auditors are not permanent employees. Auditors have long demanded some form of government ID that they can display to prove their positions as state officers when they enter a village.[42] However, the SSAAT refuses to issue IDs because of its policy of keeping the auditors as activists and outside the state system. While the policy exists in principle to ensure that auditors do not have any special privileges, performativity also comes into play. The audit leadership wants workers to identify with the auditors. They want workers to see auditors walk into a state building without any state ID and get access to government documents. If the auditors can do that, so can the workers. That is the point of the no-ID policy, which is an amalgam of complex, competing interests.

Yet, the auditors are paid by the government. They are hired through temporary contracts that vary depending on the level of the auditor. The audit team is split into the administrative staff, which is located in an office in the state capital of Hyderabad, and the auditors at large, who assemble at villages for audits. As Table 4.1 shows, the field-level staff for an audit is distributed in a hierarchy that has three levels: state resource persons, district resource persons, and village social auditors.

Audits are organized at the mandal (subdistrict) level in Andhra Pradesh. One audit covers about twenty villages. Audit teams consist of village social auditors, several district resource persons, and one state resource monitor. Village social auditors report to the district resource person, who in turn reports to the state resource monitor. Each district resource person is responsible for managing the audit in a village and the hiring of several village social auditors. The state resource person is responsible for managing the entire audit in a mandal. To ensure compliance with the law, audits are supposed to be conducted by villagers; thus, the only level of employees with the word "auditor" in their title are the village social auditors. Others are facilitators with titles such as "monitor" and "resource person."

Table 4.1 Audit Team in a Mandal

Job Title	Number of Hires	Location	Status	Responsibilities
State resource person	1	Mobile	1-year renewable contract with the state	Administer all the audits in a mandal
District resource person	Varies (5–10)	Mobile	1-year renewable contract with state	Manage and participate in a village audit; attend a mandal public hearing
Village social auditors	50–100	Mobile	Hired on demand for one audit	Conduct house-to-house interviews with workers; visit job sites; compare NREGA data with data from workers; present audit findings at a public meeting

District resource persons hire local auditors at the village level at the beginning of every audit. The tenure of village social auditors lasts only for the duration of that particular audit, after which the unit is supposed to be disbanded. In practice, however, the district resource persons maintain a list of the most hardworking village social auditors and frequently summon them again and again to participate in audits. They are informally referred to as senior village social auditors. Some of these senior village social auditors have participated in more than fifty audits in the same district.

When district resource persons consider candidates for positions as auditors, they consider the legal, strategic, and ideological ramifications of each hire. Although NREGA mandates that villagers carry out the audit, the Andhra Pradesh social audit team recruits auditors from the sons and daughters of the workers who participate in the NREGA program because the law says that audits should be conducted by the gram sabha. However, the audit unit in Andhra Pradesh also added layers of management and effectively retained control of its own unit. In theory, having the audits conducted by the workers themselves or by their sons and daughters would make it possible for the social audit team to train young people to be a reserve army of transparency activists to effectively audit NREGA and other government programs on their own in the village. However, it is crucial that actors from outside the village control the audit in order to create autonomy from local political elites. Compromise is ongoing and there is a constant concern among upper-level NREGA bureaucrats that the audit institution will become part of the bureaucracy that it is aiming to monitor and reform.

While the state supplies the hiring budget, the SSAAT governs the hiring process. The state has significant influence in hiring the director and the senior audit management team, but the director has discretion on hiring officers below that rank. District resource persons are hired in Hyderabad; these people have usually risen through the ranks after starting as village social auditors. Clear guidelines govern the process of hiring district resource persons: they must complete a written test and an interview with the management. In my chats with village social auditors, I learned that those who had applied to be promoted to the level of district resource person did so by first expressing their interest to their current district resource person. Village social auditors thus usually have strong recommendations from a current district resource person and are then shortlisted for a district resource person position. A written exam tests their understanding of the law and the purposes of the audit. The interview usually focuses on an applicant's commitment to the cause. I have attended a few interviews that served more as avenues for communicating the ideology and the rhetoric of social audits than as actual interviews.

Most of the hires at the senior level are made by reaching out to NGOs. The process of hiring village social auditors, in contrast, happens at the village level.

The auditors have to be literate, a requirement that eliminates a number of people in every village, and they need to be able to write, preferably in English. Village social auditors are paid the minimum wage. Each audit team is headed by one state resource person. The audit is done at the mandal level. The number of district resource persons depends on the size of the mandal and its prior auditing history. Typically the range is five to ten district resource persons per audit.

On the first day of the audit, the district resource persons complete the recruitment of the village social auditors by going to the villages and finding literate young people. I describe this more extensively in Chapter 5. The senior management knows the importance of hiring the best village social auditors. I have attended workshops coordinated by the audit team in which discussions about the hiring process are dominated the agenda. As previously stated, NREGA rules mandate that care should be taken to hire sons and daughters of NREGA workers who are not part of any power structure.

Once auditors are hired, they are given assignments that are restricted according to where they are from. The rules depend on the hierarchy: state resource persons are not allowed to work in the district they are from; every six months or so, they rotate to different districts. District resource persons are not allowed to work in their own mandals, but they can work in the same district. Finally, village social auditors cannot be assigned to audit their own villages and are instead assigned to different villages in the same mandal. The policy was designed to prevent collusion and political pressure. As a result, district resource persons and state resource persons constantly travel from one place to another. There is no guarantee that they will come back to the same place again after six months. In many cases they do not come back, and if they do, they certainly do not work with the same teams. Although state resource persons want to develop teams with recognized and familiar cultures so that they can more easily manage the district resource persons under them, such efforts are undermined by the fact that they continually move to different towns and form new teams. This is to ensure there is no possibility of collusion between the audit team and the lower-level bureaucrats.

The current social audit mechanism consists of three stages. First, social auditors "open up" government documents that were previously not publicly available to workers, such as the muster rolls that record attendance and the measurement books that record details of NREGA works and their locations. In the course of an audit, auditors measure worksites to match their dimensions to records, read muster rolls aloud to workers to verify that the details in these documents match what the worker recalls, and record all discrepancies between the official records and what the auditors have learned.

In the second stage, the auditors conduct household surveys of workers, during which they initiate private discussions to give workers a chance to articulate their grievances about the NREGA program. They also solicit written testimonies that challenge details in the government records. When workers are willing, the private discussions are recorded in an audit document that bears the worker's signature or thumbprint.

In the third stage of the audit, the audit team presents their findings from all the villages of that mandal in an open public hearing. This hearing is typically held outside the mandal NREGA office. The auditors read out each audit finding publicly. Then members of the public are given a chance to speak. A district-level senior NREGA bureaucrat presides over this meeting and levies penalties in the form of fines, suspensions, or termination against bureaucrats who have been found to be corrupt. In some cases, representatives from the media are there. In troubled regions, police also attend. Social audit report documents are presented in public at the village level (gram sabha) and then at a mandal public hearing at the regional administrative hub. The latter is often more convenient for district bureaucrats to attend. These public hearings offer new opportunities for workers, through the audit process, to mount a critique of the state.

Gaining the trust of the workers is crucial. Because of this, it is important to show that the auditors are independent entities. A number of rules govern their actions in order to guarantee that they remain objective. This is not new; bureaucrats have always been subjected to rules that create a sense of procedural fairness. I was surprised, however, to find that the rules of social audits go beyond typical budgetary and procedural considerations. The rules for auditors focus on managing how the workers perceive them. MKSS had developed an elaborate set of micro-practices that were encoded as norms in Andhra Pradesh (Foucault 1977). These norms dictated where the auditors should stay in the village, what they should be seen eating during the audits, and even what sort of transportation they should be allowed to take. The auditors were to take public transportation when available or use shared auto rickshaws to commute to the villages. An activist (who was now an auditor) I interviewed recalled: "We had been instructed to stay only at the panchayati office or the school building. The government had given us money, but we had to find our own food. They wanted us to eat food at the laborers' houses."[43] These practices were intended to send a message to workers that auditors were outside the ambit of local power structures.

Although the auditors (even the district resource persons) come from modest backgrounds, they are supposed to dress professionally to bring respectability to the process. They are discouraged from eating meat and consuming alcohol during the audit. Meat eating is particularly a thorny issue for the auditors, as most of them are carnivores, and occasionally they do find a way to eat meat. One of the senior bureaucrats joked that the ban on meat eating is a Brahmin (upper-caste) conspiracy. A senior member of the audit team told me that the policy existed partly due to economic considerations, as meat is considered a luxury in the villages. In addition, there is a signaling issue: an auditor who eats meat and drinks alcohol is indicating that he or she has been co-opted. But, as the senior bureaucrat pointed out, the restriction of eating meat also signals that the audit process is controlled by upper-caste norms.

Similarly, rules specify where auditors can spend the night. In the initial phase of the audit, arrangements are made to ensure that the auditors stay at the mandal (subdistrict) office. When they go to the villages for the audit, they are supposed to stay only in a government building, such as a school or the local panchayat building. Negotiating access to these buildings is mediated through local bureaucrats.

Several auditors complained that these restrictions made their life difficult. While they grudgingly agreed to live in government buildings during the time of the audit, they found it challenging to follow the rules about modes of transportation and often borrowed motorcycles from lower-level bureaucrats to commute to villages, particularly during the process of hiring village social auditors. They also did not follow the practice of eating only at workers' houses; instead, they bought food from shops.

The question of whether or not the auditors are activists was constantly raised and had to be answered frequently in the meetings. It also came up in training workshops at the district level, in the content of the training, and even in private conversations. The official rhetoric is that the auditors should view themselves as activists. However, in one audit I observed, a senior member of the team asked a room full of district resource persons to raise their hand if they considered themselves activists. Much to my surprise, no hands went up, and the senior auditor then continued,[44] "Good. Let us keep it real: auditing is a job that you all are getting paid for, so you should all work hard to earn your living."

This discouragement notwithstanding, when auditors do think of themselves as activists, that mindset has real effects that motivate them to exert power and authority during audits. Activist auditors are able to do this throughout the audit. Their power wanes, however, as soon as their audit is finished. I have seen them realize that they have lost their power when the public hearing ends and local bureaucrats turn hostile. One auditor quipped, "We don't even get water afterwards, so better get it now."[45] Reflecting on the condition of the audit itself, the director of social audits told me:[46]

> When I compare MKSS and Andhra Pradesh, [there are few similarities] except for the fact that we have state support, we get information really easily, and we have public hearings and some form of follow-up action. I think what is missing from our side is that real streak of activism. MKSS will never ever compromise on going and eating at a worker's house. We never do that. No matter how difficult it is individually, they go to each house and eat, whereas I have not

> been able to enforce it at all: no matter how much I pushed them, saying each person should eat in a laborer's house. That's what makes the personal connection. But that's not what happened. I don't think it is just a question of scale. It is also a mindset. You also feel sarkari hai [part of the government]. Since they feel sarkari they prefer to eat in a hotel. That is something that bothers me.

Such reflection from the social auditor director is encouraging. While NREGA audits come up short in comparison to MKSS-style audits, they should also be compared with the financial audits that are part of the routine of any state bureaucracy, where state officials check the veracity of government documents in private. While NREGA social audits might not generate the same level of participation and contestation that an MKSS audit produces, they are consequential. The findings from the audit process are considered legitimated. They are scrutinized in public meetings where state officials are present and take action in response to the auditors' findings.[47] The fact that audits are held regularly (and the state acts on their findings) deters acts of corruption at the local level (Pande and Dubbudu, 2017). An activist who had been lobbying for decades in Andhra Pradesh on the issues of public transparency and accountability summarized one key difference: "Auditing is not a new thing, it has been happening for fifty years. It has always been behind closed doors. But in social audits the whole thing is going in the public for the first time. This is a revolutionary element."[48]

Conclusion

This chapter investigates the only state in India to regularize social audits: Andhra Pradesh.[49] It is a case of how a state government learned from a social movement how to audit a public works program, with an open process that would involve the broader society, and especially marginalized citizens, to keep the state system accountable. In particular, the chapter has traced the process of patching a distinctive form of an audit process that I am calling participatory bureaucratic audit institution in the state of Andhra Pradesh. The patching included: who has control of the audits, how many audits take place in a year, what the scale and coverage of a single audit is, who should preside over the public hearing, how should the auditors be hired, and most importantly, the ambiguity in how the audit was perceived. The audit structure that developed in Andhra Pradesh was not the result of a social process that found support in the bureaucracy; instead, it was an initiative by reformist bureaucrats in the state who imported the idea of social audits from a social movement (MKSS) in Rajasthan. The process started with recruiting one key activist (Sowmya Kidambi) from MKSS to run the social audit team (who as of this writing, fifteen years later, heads the Telangana social audit institution), as well as to retain two other activists from MKSS (Aruna Roy and Nikhil Dey) as part of the social audit board. As the weaknesses of existing implementation systems became clear, what was initially a consensual system involving state and civil society actors became a conflictual system exclusively run by the state. However, introspection by senior bureaucrats reintroduced civil society actors, in the form of temporary staff pulled from activist groups (in particular, MKSS), but with state-sanctioned authority to run social audits. Overall, what Andhra Pradesh has consolidated is a limited but effective institution that I call "participatory bureaucracy" (Moffitt 2014).

One key part of the process—and the patching—was how the ambiguity is maintained and engineered throughout the process, which plays a key role in maintaining objectivity. Instead of seeing activists as fundamentally outside the state, I have highlighted the possibilities that develop when activist bureaucrats are able to create institutions that create space for civil society actors to have a lasting influence.

This explained the transition of public hearings from a social movement protest audit that the MKSS conducted in Rajasthan to the participatory bureaucratic audit institution that is part of the state process in Andhra Pradesh. These audits are the result of the combination of a conducive political climate and experimentation by reformist bureaucrats who partnered with MKSS. The eventual form the NREGA audit institution took is a state-sponsored, embedded but autonomous institution that constitutes a civil society presence in the state. The process of institutionalization is a result of negotiation and compromises between key activists and upper-level bureaucrats, tempered by the political realities of Andhra Pradesh. As a result, social audits are regular events in every village in the state of Andhra Pradesh. A team of auditors scrutinizes NREGA documents and worksites every six months and opens up state accounts publicly in a village meeting. NREGA bureaucrats consider the audit findings to be official, and these findings become part of the bureaucratic record. Thus, the audit process is about "writing the state," a concept that I further explore in Chapter 5.

There is always the danger that the state could co-opt the audit institutions it has sanctioned. But so far this has not happened. As I have shown, this is partly because of the ambiguity of how the audit institution is seen by different actors. The upper-level bureaucrats see SSAAT auditors as activists. The lower-level bureaucrats see the SSAAT as a powerful independent actor that exerts authority. NREGA workers and other villagers think of the audit team as representing the state. The field-level auditors want to be part of the state, but the audit leadership want to retain their independence from the state. Perceptions matter.[50] However, much of the legitimacy of social audits in Andhra Pradesh comes from the fact that workers participate in them.[51] That is the topic of later chapters.

5
Public Meetings at the Last Mile

While the previous chapter showed how the institutional design evolved to facilitate audits in Andhra Pradesh, this chapter shows how social audit meetings were further shaped by political realities at the last mile. The participation of marginalized citizens in public meetings is essential: they can validate the auditors' findings. The promise of social audits is that, if performed in the open, they will lead to greater participation of marginalized citizens and prevent co-optation by local political actors. However, fully open meetings in unequal settings may lead to the capture of the process by local elites, rather than increased participation by marginalized citizens.

Social audits in Andhra Pradesh face an ongoing conundrum: How can they increase participation from NREGA workers while minimizing confrontation with hostile local elites? To answer this question, and to further explore the politics of state transparency at the last mile, this chapter analyzes three different types of public meetings, all aimed at increasing participation from marginalized citizens at the village level. These three meetings are (1) a mandatory village meeting known as a gram sabha that in Andhra Pradesh was organized by the local bureaucrats; (2) a meeting organized by a political party, called the rachabanda; and (3) an experimental social audit meeting organized by the audit team. The social audit meeting that is part of the NREGA will be the subject of the next chapter, but the discussions of public meetings in this chapter will help us understand the possibilities and limitations for outside actors to conduct these meetings.

The chapter begins with a discussion of gram sabhas. In 1992, an amendment to the Indian Constitution decentralized governance in India by increasing the role of village councils. Panchayati raj, as such decentralization is known, has been part of the national discussion ever since India gained independence from the United Kingdom in 1947. Yet, it was not until 1992 that the panchayats (village councils) were recognized as democratic bodies and were given a formal role in rural governance. The constitutional amendment created the institution of the gram sabha, a meeting at the village level.

I then discuss rachabandas, another type of public meeting in India that is coordinated by the ruling political party. My research shows that when public meetings are politicized, they are well attended. Participants attend largely as groups identified with a political party; in addition, the party is able to mobilize bureaucrats to be present. The combination of the strength that individual citizens acquire through membership in a political party and the fact that bureaucrats who have the power to address grievances attend rachabandas ensures that the concerns of the people will be addressed.

The chapter ends with an experimental social audit meeting organized by the social audit team I actively participated with in one village. We recruited members of a Dalit union, political party leaders, and local elites to attend the public NREGA audit meeting. We had hoped that membership in these different social groups would, first, motivate the workers to attend and, second, empower them to actively participate because of the strength derived from being part of the social groups. Instead, I found that the organizers of the meeting were unable to cope with this broad form of politics and that preexisting political rivalries derailed the possibility of focusing on the material goals of marginalized workers.

Gram Sabhas: Conversation without Conflict

In 1992, India passed a constitutional amendment that set in motion the decentralization of power to the village councils, or panchayats (Rao and Sanyal 2010). The amendment mandated that villages hold periodic public meetings called gram sabhas to increase "the scope for [citizens'] voice and agency" (Rao and Sanyal 2010, 147). The state's vision for gram sabhas was that they would function as citizen referendums on the decisions of the gram panchayats (village councils) regarding who is chosen as beneficiaries of antipoverty programs and how the resources of development programs should be allocated and distributed. The concept of discussion is central to this ideal vision of how gram sabhas should function: through dialogue about the decisions and actions of village councils, ordinary citizens would become active participants in democratic governance (Rao and Sanyal 2010). This section deals with the efficacy of the gram sabha as a public space for improving the accountability of Indian states to their citizens, particularly with regard to management of public services (Sanyal and Rao 2018).

The origins of the gram sabha derive from the former practice of having village elders arbitrate in local affairs. While it may not seem particularly democratic for five old men to make decisions for an entire village, the central government has reformed the current model of the gram sabha to serve the democratic function of increasing citizen participation in government procedures.[1]

Sociologist Paromita Sanyal and economist Biju Rao evaluated the empirical possibility in a comparative analysis of the four southern states of India, which includes Andhra Pradesh (Sanyal and Rao 2018). Their analysis of nearly 300 gram sabhas finds that the poor have indeed found a way to participate in the functioning of the state. They introduce the idea of "oral democracy," that is, the opportunity that gram sabhas give the poor to participate in state functioning through speaking in these assemblies. They show how some state governments were able to use public meetings to announce state policies, choose beneficiaries of public programs, and seek public input. The poor learn to experience the state by learning to articulate their private grievances as public issues the state needs to address. They conclude that "[gram sabhas] show that democracy can be strengthened and deepened by the simple but profound act of giving citizens the chance to speak and to be heard" (Sanyal and Rao 2018, 175). Most important, they find that in the four states where they conducted their research, marginalized citizens were generally not afraid to speak out in public meetings. However, they found that two factors seemed to be preconditions for the participation of ordinary citizens: gram sabhas should be held on a regular, predictable schedule and they should have "clout," i.e., the possibility that citizens' concerns and problems would actually be addressed and solved (Rao and Sanyal 2010, 168). This section relies on my study of the state-mandated gram sabha meetings. Because of Rao and Sanyal's findings (as well as the history of social mobilization by Dalit groups that I outlined in Chapter 1), I took for granted that citizens in Andhra Pradesh would be able to participate effectively in gram sabhas. I wanted to study the process of organization, i.e., learn how citizens are recruited to attend these meetings, where meetings are held, how easy it is for members of "lower castes" like Dalits to attend, and the attitudes of state bureaucrats toward conducting gram sabhas.

NREGA social audit meetings in the villages are a subset of state-mandated gram sabhas. The NREGA law mandates that gram sabhas be held to obtain citizen input on variety of issues concerning the program. Gram sabhas are supposed to be conducted to solicit citizens' demands for work, to decide where work should be conducted, and also to determine what the work schedule should be. However, as far as I could tell, the NREGA gram sabhas did not include participation from workers during the time of my fieldwork in Andhra Pradesh; they existed mostly on paper. Up to this point, I hadn't actually witnessed a NREGA gram sabha but had only seen photos of the meeting with a time stamp to prove that it indeed had taken place. While I am not implying that every NREGA gram sabha exists merely as a photograph, I did seek to highlight the possibility that what I saw in the mandated gram sabha could reflect a larger reality. There was a divergence between the institutional goal of enabling marginalized citizens to speak out and organizing gram sabhas in such a way as to inhibit or facilitate actual participation.

During my fieldwork, I administered a modified version of Rao and Sanyal's survey in fifty villages. This encompassed all the villages in two mandals. I chose these mandals because they were part of Rao and Sanyal's study and also because

I had already spent time in one of them and was therefore familiar with its social dynamics. I assembled my survey team from among NREGA's social auditors. It consisted of one woman and nine men, most in their early twenties. I translated Rao and Sanyal's questionnaire into Telugu, the local language. I ensured that none of the auditors on my team conducted the survey in his or her own village. In addition to the door-to-door work of my survey team, I personally administered the survey to participants at three gram sabha meetings.

In my discussions with economist Vijayendra Rao prior to attending my first gram sabha, he advised that I speak to inhabitants of the village, who would be able to help me discover the meeting. I did not understand why a public meeting like a gram sabha would need to be "discovered." However, I soon learned. It took two months of diligent tracking to find out when and where the meeting would take place. Obviously, a mandatory meeting of this kind was a rare event and missing it might mean losing the opportunity to observe one. In my efforts to obtain information, I followed the bureaucratic hierarchy down from the state capital to the district headquarters, to no avail. Even the district program directors did not seem to know whether the meeting would take place. They said they had not yet received the government circular informing them of the details. The social auditors I accompanied also knew no particulars about the meeting nor did the people in the village.

It was only several days before the meeting when I finally saw the government flyer. The mandal program development officer (MPDO) had received similar notification but said she had only skimmed it; after all, it was one of many circulars that she receives from the state. She was initially worried the state had sent me to ensure that her gram sabhas were conducted properly, but after witnessing my close relationships with the auditors, she came to accept that I was there from the United States to do fieldwork. It was at that point she confided to me that the meetings were a headache but had to be done because they were part of her job. The Andhra Pradesh government had further burdened the bureaucracy at this time because the current term for elected political representatives had expired but new assembly elections had not yet taken place. So the task of administering the gram sabha fell to local bureaucrats.

I was at the mandal office when a group of panchayati secretaries gathered to plan the gram sabha.[2] One of them later told me they were meeting to determine the schedule of the gram sabha, which was done without any input from villagers. To me, this was evidence that the meetings were not really about facilitating citizen participation. The secretaries divided up the mandal and appointed several senior bureaucrats from different departments to serve as observers.[3]

The protocol of announcing the gram sabha was the same in each village: someone with a tom-tom drum walked through the main areas of the village, yelling out the date and time for the meeting and announcing that bureaucrats from the mandal would be in attendance. All the gram sabhas in the mandal were to be held on the same day, making it exceedingly difficult for presiding bureaucrats to ensure they had people covering all the meetings (as it was for researchers also).

The meetings took place throughout the day. Levels of attendance varied, depending on the time of the meeting and the size of the village. Moreover, because the meetings tended to be held in government buildings in upper-caste areas, it was difficult for Dalits and members of the backward castes, who lived in distant neighborhoods, to take part. In a few meetings, the only people present were the bureaucrats. I attended one of these "empty" meetings and observed the responses from the bureaucrats. The presiding bureaucrat asked the panchayati secretary why no one had showed up. The panchayati secretary replied that it was not his village; he was simply filling in for somebody else. We stayed for twenty minutes, hoping somebody would appear, but despite the fact that the panchayati secretary asked a few villagers to join us, they all apologized and said they had work to do. A few people wandered in and the panchayati secretary immediately got his camera and took a photo to confirm "attendance" after asking those few to please stick around for a minute. The presiding bureaucrat recorded some impressions in his notebook to prove that the meeting had taken place. It was clear that the official government account bore no relation to reality, nothing to indicate the complete lack of attendance and the fact that nothing had been accomplished. This gives a clue to how some government bureaucrats handle gram sabhas.

It was clear that bureaucrats at the mandal deputized to run these meetings did not want to conduct them and were going through the motions simply to satisfy protocol. While their lack of interest is partly attributable to the fact that they were not supposed to be conducting mandatory gram sabhas and had been recruited at the last minute, rushed meetings are more the norm than the exception, as Gupta (2012) points out.[4] The minimal planning and foresight provide further evidence of the bureaucrats' lack of enthusiasm. This attitude is also common among higher-level bureaucrats. Under such circumstances, the probability of having a productive meeting is very low.

The content of the gram sabhas I attended varied depending on the interests of the people running them. Surprisingly, higher-level bureaucrats issued no instructions about meeting agendas. Often, the time was used to lecture villagers about citizenship without taking into account the issues that concerned them. In one meeting I attended, the panchayati secretary gave a state-of-the-village address in which he discussed various issues that concerned the village but also used the opportunity to give a civics lesson:

> If we want our streetlights to be fixed, water pumps fixed, when we don't have money in our panchayatis, where will we go? Everyone should pay taxes. If a motor burns out, where will the funds come from? . . . Say you buy a land with one lakh; in that, 4 percent is given by the government to our panchayati. So that money we should utilize only for lights, hand pumps, and similar items. We should not use it for other things. . . . Who has paid taxes? No one has paid. Only when everyone pays can we get things done, fixing the lights, the pumps etc. . . . Where will we get all the funds? The government will not give all the funds. We are given only so much, on the basis of our population. That we should remember.

He also gave a tutorial on cleanliness, declaring that it required the cooperation of many people:

> What is cleanliness? We should keep our lanes and our panchayati office as clean as we keep our houses. We spend INR 10,000 to have the municipality people clean our village, the very next day it is covered with dirt again. Can I get this done all by myself? Only when all of you support me can I do something about it. . . . Only if all you cooperate can I do something. Putting money in this is not a great thing.

Throughout his speech he emphasized the responsibility of citizens to take care of the village. I was struck by the fact that no one challenged his assertions, even though they went on for some time.

Actually, people didn't seem to pay close attention to what was being said. Some tried to get up and leave but were told to wait. They reluctantly sat down but then appeared to have questions of their own. A man (who lived in the Dalit habitation) raised the issue of why a well had not been drilled in his village: "Why is it that we still don't have that facility in my neighborhood when other neighborhoods have it?" The question clearly touched on the sore subject of caste differences, but the panchayati secretary skirted this by replying that there had been no funds for it. He reassured the man that when there were funds, the well would be first on the agenda.

After the meeting, I caught up with the man who had asked the question. He told me, "Even ten years ago we would not have dared to bring up an issue like this. Things have changed now. It is a different generation now. We don't talk to them [upper-caste village residents] unless we are given respect. We are not dependent on them for work. There is no dependence." I also asked the surveyors for their impressions of the willingness of Dalits to speak at gram sabhas, and before I had even finished my question, several of the surveyors were responding: "People are not afraid. They are talking in groups. The women are particularly effective in talking. Ladies make the officers stand and talk." I sensed that my survey team, many of whom were from the Dalit caste, were eager to portray a changing world. They clearly desired to paint a picture of a society in which caste had been overcome. But as soon as I asked about marriage and inquired whether people could marry across castes, they said, "No way. That is not happening." One of them added, "Even if you wait 5,000 years that will not change. Feelings are not there on our side, and the upper castes won't allow it. Only love marriages are a way to achieve it." This is a stark reminder that even though there have been significant transformations in Dalit rights, caste relations continue to define village life.

To get a better sense of where governments meetings happen, I asked my survey team if it was a problem that the gram sabhas often take place in the panchayati office or the school building, typically upper-caste establishments. Several nodded, saying, "Yes, that is a big issue," although they had not mentioned it to me before. It was taken for granted that the formal meetings organized by bureaucrats would always be situated in areas where Dalits cannot come. One of them said that the reverse is true, too: if the meeting takes place in a Dalit area, nobody from the upper-caste areas will come. If the meeting is held in an upper-caste area, he added, there is a chance of attracting a few Dalits but not the other way around. Significantly, the bureaucrats seem to give no thought to these considerations. Such practices have been routinized and solidified, thereby excluding the participation of certain social classes entirely. One of my surveyors suggested that meetings be conducted at the neighborhood level rather than the village level. While a few expressed support for this idea, all agreed it would be difficult to implement as each village typically consists of ten to twenty neighborhoods. One of the surveyors pointed out that if the state attempted to conduct neighborhood sabhas, the process would become too political and too difficult to organize.[5]

The surveyors and I were quickly able to identify which powerful figures in the villages were missing from the meetings. Representatives of political parties and sarpanches (village heads) were largely absent. The sarpanches are no longer in power, and in a few places the villagers were aware of the significance of this. The sarpanches who did show up asked questions, hoping that some of their complaints could be resolved. The mandal bureaucrats who presided over the meetings were given clear instructions; one surveyor overheard a conversation between officers in which the mandal program-development officer said, "Any problems that people are raising, just reply that we will solve them." Such pat assurances were not necessarily empty; in some cases, the MPDO would call the department responsible for the issue in question and ask why it had not been resolved. I was excited about the possibility that the meetings were actually being used as forums for solving problems. But one of the surveyors quipped that the real gram sabhas were in fact the rachabanda meetings. As soon as rachabandas were mentioned, several members of the survey team lit up with enthusiasm. When I asked what the main difference was between the two types of meetings, they responded in unison: "It is the presence of the political party people."

The state of gram sabhas is as much a story of bureaucratic calculation as it is a story of bureaucratic ineptitude. In Andhra Pradesh, there has been a systematic undermining of the local gram sabhas as an institution because of the views of the higher-level bureaucrats who sought to centralize power. I agree with Sanyal and Rao's assessment (Sanyal and Rao 2018) that state support is important to ensure that these gram sabhas are functional, but would add that there seems to be no possibility of that in Andhra as the entire state apparatus in Andhra Pradesh—higher-level bureaucrats, lower-level bureaucrats, and the political party in power and in opposition—rejects this forum.

A Rachabanda Meeting: Public Display of Political Party Power

The political party in power organizes rachabanda meetings as a public display of power. All the local mandal bureaucrats who are present in a village attend. The meetings are political in the sense that they are organized to show that the political party is responsive to the needs of citizens and can solve concrete problems by assembling the entire bureaucracy of various departments in the mandal. The purpose of a rachabanda meeting is to ensure that people's complaints are heard and resolved. Normally, the bureaucrats stay put in the mandal offices; thus, seeing them together in the village is a rare sight. The meeting elicits the maximum participation from village residents because political leaders come and also because the bureaucrats are forced to address or at least listen to the concerns of the village.

Within minutes of mentioning the rachabanda meetings, I was informed they were not a creation of the current political party but had been started by the Telugu Desam Party (TDP) leader. When I asked one of my interviewees at a gram sabha about rachabanda meetings, he said, "Everybody comes to those meetings. The political party people, all the department people are there. The earlier version of the rachabanda program used to be called Janmabhoomi when the TDP were in power. Now they have changed their name. Fighting will happen in those meetings. Rachabanda is the true gram sabha; this [gram sabha] is not real."

Rachabanda meetings mobilize entire bureaucratic offices at the mandal level to travel to the villages in an attempt to impress the locals and reduce coordination costs among the bureaucrats. When I attended a rachabanda gathering, it was easy to see that it resembled a political rally. The meeting started off with a speech written by the chief minister, read out by one of his representatives:

> From the previous rachabanda program, we have understood what you are expecting from our government, we understood what you want and need. Those who work for you wholeheartedly, those who respond to your problems, they have seen how much you appreciate them firsthand. That appreciation of yours is what is encouraging us to come to you again and again. For this new rachabanda program, you are the inspiration. To fulfill the promises made in the first rachabanda program, we have listened to your problems and have promised to solve them. As we are those who serve you, it is our responsibility to solve your problems, and it is for that we are holding this second rachabanda. In the first rachabanda, with 2,500 crore rupees, 26 lakh people have benefited with ration cards, pensions, indiramma houses, 0.25% interest. . . . All these services were delivered. In that rachabanda, whosoever was eligible for these schemes, we took applications from them. All those applications were screened, and the eligible ones were recognized. . . . More schemes and more programs. For the benefit of farmers, there will be no interest for loans up to 1 lakh. . . . In the state, with a goal of having no poor person striving with hunger, we have started a great and humanitarian scheme of providing 1 kg of rice for 1 rupee. To make this program available to more people, through this rachabanda we are going to issue new, 24-lakh ration cards to eligible poor people. . . . Come, participate in rachabanda and make these schemes and programs a success. Enjoy the benefits of these schemes, and we are hopeful that you will bless us who are working day and night to fill your lives with light. Your Kiran Kumar Reddy garu, CM [Chief Minister] of AP.

The meeting thus began with the political party taking credit for solving the problems of the citizens while conveying that elected officials were listening to its members. It also served as an opportunity for the political party in power to announce new development programs and to identify and resolve problems with the delivery of public services. Typically, the politicians who ran these meetings used them to pinpoint failures in the bureaucracy. One politician from the Congress Party said:

> However much we do, we will have shortfalls and more requirements, and the responsibility of fulfilling those is on us, specifically on the bureaucrats. . . . In the first rachabanda, no matter how many homes were given, more will still be needed. In a similar manner, ration cards, livelihood measures, all these issues need to be addressed in this rachabanda, and I am reminding the bureaucrats.

The reason for the high level of participation among the villagers was the presence of political support plus the fact that since all the mandal bureaucrats were present, they could solve problems on the spot.[6] Nevertheless, not everybody agreed with the claim that the party in power was solving new problems. One activist said, "The meetings are a way to ensure that the state gets credit for work they were supposed to have done already." Due to the political nature of the rachabanda meetings, people associate them with the chief minister of the state. Thus, the politicians are there to be seen getting things done.

I attended two rachabanda meetings. One had a bigger political presence and was organized like a rally. There were booths tended by lower-level bureaucrats who were collecting petitions. The state issued receipts to acknowledge that they had collected these petitions, but speculation on their impending fate varied, depending on whom I spoke to. One person claimed there was no way the petitions would be looked at systematically, and another insisted they would immediately be dumped in a wastebasket. In some cases, local politicians who served as intermediaries between the bureaucrats and citizens backed some of the petitions to give them additional weight.

Multiple conversations took place simultaneously. Each bureaucrat had a group clustered around him, and political party members served as representatives of citizens and spoke on their behalf. Police intervened to keep the meeting from becoming unmanageable. At the rachabanda, bureaucrats who are used to dealing with individual complaints from the comfort of their offices have to deal in public with workers mobilized by political groups.

In many ways, the rachabanda meetings I witnessed were huge successes. This was certainly the case with respect to the attendance of all concerned parties. They are very different from the NREGA audit meetings, from which political parties are excluded. They are also a distinct contrast to the state-mandated gram sabhas I attended in fifty villages, which are merely ceremonial exercises that do not have much to offer citizens. Rachabanda meetings demonstrate that, if there is political will, local bureaucrats can be made to attend at the beckon of the political party. But they are one-off events, intended to show political power but not to dig up corruption in public programs. In addition, rachabanda meetings take place at the whim of the party in power and are therefore not a regulated, reliable tool of governance.

Uncontrolled Participation: An Experimental Audit Meeting

In this audit, I was engaged as a researcher in participant observation who sometimes encouraged the auditors to ask questions that went beyond the audit script. Usually, I was able to retain my identity as an independent researcher when not shadowing the auditors. However, when I accompanied the auditors as they did their work, people sometimes assumed I was part of the audit team. This confusion, however, often led to productive conversations that I exploited in the interest of learning as much as possible about the auditing process.[7]

I wanted to understand how workers are embedded in a village as members of different groups and to gain their participation as members of these groups, while at the same time approaching them as individuals. A typical NREGA audit expects individual workers to talk to outside auditors without any intermediaries; in other words, workers are summoned as individuals to participate in audits (Shankar 2010).

But these encounters often require a lot of faith on the part of the workers. We wanted to see whether we could communicate with them through a trusted political intermediary who could support the workers who were willing to talk to us. We looked for groups that these workers were part of, such as Dalit worker groups and political party affiliations that would encourage workers to speak out not just as individuals, but as people with the power and backing of a group.

We also wanted the meeting to be well attended by the entire village, and thus ensured that it was scheduled at a time that made it easy for marginalized workers within the village to attend.

The audit team is guided by rules and norms established in the training sessions and periodic workshops I described in Chapter 4. Some rules are difficult to follow in practice, especially the mandate that auditors maintain a distinct identity from NREGA field bureaucrats. The purpose is obviously to prevent collusion between the two units and to maintain the image of an objective audit so workers will come forward without fear. But in reality, auditors sometimes depend on the help and support of NREGA bureaucrats and are inevitably identified with them in the eyes of the villagers.

The first task in the audit is to recruit local auditors from throughout the mandal. The audit team includes a senior resource person, who heads the entire audit for the mandal, and the district resource person, who heads at the village level. Each audit team typically has one senior resource person and a number of district resource persons, depending on the size of the mandal. Each district resource person is responsible for hiring local social auditors. Typically, the village is located within a radius of twenty miles from the mandal office, and the lack of adequate transportation and poor road conditions make travel difficult. Local bureaucrats know the terrain and also where to find potential auditors. Thus, while delegating some tasks to NREGA bureaucrats violates the regulations of the audit, even the best-intentioned district resource person usually asks the local field assistant for help in finding local auditors. The most common practice is for the district resource person to travel with the field assistant by motorbike to each village. I traveled with them on a few occasions, and in each case the field assistant took us to the village square, where the district resource person asked around to find a literate person interested in working for the audit.

There are only a few literate people in each village. One of them told me literate people are the default participants in the village for every government project. A number of state-run initiatives only hire local people to conduct surveys, since it is cheaper and more effective to recruit individuals familiar with the local area. As a result, the few educated youths in each village are used to carry out surveys.

The interview for the job of auditor is very brief. It consists of the following questions: "Are you interested in working as an auditor for a period of two weeks? Do you know how to read and write? What are you doing now? Do you have any connection to the field assistant or to the local political party?" Technically, if the potential surveyors are connected to the field assistant or the local political party, they cannot be hired. In practice, however, political connections are so common they cannot be avoided. The real safeguard in the audit process is appointing auditors to work in villages other than their own.

The number of district resource persons assembled for an audit varies depending upon the size and complexity of the audit.[8] District resource persons divide up the villages among themselves and recruit local auditors. Once all the auditors have been hired, four or five of them are assigned to a particular district resource person for the duration of the audit. Typically each district resource person is required to conduct the audit in two villages. I noted a marked range in the sincerity and motivation of the district resource persons and their teams. The district resource person I shadowed—"John"—appeared very enthusiastic about the audit process, and I soon discovered he had a reputation for being a hard-working auditor.[9]

John emphasized how critical it is to pick the right social auditors from the village for the job. Significantly, women are not the first chosen. According to John, the presence of female auditors creates complications for district resource persons. Sometimes, he said, the women complain they cannot walk for long distances. In addition, the district resource person is responsible for their safety. Because the audit requires local auditors to relocate to the mandal office and stay with the audit team overnight in order to safeguard them from pressure from villagers, the absence of gendered facilities often becomes a problem.[10] I have seen cases where interested female recruits were forbidden by their parents or by the village head to work with the audit team. Despite these constraints, however, in the audits I witnessed a small number (around 10 percent) of the auditors were women.

As this discussion shows, these seemingly mundane decisions about where to stay, the politics of selecting auditors, gender, and the connections to power have consequences. In the state-level training meetings I attended, the higher-level auditors brought up such issues frequently to emphasize how crucial these decisions are to the ultimate success of the audits.

After the teams were selected and the auditors did an initial inspection of the mandal's documents, we were ready to leave for our assigned villages. The journey was not inconsequential, even though the village was not far away. The team I was shadowing waited for an auto-rickshaw to transport us. Bus service is infrequent, so auto-rickshaws are a more reliable form of travel. These were "share autos" and the team far exceeded the allowed capacity in weight, but the charge was nominal.[11] Each team was given a bag to carry their files in, including the consolidated reports, muster rolls, and payment vouchers. An auditor usually carried the bag, which was quite heavy.

The auto-rickshaw dropped us at the village square, where the field assistant was waiting. He took us to an empty house which he said was ours for the duration of the audit. However, the district resource person did not seem happy about this and told us we couldn't stay there. I was aware of the rule specifying that auditors be housed in public buildings but was curious to know why the district resource person was concerned, as it was an empty house. When I asked about this, he said the field assistant had chosen the house and that it belonged to one of his associates, which made it unsuitable. The district resource person was concerned about the appearance of being co-opted and wanted to avoid any impression that the audit team was associated with or influenced by the field assistant. While his concerns were in line with the NREGA policy, I sensed something else simmering below the surface regarding the field assistant. I would later learn my suspicions were correct.

We lugged our bags to the school building. Within minutes, the former sarpanch arrived on his motorbike. The district resource person introduced the audit team to him, explaining that we had come from the state government to conduct a social audit of NREGA. After talking on the phone, the sarpanch handed him the keys to the school, which was very modest. The village, like other villages in Andhra Pradesh, was segregated along caste lines. NREGA work in the village was done mainly by Dalits and the backward castes; thus, the school we stayed in was in the Dalit neighborhood.

The auditors started getting their documents in order, and even though it was growing dark, I ventured out to talk to the villagers. The school's veranda seemed to double as a hangout for local youth, all men in their twenties. They had a television with them and were watching a cricket match. This particular group had a tough reputation and played their part, talking loudly and catcalling. I couldn't resist watching the game with them on the veranda. After a while one of the men asked why we were in the village. I told him about the audit and also about my own research. He nodded and returned to the game. Then, gradually, the rest of the men started talking to me. They had seen the auditors before in their village;

in fact, this was the fourth round of audits in this mandal.[12] One of them said, "We know everything that happens in the village with respect to NREGA, but we won't be talking to the auditors." In their view, the audits were all shams and they wouldn't waste their time and compromise their position in the village. They worried that being seen cooperating with the auditors would upset the local elites. I was a bit confused as to why these men were summarily dismissing the audit team. It would only be apparent to me after the audit how delicate the political divisions were in the village.

The audit started at 6:00 a.m. in order to catch workers before they left for the day. It was hot even then and would become unbearable later. The four auditors split into two pairs. They were tasked with talking only to workers whose names were on the muster roll. And they were to interview these people in their homes, as they needed to see an NREGA job card to ensure they were speaking with the right person. The auditors asked for other documents, too, such as bank passbooks and payment slips, which serve as additional proof that the worker had in fact been working.[13] Asking for these documents signaled that the auditor was part of a state enterprise; there is a thin line between information and surveillance in the audit. Because of the importance of these documents, the auditors often tell the workers: "Do not give the documents to anybody. Keep them safe. They are your proof." In the interactions I witnessed, the request for documents served both as a conversation starter and as a focusing gesture to establish the authority of the auditor.

The auditing process is fairly routinized. Each district resource person has supervised many audits, though for most village social auditors, the audits occur only every six months.[14] In each interview, the auditors asked the workers how much they had worked, where they had worked, and if they had been paid the amount listed on their documents. Despite the ordinariness of the questions in the household survey, asking them is a substantial task. One ambiguity involves translation: the auditors have to convert survey questions into language that uses local references the villagers easily understand. This process of mentally converting the language of written questions is time-consuming, at least for the initial interviews. The need for the process is especially acute when discussing the nature of particular jobs. The term on the official documents is often not the term the workers use. Further ambiguity arises because workers' recollection of time is often difficult to pin down, which results in confusion when they are asked to recall how much work they did. This is also true with regard to wages: workers often do not remember precisely how much they were paid for a particular task, and their memories become less reliable the further back in time the auditors' questions go.[15]

Asking so many questions often takes time, but the auditors also need to rush to reach all the workers in the muster roll. They are required to interview every single one; there is no sampling strategy. This requirement puts enormous pressure on them to move quickly from house to house, and if a worker is not at home when the auditors visit, they are usually marked as "no shows" in the audit report and are forgotten.[16] The auditors optimize their time by developing shortcuts, quickly jotting down the essentials during door-to-door visits and then completing the reports in longhand later, when they are back at their village headquarters or the mandal office.[17] Because speed is essential, there is a range in the attention auditors give each worker that depends on the level of reciprocity he or she senses. The district resource person constantly reminded me that just visiting every worker and checking every worksite is a herculean task, and my experience of it was indeed physically exhausting.

Once in a while, auditors would talk about entitlements and ask the workers if they were satisfied with the NREGA and receiving the non-monetary benefits offered to them by law. While the district resource person was waiting for someone to answer the door, he or she would send a village social auditor ahead to the next house to inspect the next worker's job card.

John was trying hard to impress me. He would often ask, "What should I do differently? You are an independent observer, why don't you tell me what to do?" He had heard my conversation with the local youth and noted their comment that the audits were a sham. Slowly, with my encouragement, he began deviating from the script for the interviews, talking more freely to the villagers. We also paused and conversed with people who were not on the muster roll, asking questions that enabled us to better understand local political realities. We talked about the local elites, who were the big landlords, which political party controlled the village, and the divisions in the village. We found that the village was divided into political factions and the details of that conflict were overwhelming, and we as auditors from the outside could barely keep up.

Our deviations slowed the audit process considerably. John had been assigned to cover two villages in this audit, but at the speed we were going, we would have trouble covering even one. I recalled a conversation I'd had earlier with the state resource person, John's boss. He had worked at an NGO for several years and complained to me about the number of audits they had to finish in one term and the time pressure that pervades the audits as a result. Because of the rush, he said, they were not able to do a thorough investigation in each village. I also remembered previous conversations with the social audit leaders back in Hyderabad. I had asked about the limited time assigned for each audit, and the audit director told me:

> You have to create the time. Nobody is telling you to complete the audit in a certain time period. I say if you need 20 days for an audit, spend 20 days in the field. I have never stopped them [from] spending more time in an audit. Planning is

> in their hands. How many days are required to do an audit is in their hands. Expenditure I question, however. If it is going to take longer, I want you to tell me why you are taking more than ten days. Expenditure tabs should be there.

Confident that I had full support from the director, the senior resource person, and, most important, the district resource person (John), I suggested we spend more time in the village to get more detailed information.

Clearly, more time in the village meant we needed more auditors. We reached out to the state resource person, John's boss, who oversaw the audit, and he immediately agreed to find somebody else to survey John's other village. We now started extending the conversation at each house. Outside one residence was an oversized poster of the famous leader Ambedkar.[18] Gesturing toward it, I asked the homeowner if he was a union leader. He said no, but offered that he was president of the Ambedkar Association. Many villages, particularly in Dalit neighborhoods, declare their allegiance to their hero with a statue, but there was none in this village. The homeowner/Ambedkar Association leader told me there had been a dispute over who would pay for the statue and who would dedicate it, an indication of division among the Dalits.

As soon as he learned that I had come from the United States, he began speaking in a different tone.[19] He was a literate man in his late thirties, though in appearance he looked to be in his fifties. He told us the field assistant had come to the village the previous day and had instructed everybody not to cooperate with the auditors. He had also warned that if they did allow themselves to be interviewed, NREGA might be canceled. But, then, the Ambedkarian leader said, the field assistant had added, "Don't worry, I will get your testimonies."

To our surprise, people started slowly trickling into the house. The Ambedkarian asked them if they were happy with their NREGA wages. The first group of women who arrived looked hesitant, but when the Ambedkarian's mother urged them to talk, they let us know that the field assistant was biased and did not give work to them. The district resource person said, "I cannot take your testimony unless I can see your job card." A few returned to their homes to get the cards. Some were workers we had already visited. One said, "I did not know that you were connected with our leader," meaning the Ambedkarian. Soon we heard that NREGA work was not being given to some workers and that those who did work were not being paid adequately. Some workers had paid bribes to obtain job cards in the first place. We began hearing things that had not yet been mentioned in the audit. We had initially approached the workers as individuals. But, when we explicitly approached them as members of a group, in this case members of the Ambedkar Association, they opened up and began giving testimonies that were recorded with their thumbprints. I felt vindicated. My strategy seemed to work. The auditor seemed pleased with what we had found. But I was not ready for the backlash we were soon to be facing.

As we left the house, we noticed we were being followed. News of the spontaneous meeting at the Ambedkarian's house had obviously traveled quickly in the small village. I saw the field assistant glaring in our direction. The district resource person instructed him in a loud voice to go away or he would call the police. The field assistant shouted back that he was not doing anything wrong and reminded John that it was his village and he could stand anywhere he wanted. Eventually the field assistant passed the task of intimidation to his friends, although we managed to get written testimonials with thumbprints or signatures from a sizable number of the workers who had been speaking with us.

The atmosphere quickly grew menacing and the auditors became nervous. I asked John, "What have we done? Should we back out?" He replied, "No, we should press forward." The field assistant and his men constantly asked us what we had found out. John gave the standard answer: "Come to the gram sabha to find out." By the third day we had a clear sense of strong political divisions in the village. The Dalits were divided, and I discovered later that even the Ambedkar Association, which had tried to unify them, was itself split. We heard more stories, some of which concerned a recent chemical plant spill that village leaders had ignored. The company had gone so far as to bribe the Dalit leaders to say nothing, even though the village's drinking water was polluted. Our uncovering of these matters bred increasing animosity with the field assistant, his supporters, and the sarpanch. It was clear the field assistant was connected to people in the political party. Typical audits do not come close to revealing such controversial issues.[20]

We were traveling in the Dalit neighborhood on our motorbike when the sarpanch appeared on his bike and signaled for us to stop. He asked, "Why did you spend such a long time in the house of someone in the opposition party? You should not believe what they are saying. Is there no other house left for you to finish?" The district resource person, putting up a brave front, replied, "I am here to do my job, and if you have any problems with the audit, you should report it to my manager." The sarpanch softened and said he was just ensuring that the auditors got the full picture and weren't caught up in dirty local political fights. He added, "You are here to talk to people who have worked in NREGA, to ask them a few questions and then leave." I didn't think much about this exchange, and I certainly did not anticipate what was in store for us later in the audit because of our "minor" deviation from the norm.

In the village that evening, we encountered the cricket-watching youths. They were now eager to initiate a conversation, and we held an impromptu meeting with them at a public outdoor area. They quickly got to the core issue—the inability of villagers to speak against local officials. One of them said, "Ravi [the field assistant] is ultimately one of us. Even if he has taken money, he lives here. It is not going to be possible to mobilize against him. He is our relative." After our discussion, they warned us to finish the report soon and leave the village immediately afterward. This was an important revelation. The field assistant is part of the lower-level bureaucrats who were hired from the village as part of deliberate state policy to ensure that the social distance between the marginalized citizens and the local state was not high. As we will see in Chapter 7, the low social distance between the lower-level bureaucrats and NREGA workers allows for private settlements beyond public meetings.

The last step in the audit process was the village meeting. Typically at this stage, the auditors are tired and still have a second village to visit. The gram sabha is thus not a priority and they do not look forward to it. This particular gram sabha, however, was different. The district resource person was keen to hold a productive meeting. He knew we had recruited workers from the Ambedkar Association to attend and that they would be able to support the audit report. The worry in a typical NREGA gram sabha is that very few workers present will be able to support the auditors publicly. This is important as the auditors are not in a position to directly challenge the field assistant. I told John that we should ask members of the opposition political party and other village residents to attend. We soon realized that the location of the public meeting would be critical. The field assistant told the district resource person that previous meetings had been held in the upper-caste area of the village, not the Dalit neighborhood.[21] The statement seemed strange coming from him, since he himself was a Dalit, but he preferred not to hold meetings where the bulk of the NREGA workers lived. However, John insisted that the meeting be held in the Dalit neighborhood.

The debate now shifted to where exactly it should be held in the Dalit neighborhood. The Ambedkarian leader had alerted us that the precise location would matter. He tried to sway us toward his side of the neighborhood, but the field assistant insisted that there would be chaos if we held it there. Eventually, the district resource person settled on a compromise that seemed acceptable to both sides: an open temple decorated with an array of spears.

The next decision was when to hold the meeting. Normally, gram sabhas took place at times that were convenient for the auditors without taking into account the convenience of the workers.[22] I insisted we schedule our meeting for the evening, after the workers had returned home. However, the auditors feared things would become unruly at night because of people getting drunk. Eventually we decided on 5:00 p.m.

That afternoon we went to inspect the NREGA work being done in the hills surrounding the village. We got back to the village at 5:00, and the auditors walked around to round people up. Most of the Dalit neighborhood was empty because the workers were not yet back, so we decided to postpone for a bit. The sarpanch showed up at 5:15, asking why the meeting had not started. We explained that the workers were not yet back, and reluctantly he agreed to return later. Slowly the meeting space began to fill up. One drunken man kept asking for a separate passbook. The sarpanch drove up on his bike twice more to see if the meeting had started. Finally the district resource person informed him the meeting would now start at 7:00 p.m. Soon after, the state resource person arrived from the mandal. People continued to trickle in; the open temple was getting packed and the sky was darkening.

So far, those gathered were all workers from the Dalit neighborhood. Had the meeting been held in the upper-caste area of the village, the likelihood of these men attending would have been very low. In a segregated caste society, mundane decisions about the locations of meetings become an important precondition for participation. However, meeting organizers typically do not give this much attention. When John invited me to sit with the auditors, I told him I needed to take photographs and record the proceedings. However, I was hesitant to leave, suspecting he might need my help, and as it turned out, I was dragged into the discussion anyway.

The audit meeting started off in the usual way, with a speech proclaiming that the NREGA was designed to preserve the right of the workers to work. John stressed that the number of workdays for Dalits was unlimited.[23] Next he gave a dry presentation of the demographic statistics of the village. He announced that twenty-six work projects had been completed in the village during the previous year. He also announced the total amount of money spent in that period on NREGA works. At this point, people started interrupting with a range of complaints:

> "I don't have a job card so I was not allowed to work."
> "I had to bribe the mates to get my payment."
> "The field assistant's family do not go to work but they still get paid."
> "I gave my name to be added to the work group but it was left out."
> "NREGA is a waste, please take it away."

One person shouted, "NREGA work is done mainly by women, and yet there is not a single woman here at the gram sabha." In fact, a few women had appeared, and one asked, "Why do I not have a passbook in my own name? Why do I have to work under somebody else's name?"

The field assistant was initially silent. But then the Ambedkarian leader said, "Forty percent of the people in this village do not have passbooks." Clearly this was a political statement indicating the split in the village. The allegation irked the field assistant, who said, "So what if you don't have documents? You are still able to get work." He was upset that people were using what he regarded as a technicality to attack him.

By this time, multiple conversations were under way. I had been observing the meeting from the periphery, believing I could avoid notice if I did not stand on the platform, but suddenly I became the object of attention. Three people I had seen earlier with the field assistant pointed at me, asking, "Why did you spend one hour and fifteen minutes with the opposition party?" Though we had known our movements were being shadowed, we did not anticipate it would become an issue at the meeting. I ignored the question.

Meanwhile, the field assistant was claiming he would settle the passbook problem soon. He added, looking at the most outspoken woman, "I will feed you the passbook in your mouth." This derogatory remark upset the women and many of the men. The woman replied, "Mind your language. Do not degrade yourself." Soon after this, a fistfight broke out between the sarpanch and several men from the Ambedkar Association. The youth whom the auditors and I had spoken to earlier formed a circle of protection around us. The NREGA program officer, who manages NREGA at the mandal level and is the boss of the field assistant, tried to intervene, but somebody attempted to attack him. The sarpanch immediately shouted not to attack the NREGA program officer. The situation was spiraling out of control and the villagers were becoming increasingly agitated.

There was a clear split: some attendees approved of our unorthodox behavior as auditors, and others sided with the field assistant and the sarpanch's men and wanted us to leave. One auditor mentioned that the field assistant was related to the sarpanch, which violated the rule stating that a field assistant cannot be related to any member of the political party. When the state resource person heard this, he announced he would report the situation to higher authorities and have the field assistant removed. That was the last straw. The field assistant, visibly upset, began shouting insults at all who were speaking out. Once again, attention shifted to me and the auditors, and again people demanded to know why we had spent so much time with a member of the opposition party. More questions followed about why this meeting was being held so late and why at this spot. The implication was that the entire audit was politically motivated.

The conflict was no longer about the content and veracity of the workers' testimonies. The meeting had triggered a preexisting feud between two political factions. We, the auditors, became tools of the contestants in a political battle.

By this point, discussion had completely broken down and scuffles had broken out. Someone hit the sarpanch and the situation became even more chaotic. Although a few young men pushed me around, the wall the youth had built around the auditors and myself held. Eventually, I was whisked away. It was very dark and I could not even see the faces of the people escorting me to safety. I found myself on a motorcycle, accompanied by the state resource person and

John. We raced out of the scene and saw that the other auditors had also escaped on motorcycles. In the distance, I could hear the fight continuing. Suddenly somebody noticed that we were fleeing and yelled. The person driving our motorcycle told me to hold on tight and accelerated to maximum speed. Thus, the auditors and I were literally driven from the meeting with our official documents. All we had achieved was the rekindling of a preexisting political fight.

We did not speak much that night. We were happy to return to the mandal office and after the long day we soon fell asleep. I woke early in the morning wanting to go back to the village, but the other auditors looked at me as if I were out of my mind. They said they had work to do: finishing their paperwork. I called the field assistant on the phone. He answered immediately and I told him I wanted to come to the village and talk to people. He said tempers were high and that anything could happen. He added, "I cannot be responsible. You should know that you were warned." He also said nobody would talk to me.

Despite his admonitions, I took a bus alone to the village. It was late morning and I was confident I would be safe. I walked down the main street. Everybody was busy doing their work and, although a few people glanced at me, no one came forward to talk. I sensed everybody watching me and found it increasingly difficult to stay. The Ambedkarian Association leader was not there. I met with another person from the local media, a writer for the opposition-party newspaper who was sympathetic to what we were doing in the audit.[24] He asked me to leave. He said the village would not be safe for me until several days had passed. He said, "All this will calm down in a few days." But he also said, "Nothing will come out of this."

The experimental audit had exposed issues that a typical audit would not uncover. The purpose of the audit meeting is to record discrepancies in NREGA and have them debated in the gram sabha. The recruitment strategy of this audit, which recognized the social groups that workers were part of, created an environment in which workers were supported and thus participated in the audit. However, the meeting also brought other social groups with differing interests into focus. As a result, it became another occasion for in-fighting, bringing existing rivalries to the foreground and ignoring workers' grievances about NREGA entirely.

Conclusion

This chapter has compared three meetings organized at the village level in Andhra Pradesh. The gram sabhas—run by the lower-level bureaucrats—are at worst "paper meetings" that serve as a "check box" bureaucracy to effectively conduct a meeting; more specifically, they are mandated but with no real outcomes

(Mathur 2015). Apolitical and of very little use, the gram sabhas as practiced in Andhra Pradesh can be seen as the case of an "anti-politics machine" that serves only to fulfill a bureaucratic requirement. By contrast, the rachabanda meeting coordinated by the political party is useful in bringing state-level bureaucrats closer to the village and helping citizens "see the state," yet fail to offer a deliberative platform (Corbridge et al. 2005). The experimental audit meeting shows the limits of outside actors intervening in local politics when things spiral out of hand, creating chaos.

The chapter then explored how the social architecture of a social audit meeting affects its capacity for marginalized people to "read" the state. This social architecture includes who organizes it, who is recruited to participate in it, how participants are recruited (i.e., whether people are recruited as individuals or because they are members of a social group, like NREGA workers, state employees, or members of a political party), and how open these meetings are to people who are not recruited to participate. Being collectively present as part of a social group could enable marginalized individuals to exercise power in a public meeting where it is hard for the marginalized to fully participate as isolated individuals. A key part of the social architecture explored in this chapter is the possibilities of empowerment that recruiting workers to attend NREGA public meetings in social groups provides. Drawing on group membership has the potential to enable NREGA workers to be active participants in the meeting. Yet, drawing on social group membership as a source of empowerment at an NREGA audit might backfire in rural India by bringing out issues that reflect rivalries among social groups and, as a result, makes it difficult to focus on the topic of the meeting.

Considered together, the open, state-run meetings that take place in villages operate on a spectrum from fully bureaucratized, non-politicized meetings to fully politicized meetings. The state-mandated gram sabha discussed in this chapter operates at the fully bureaucratized end of the spectrum. The rachabanda meeting organized by the ruling political party operates, by contrast, at the political end. Attempts to fully contend with local politics backfired, as the experimental audits showed.

Thus, the organizers of the meetings need to recognize and acknowledge the barriers to meaningful participation and design meetings to encourage and ensure participation by the marginalized. But how might they do this? Could the meeting be organized by a political party? As is evident from the example of the rachabandas, when a political party organizes a meeting, it is well attended. Yet those forums are not meaningful spaces for participation. It is important to note the difference between good attendance and the ability of attendees to raise critical questions about sensitive topics. This dichotomy occurs because rachabandas are structured to make the political party in power look good, and political parties are likely not interested in organizing a meeting where their own actions might be questioned. In any case, the political party in power has not come forward to conduct NREGA meetings, and it is not clear that they would be willing to do so if there was a possibility that they would be implicated in the handling (or mishandling) of NREGA at the local level.

Both the gram sabha and the rachabanda preserved hegemony because their organizers treated them as rituals that did not challenge existing power relations. In contrast, the meeting that was part of the experimental audit attempted to interrupt local power relations and encourage participatory democracy but ended up creating too much friction, which the social audit team was unable to handle. So, how social audits are structured to deal with the messy last mile and avoid these problems is what we turn to next.

6
Reading and Writing State Records

Where are you?... What is the name of the district, mandal, and village you are in? What is name of the sarpanch [village political representative]?... Give the phone to him.... [With a raised voice, addressing the sarpanch] Do not dare to do anything to our official!... We will get the police!... What do you think you are doing? No! Stop, stop, listen to me, just let them go!... Give the phone back to our official.... [Now addressing the social auditor] Are you safe? You do not panic. You immediately leave the place. Do not give any of the documents to them.

This excerpt from a phone call a senior auditor in the social audit institution made to a field team in a village in Andhra Pradesh reveals the struggles and dangers auditors encounter when they attempt to open up government records publicly. Social audits in Andhra Pradesh depart fundamentally from financial audits of public programs. Unlike a financial audit, which professional accountants conduct behind closed doors, social audits are designed to be an open process that accesses government records and solicits the participation of marginalized citizens.

Although the national NREGA legislation mandates social audits, Andhra Pradesh and Telangana are the only states that conduct them.[1] As I described in Chapter 4, the Andhra Pradesh government created an independent social audit institution, the Society for Social Audit, Accountability and Transparency (SSAAT), to conduct social audits of NREGA activity. Creating the institution was only the first step. In order to successfully conduct NREGA audits, social auditors had to overcome many problems at the last mile by continuously patching the institution. The follow-up actions by the upper-level bureaucrats are limited by several factors that include lack of cooperation among lower-level bureaucrats and the lack of political will to enforce NREGA policies (Afridi and Iversen, 2014; Aiyar and Mehta 2015). But as Suchi Pande and Rakesh Dubbudu argue, "we [need to] distinguish between the transparency role of social audits from the follow-up measures needed for full accountability. We also view the investigation of fraud as a different area of oversight than detection" (Pande and Dubbudu 2017, 21).

The chapter is focused on thinking about how the *transparency* that social audits create in theory leads to a practice that enables marginalized citizens to demand accountability from the state (Jenkins and Manor 2017). The key part of the strategy is how auditors mediate marginalized citizens' access to NREGA records.

My analysis in this chapter is inspired by the work of Stuart Corbridge, Glyn Williams, Manoj Srivastava, and René Véron, who used the idea of "seeing the state" as a way of examining changes in relations between state and society in India" (Corbridge et al. 2005). Their book looked at the "developmental state" from the vantage points of different groups of poor people in India. They noted that a big problem for the poor is that they rarely see the state—that is, interact with state institutions—because the state does not see them. They argue that one of the achievements of state antipoverty programs is that the "institutional surface area of the state" which the poor "see" has increased; that is, "poorer people often see the state, because the state has chosen to see them" (Corbridge et al. 2005, 10; Heller 2012, 647). They urge us to focus not just on whether development programs succeed in terms of what they sought to achieve, but also on how much the developmental state increases its presence in the lives of the poor. They argue that the opportunities that development programs offer the poor to have "sightings of the state" could pave the way for more active forms of citizenship, leading to better material outcomes for the poor.

Paromita Sanyal and Biju Rao take this argument further in their comparative analysis of the four southern states of India, which includes Andhra Pradesh (Sanyal and Rao 2018). These states have built local state institutions such as the gram sabha (village assembly) that solicit feedback from the poor. Their analysis of nearly 300 gram sabhas finds that the poor have found a way to participate in the functioning of the state. They introduce the idea of "oral democracy," that is, the opportunity that gram sabhas give the poor to participate in state functioning through speaking in these assemblies. They show how the state uses public meetings to announce state policies, choose beneficiaries of public programs, and seek public input. The poor learn to experience the state by learning to articulate their private grievances as public issues that the state needs to address. They conclude that "[gram sabhas] show that democracy can be strengthened and deepened by the simple but profound act of giving citizens the chance to speak and to be heard" (Sanyal and Rao 2018, 175). This mechanism by which the poor see the state and can hear and speak to the state was not available to them until recently.

The social audits in Andhra Pradesh go further. As Yamini Aiyar and S. Mehta write in their analysis of social audits in Andhra Pradesh, "These interactions [audits] are different from deliberations in other public spheres, where the discussion between the state and citizens is mostly in the framework of the latter petitioning the state and competing to stake claims in programmes and for benefits. In these interactions, the state is not obligated to justify its decisions. The social audits change this equation" (Aiyar and Mehta 2015, 71).

It will be useful to understand how exactly the social audit process changes "this equation" between state and society. To do this, we need to recognize the central role that documents and the act of documentation play in governance. Recently, anthropologists have examined the practices of how a bureaucracy functions and have argued that *writing* is how power is exercised (Hull 2012b; Hull 2012a). Anthropologist Akhil Gupta writes that "one has to shift attention away from writing's instrumental function in helping run the government to its constitutive role as that which defines what the state is and what it does" (Gupta 2012). Anthropologist Nayanika Mathur documented bureaucratic writing as "a process that requires the hard labour of writing, interpreting, reading, drafting, redrafting. [. . .] Performance of this labour is critical for the state and its project of welfare to remain alive" (Mathur 2015, 115).

The upshot of this attention to writing is that it is not merely a function that the state performs. Gupta, Mathur, and others argue that the writing and production of documents are what actually constitutes the state. Anthropologist Mathew Hull traces the origins of bureaucratic writing to colonial motivation to surveil and control local native functionaries who were the lower-level bureaucrats. He writes, "British officers in India were frequently transferred among different posts. They lacked knowledge of the locales they administered and of the permanently posted native functionaries on whom they helplessly depended. In response to these uncertain loyalties, the British, building on the elaborate written procedures of the Mughals, expanded their graphic regime of surveillance and control" (Hull 2012b, 10). In discussing the contemporary government in Pakistan, Hull writes, "if you want to understand bureaucratic activities, follow the paper" (Hull 2012b, 22).

While Hull focused on how documents mediate relationships, the documents were tethered to internal government processes and were controlled by the bureaucrats. But social audits bring in new possibilities for circulating formerly closed government documents beyond the confines of the state bureaucracy.

In Andhra Pradesh, the social auditors go beyond merely circulating existing government documents; their objective is to help the poor *write* new documents that destabilize state accounts and enable citizens to be directly involved in how the state is accountable to them. Beyond the real-time implications of marginalized citizens correcting errors and misinformation in state-issued records, in a larger sense, social audits create the possibility of reshaping relations between the state and society with a more equitable distribution of power. Thus, social audits need to be evaluated not just in terms of the outcomes of NREGA, but also

Table 6.1 Design of the Three Stages of the Social Audit Process

First Stage: Household Survey (Private)	Second Stage: Village Meeting (Open)	Third Stage: Mandal Meeting (Open)
Workers see the records and give testimony; auditors write the record; workers sign the record.	Auditors read the records out loud in public so that workers can see where discrepancies exist.	Discrepancies are resolved: workers receive compensation, and sometimes lower-level bureaucrats are fined or suspended.

in terms of how they change relations between the Indian state and society and their potential to further democratize the state.

The struggle to make NREGA administrators fully accountable centers on questions of who has *read* access to NREGA records and who has *write* access to them. This chapter details the process of how the auditors rewrite NREGA records when there are discrepancies in the administration's official records. How do upper-level bureaucrats both facilitate, yet ultimately limit, this rewriting?

The social audit process has three stages. As Table 6.1 shows, each stage brings with it the possibility for seeing more of the state, giving NREGA workers greater engagement and voice and holding the state accountable, while at the same time each stage has its own impediments caused by omnipresent power struggles to realizing that goal. In what follows, I detail how social auditors mediate *read* and *write* access of NREGA records to NREGA workers in each of these three stages, and how they respond when lower-level administrators contest their findings.

The Household Survey and the Worksite Inspection

During the first stage, the household survey, SSAAT auditors give workers *read* access to their documents. The auditors visit all NREGA workers in the survey area so the workers can *read* NREGA documents for themselves. When workers are not literate, the auditor reads the records out loud for them. Typically the documents include the NREGA muster rolls for each worker: how many days they have worked, when they worked, where they worked, and (most important) how much they were paid. The household survey also gives workers *write* access to their documents when they find discrepancies between what they think happened and what the official record says. They direct auditors to change NREGA records to correct the number of days they worked, where they worked, and how much they got paid. Workers are also able to add a petition that may add more context to the changes they have made. In addition, the auditors inspect all of the NREGA worksites to check for problems in the implementation of NREGA projects.

Social auditors prepare for the audit by accessing NREGA records. Upper-level bureaucrats ensure that social auditors have full access to both the digital records and the paper records that are maintained at the local mandal offices. During my fieldwork, while the visiting audit team occasionally complained about not getting the full set of documents from lower-level bureaucrats, they were able to resolve this by calling the SSAAT leadership, who had the backing of upper-level bureaucrats to intervene.[2] The digitized NREGA records enabled the social auditors to organize the records so they could start the audit efficiently. They used software to consolidate all the information about the NREGA work a worker had done, which made it easy to cross-check information during the face-to-face visit.

Once the village social auditors are hired, the household survey starts. Auditors are required to interview every NREGA worker whose name appears on an NREGA muster roll; there is no sampling strategy. They interview workers in their homes. Auditors ask workers to show them their NREGA job cards to ensure that they are talking to the right person. They ask for other documents as well, such as bank passbooks and payment slips, which serve as additional proof that the worker has in fact been working. Because they must visit so many workers and verify so much documentation, auditors are under enormous pressure to move from house to house quickly. If a worker is not at home when the auditors visit, auditors usually mark them as a "no show" in the audit report and do not attempt to visit them again.[3] Because of the need for speed, the attention auditors give each worker depends on the level of response they expect from the worker.

During interviews, auditors ask the workers how much they have worked, where they have worked, and if they have been paid the amount listed on their documents. Despite the routine nature of the questions in the household survey, the act of asking them is a substantial task. One difficulty involves translation: the auditors have to convert survey questions into language that uses local references that villagers can understand. The process of mentally converting the language of written questions is usually time-consuming, at least for the initial interviews. For example, when asking questions about whether the worker worked on a particular worksite, auditors must learn the colloquial name for that site that workers use, which is often not the term on the official documents. Workers also frequently do not remember precisely how much they were paid for a particular task, and the further back in time the auditors go, the less reliable their memories become.[4]

At this stage of the audit, the auditors also visit worksites. Inspection of the worksite varies depending on the type of work that is being audited, but there are a shared number of features. First, auditors, try to visit the worksite to ensure that there are no "*benami* works," works that are mentioned on paper but are actually not done. Second, the auditors verify the location of the work to ensure that the work was done at the location marked in the document. This is to confirm that the work was done on public lands and not on private property to benefit a local politician. Third, the auditors take measurements to ensure accuracy. For example, if the task at a worksite is digging a pit, the auditors use a tape measure to authenticate the depth, width, and height of the pit and compare their measurements with data in the official records and write down discrepancies. Fourth, they will visibly check the work to assess the quality of the completed job and get a sense of materials used. Finally, they make sure that the work was done by a human rather than by a machine; NREGA bans the use of machines.

Traditionally, many development programs have been hijacked by contractors, who use labor-displacing machinery to do the work and claim development funds. Auditors will look for telltale signs of machine marks at the worksite. On my visits to the worksites with the auditors, they have pointed out when markings on the structure indicated evidence of work done by machines. Typically, they include tire marks and distinctive scratches left by the machine scraper, as well as the shape of the structure of the pits that were dug. The auditors have learned to visually detect cases where the machines have done the majority of the work and workers were employed to do the final touch-up to hide the machine tracks and make it seem that the entire job was a human endeavor. Auditors learn this through the sheer number of worksites they examine, as well as by soliciting feedback from workers. They add information about discrepancies to the audit report. To recall, NREGA has two goals: to ensure workers get paid and to ascertain that the work itself has been done according to specification. Visiting the worksite gives social auditors critical context they need about the work and, based on that, they then solicit worker testimonies to understand and document the extent of misappropriation.

The following snippets are a selection from the household surveys I participated in. Besides editing the transcript for clarity, I have removed details that would identify a particular worker, such as name, job card number, and the village where they live. The interchanges illustrate what happens at these audits and the diversity of issues audits bring out. They include instances where auditors found examples of workers not getting paid, workers not getting paid the full wages due them, workers who were paid through a proxy who received a commission for each payment, workers who could not remember precise details, workers on the NREGA books who had died, workers on the books who had migrated to a city, and workers who were not allowed to work.

Workers not getting paid

AUDITOR: *How many days did you work in NREGA?*

WORKER: *Three days.*

AUDITOR: *Do you remember when you worked?*

WORKER: *In June.*

[Auditor reads the record that this worker received the payment of Rs. 325.]

WORKER: *I have not received the payment.*

[Auditor collects the worker's thumb impression.]

Worker unable to remember where he worked

AUDITOR: *Did you get the money?*

WORKER: *Yes.*

AUDITOR: *Where did you work?*

WORKER: [laughing] *Whatever the document says, I worked there.*

AUDITOR: *You do not remember.*

WORKER: *It has been such a long time. You are coming after a long time to ask us.*

AUDITOR: *Audits happen every six months.* [Auditor moves on, noting down only that he talked to the worker and worker did not remember.]

***Benami* [Fake] Worksite**

AUDITOR: *Did you work on the canal bund project?*

WORKER: *Yes, I did work on it last year.*

AUDITOR: *But did you work on it again this year? The record says you got paid 1,016 rupees.*

WORKER: *No, I did not. Clearly somebody has eaten that money. I did not work and I did not get the money.*

Money shown as paid to a dead man

AUDITOR: *Did your husband get paid 2,150, as per the records?*

WORKER'S WIFE: *My husband died two years ago.*

[Auditor takes her thumb impression.]

Work shown as done by a person who has migrated to the city

AUDITOR: *Did you son Naga work on these different works and received the payment of 5,330?*

WORKER'S FATHER: *Naga went to Hyderabad for police coaching then. So he did not work and did not receive the payment.*

[Auditor convinces the father to give a statement.]

Fake record of worker living at a house

AUDITOR: *Amma, have you worked on Upadhigami padhagam [NREGA]? Did you work at Kakiramalu [name of a worksite]?*

WORKER: *Yes.*

AUDITOR: *How many days do you work?*

[Kids are crying in the background and the auditor has to work to regain her attention.]

WORKER: *I do not remember.*
AUDITOR: *Do you get the receipt for the money?*
WORKER: *No.*
AUDITOR: *There is a record under Suvarna from this house, who seems to have worked for 25 days and have got paid Rs. 2,650. There is nobody called Suvarna in your house?*
WORKER: *No.*
AUDITOR: *There is nobody like that here?*
WORKER: *No, there is nobody like that here.*
AUDITOR: *Put your sign, to show that I talked to you. [Auditor records the discrepancy in his audit report and the worker provides a thumbprint.]*

Sometimes the household survey is not a one-on-one interaction and the people who live in nearby houses join in.

Group Interaction: Testifying against the Field Assistant

WORKER: *This is our time to get back at the field assistant.*
[They know that the field assistant is going to be in trouble and start badmouthing him. Although the field assistant was not present, speaking against him to the auditors, who are outsiders, is a sign of change.]
ANOTHER WORKER: *He needs to pay us back for all what he has done.*
ANOTHER VILLAGER: *Please write that we have not been given a job card.*
[Workers need a job card to participate in NREGA.]
ANOTHER WORKER: *He does not open up work when we ask him to give us work.*
[The auditor writes a group petition and then reads it out loud.]
AUDITOR: *Can you sign this?*
[Auditor records the name of the village, the names of the workers, the workers' job card details, and the workers' specific complaints. Each worker provides a thumb impression. One carefully writes his signature on the document.]

Audits allow workers to go beyond just seeing the official record; they also offer an opportunity to question it. In each household, the auditor reads out the information from the digitized government record and asks the worker to confirm that data. If there is a discrepancy between the worker's version and the official record, the auditor solicits testimony from the worker. If the worker is willing, the auditor writes that testimony down as part of the audit record. The household survey thus gives the worker an opportunity to both read the actions of the state and to write in that record to correct details and add corroborating information. The document produced at this stage is not yet part of the official record. It must pass through two more audit stages first. However, these workers, who are marginalized citizens in Andhra Pradesh, are able to testify openly about what they received and did not receive in NREGA. I observed this happening over and over again in many villages.

The fact that NREGA workers are able to participate in challenging official records and contributing to changing them must be seen in a historical context. Giving testimony to outside auditors that will soon be seen by the field assistant does not just happen; a long arc of social change preceded those moments. When a worker takes that step, it is a continuation of a decades-long struggle for empowerment that is finally finding a moment of expression.

It was clear to me that these workers were empowered. Audits work well when the workers are not afraid to speak up. But not all workers chose to cooperate fully, a topic I will explore in the next two chapters.

Auditors avoid approaching any union or political party for support. One senior auditor explained why approaching an opposition political party would be a bad strategy. He said, "If we get their involvement, their evidence would not stand in the public meeting. These political parties speak in generalities. We don't need their help. We go directly to the workers. We look at musters, we talk to people. We ignore the political people. We actively keep them out."

When I asked him whether there is any use for a political party in the social audit process, he said, "If they have something to say. They can give the clue [of any corruption that know about]. But we will go investigate ourselves. We will talk to the workers and will go to the worksite and do our measurements." The social auditor insisted that talking to the political party was counterproductive.

At this first stage of the audit, workers carefully regulated how much they revealed to auditors. They carefully calculated how much to say based on what they felt their testimony could achieve. In Andhra Pradesh, this was not due to the fear of the local state, a significant difference from what I observed in the social audits in Bihar. Here in Andhra Pradesh, fear of the mates and field assistants was the exception rather than the rule, which points to how critical prior social mobilization is in order to make these audit processes effective.

The household survey by social auditors allowed citizens to see government records, as individuals from their private homes, and to correct state-authored accounts.[5] This was indeed a radical step, as marginalized citizens never had access to program documents before. Social auditors were able to hear directly from workers and also inspect the worksites and measure NREGA work and write new records documenting the discrepancies with the official version. In addition, social auditors allowed NREGA workers to create testimonies which were recorded. However, despite the many empowering and progressive facets of the social audit, workers remained hesitant about the power of the process to ultimately benefit their standing and their lives. Some measure of trust was still withheld—suspicions, I surmised, that were rooted in uncertainty about the next step, that is, what would be the final outcome of their "read and write access"? Would "going public" help them or hurt them? This in turn gives rise to other questions: How do you ensure that the social audit process is legitimate and that workers can trust the audit? Because if audits are held privately, how can you be certain the auditors are not colluding with the lower-level bureaucrats and will drop the audit findings? This was one reason why the NREGA design mandated public hearings, which theoretically are supposed to be the next layer of transparency. But how do they function in practice? What sightings do they generate, and for whom? Do they bolster workers' trust or weaken it? How the social auditors attempt to patch that lack of transparency is what we will turn next.

The Village Social Audit Meeting

The second stage of a social audit is the village meeting, when auditors read their findings out loud. This includes compiled data about the total NREGA expenses in the village for both wages and materials and details about discrepancies the audit process has uncovered. The village-level social audit meeting is an open public meeting to ensure that the social audit process remains transparent and to ensure that workers collectively are able to make sure that local elites have not influenced the auditors.[6] Structuring these meetings so that they won't be captured by the local elites requires going through a series of patches.

The auditors typically spend three to seven days in a village conducting the audit. The village social audit meeting typically marks the culmination of the auditors' presence. The audit meeting starts with an auditor summarizing the audit findings. In one of the audits I attended, the auditor started the meeting with this summary:

> It has been five days, coming to your village. . . . The expenditure from August 1, 2011, to till June 30th, 2012, is X Rupees. The wage component is y rupees and for material it is Z rupees. The work consisted of canal repair works, horticulture, removing mud from wells, clearing bushes, and building roads. We visited all the workers. We visited worksites and took measurements. We could not complete all the measurements, because some of the measurements were rendered inaccurate because of rain. . . . These worksites were shown to us by workers. We have tried our best to measure them. We also received complaints about some workers that they did not get paid. We found problems with workers who had not been allowed to work.

The summary included the amount of expenses and the ratio of wages to the costs of materials needed to conduct the work. He listed the major worksites and highlighted some of the problems found in the audit.

The village social audit meeting is held publicly. The supposition is that this meeting will allow the auditors to inform workers (and other villagers) about how NREGA has performed and what it has accomplished in their village. The meeting is also supposed to be a way to build workers' trust by ensuring them that elite local interests have not co-opted the audit process. However, in Andhra Pradesh, the village social audit meeting became a site where lower-level bureaucrats and local politicians challenged the audit's findings. Rather than strengthening confidence in the process, the meetings turned into a power struggle between social auditors and local bureaucrats and politicians.

The struggle for control of the village social audit meetings was not just an issue in Andhra Pradesh. The first time that local politicians exercised their power regarding this issue was in Rajasthan, where they wanted to ensure that outside actors would not be permitted to participate in village social audit meetings. But an activist from MKSS (Mazdoor Kisan Shakti Sangathan) who knew the situation in Rajasthan countered, "The social audits, if done at the gram sabha [referring to the social audit village meeting], are a waste. Whether it is Bihar or Rajasthan, they all claim to have done audits, and there are zero findings; everything is okay. Gram sabha as an institution can be misused." A report by *The Hindu* summarizes the issue well:

> This is where the amendment to Section 13, Schedule I of the act came to their aid [of the sarpanches and other local elites]. The amendment itself was done surreptitiously, and discovered much later by activists only when it was used against them. . . . It stated the social audit process shall be open to public participation. Any outside individual person apart from the gram sabha [village meeting] shall be allowed to attend the social audit as an observer without intervening [in] the proceedings of the social audit. The sarpanches gained respite with the High Court, staying the entire social audit process in the state and ruling that Section 13B had to be followed to the letter. With this, the social audits as done earlier in a campaign/participatory mode, came to a standstill.[7]

After this ruling, MKSS had to stop conducting social audits in Rajasthan. MKSS was an outside actor, and the amendment allowed them no role in the social audits in Rajasthan. The amendment to Section 13 put pressure on the SSAAT leadership team in Andhra Pradesh to ensure that they themselves, and not local village officials, conducted the local village social audit meetings. One key way they accomplished this was to keep sarpanches from being involved in NREGA. An upper-level NREGA bureaucrat told me:

> NREGA was the first implementation in AP that completely and totally bypassed the sarpanch. And that's why the scheme has worked well in AP. [The] sarpanch does not have check-writing power [i.e., they aren't involved in distributing NREGA funds]. Their only role is to ensure that work is happening. Beyond that, not giving him hold over the program is what saved NREGA in AP. Otherwise we would not have had social audits to begin with.

NREGA bureaucrats implemented the program in Andhra Pradesh, not local sarpanches. The overall role of the sarpanch was significantly reduced.

The former minister of rural development in Andhra Pradesh echoed the significance of the decision to exclude sarpanches from the implementation of NREGA there. I asked him, "If social auditors are opening public records and reading them out in a public meeting, aren't you giving ammunition to the opposition party to question your party and tarnish its image? Why would you agree to such a thing?" The former minister replied:

> Government is not afraid of social audits. That is because no political party work is involved at the local level. Whatever misappropriation takes place, the responsibility lies with the officer, the field assistant, or the technical assistant, or the MPDO of the mandal, or the project director of that particular district. Responsibilities are with them and not with the political worker, and not with the Congress Party.

Another upper-level bureaucrat echoed the former minister's sentiments. She was right in the sense that in Andhra Pradesh, the ability of political parties to influence how the NREGA was administered was significantly reduced. Informal influence continued, but upper-level bureaucrats were able to maintain control of the implementation of the program and independent auditors were used.

This upper-level bureaucrat believed that the benefits of running the program through the NREGA bureaucracy as compared to running through the sarpanch influenced the political viability of social audits. She added:

> See, it is easier for you to go after an MPDO [mandal program development officer] or an FA [field assistant] or a TA [technical assistant] than to go after a sarpanch, because if you go after a sarpanch there is a huge political backlash. There would have been Congress-TDP alliances, there would have all kinds of protests. We bypassed all of them.

She was pointing out that since NREGA is implemented through the bureaucracy, the social audits can blame the bureaucrats for any corruption. If NREGA was administered by the local politicians, then the social auditors would have found it hard to blame the politicians because that would have created political backlash. She was referring to Rajasthan, where social audits were shut down because of political backlash from local political leaders who felt threatened by social audits.

One study found that in the state of Karnataka, where the audits were run by the state government and not by an autonomous body, local elites captured the process (Lakha et al. 2013). The absence of a formal role for them has influenced the nature of the audits there and has made it easier for the SSAAT to conduct social audits. The auditors who are part of the audit team are able to go to a village and report to an independent bureaucracy that local politicians and NREGA employees do not control. However, political struggles were constant. While it is true that the formal role of sarpanches have been significantly reduced in the implementation of the NREGA in Andhra Pradesh, the struggle for control continues, sarpanches still wield power locally, and the struggle between the social auditors and the local power nexus often manifests in the village social audit meeting.

The nature of these meetings has changed considerably over time. While the SSAAT initially advocated openness and transparency and championed the village meeting, they wanted to conduct the public hearing only at the mandal level. As a result, when I first arrived in 2011, village audit meetings were held simply to comply with regulations, and the social auditors were not really interested in or invested in them. However, the next year, I noticed a change in the meeting dynamics. I observed that local politicians and lower-level NREGA employees demanded that these meetings be held, but that the social auditors were apathetic. At first I thought the auditors were simply not doing their job, but I later came to realize that the fight for openness was a power struggle between the auditors and the lower-level bureaucrats and politicians. Auditors could not avoid conducting village social audit meetings because the officers who presided at the mandal-level public hearings pressured them to conduct them. But the auditors did not want to hold village audit meetings if local elites were the only ones who showed up.

One of the meetings I attended illustrates the hesitation and quandary of the social auditors. It was attended by only a few people who did not look like NREGA workers. The social auditor who was reading the findings focused on high-level details. He talked about the total amount of money spent in the village and the amount of "deviation" (the term social auditors use to indicate a difference between the audit findings and the data in NREGA records) the auditors had found, but he left out individual testimonies. One villager, a local sarpanch, asked the social auditor to read out the names of the workers who had testified. The district resource person refused, saying loudly, "Are there any NREGA workers here? I will only read out the findings if there are workers here."

Clearly, the social auditor did not want to read the findings in the absence of workers. He knew that the people present were local elites, who had come specifically to find out which workers had testified and to what. The social auditor did not want to read out the testimonies when there were no workers present. Several attendees replied, "We all are workers. We have worked on NREGA." The auditor replied, "If you are a NREGA worker, bring the job card." A job card would have enabled him to easily check NREGA records to ascertain whether the attendees had worked on NREGA. The people gathered were shouting and demanding that he read the audit report and reveal the names of the workers who had testified. They said that they were workers and were not required to carry their job cards all the time. The social auditor repeated that he would only read out the names if workers were present. I did not understand why he was hesitant. My confusion was echoed by a question from one of the attendees: "The social audit process is an open process. Why are you afraid? How will we know what you have been doing for the past few days in our village?" In this instance, the auditor stood his ground and the meeting concluded without his reading the names.

Later, it was made clear to me that the auditor had been worried that local elites would find out who had testified so they could pressure workers to not testify at the next audit. A senior auditor told me, "They had us cornered. For the gram sabha thing [village social audit meeting], all over Andhra Pradesh they cornered us. The bureaucracy got after us, saying, 'gram sabha, gram sabha, gram sabha.' Okay, today we are having the gram sabha." She was referring to the fact that NREGA legislation requires auditors to hold village social audit meetings.

Social auditors experimented with several types of audit meetings to cope with this requirement while protecting workers and, ultimately, figuring out how to solicit their participation in such a way as to prevent capture of the meeting and intimidation by local elites. I have attended meetings where fewer than five people were present and the auditors mechanically read their findings. They gathered proof that the meeting had taken place, often by collecting thumbprints of a few workers and taking a picture of the meeting to present as evidence of compliance with the law.

Field assistants continued to demand that audit findings be read out loud at the village audit meeting. Because of these complaints, the social audit leadership and NREGA upper-level bureaucrats eventually instituted a new process: a neutral, objective party, an ombudsman, would attend village meetings. Ombudsmen are appointed by the district-level bureaucrats. The SSAAT draws up a schedule of audits ahead of time to inform ombudsmen of the times and dates of the meetings. The intended role of the ombudsman is simply to countersign every finding to confirm that it has been read out loud in the meeting.

This decision served both a transparency and a monitoring function. In principle and intent, the village social audit meeting is the venue where workers have a chance to publicly participate in the social audit process following their private conversations with auditors.[8] The requirement that audit findings be read out loud at the village meeting further ensures that the auditors represent the interests of the workers. The signature of an ombudsman on an audit report signals that it was read out loud at the village meeting. But the public reading at the village meeting also gives field assistants an opportunity to pressure workers to change their testimony. It is thus not surprising that auditors are hesitant about what they reveal in the village social audit meetings and that workers are often hesitant to attend.

To recap, the village public meeting was designed to ensure that workers collectively are able to discuss NREGA discrepancies if present. Yet in practice, as we saw, the village public meeting also allowed local bureaucrats and local elites to attend these meetings and contest the findings. More importantly, the actions of the lower-level bureaucrats were aimed at creating a chilling effect on NREGA workers and inhibiting them from testifying, as the workers know that these testimonies will become public and they will be punished or disadvantaged by the very process designed to empower them. To some extent, these issues were dealt with by social auditors employing strategies with respect to how they conducted (or not) these meetings. But there needed to be a mechanism to ensure that the upper-level bureaucrats could adjudicate between the lower-level bureaucrats and social auditors and create legitimacy both from the upper-level bureaucrats' perspective and from the workers' perspective. Andhra created a new process to do that, which was the mandal public hearing. How that process works is what we turn to next.

The Mandal-Level Public Hearing

The third stage of the social audit, the mandal-level public hearing, is the culmination of the process. It is held at the mandal headquarters, a location far away from the villages, which means that the auditors and higher-level NREGA administrators meet beyond the eyes and ears of lower-level NREGA administrators and local politicians. The meeting, which is run like a court proceeding, presents the social audit findings for each village in the mandal. After findings are read out, both the social auditors and lower-level NREGA administrators present their case. The presiding officer, an upper-level administrator, makes a ruling on what should happen when these two parties disagree.

The rationale for conducting the mandal-level public hearing in Andhra Pradesh is that NREGA is implemented by bureaucrats at the mandal level, as opposed to village-level implementation, which would have been the case if the elected village sarpanch had controlled the program.[9] In addition, it is convenient for upper-level bureaucrats to travel to the mandal from district headquarters. The mandal-level public hearing combines the audit findings from all the villages (approximately twenty) in the mandal. There is one serious limitation to conducting the meetings at the mandal: workers do not generally show up to these hearings. Thus, this process relies on the social auditors to represent adequately the interest of the workers. The meeting is largely constructed as a mobile court at which upper-level NREGA bureaucrats are the judges.

The audience at the mandal-level public hearing typically consists of SSAAT auditors, field assistants from all of the villages in the mandal, and the bureaucrats assigned to the mandal office. Politicians do attend, but social auditors make an active effort to reduce the influence of local politicians in these meetings. The auditors do not allow politicians to sit on the dais, for example.

The meeting lasts a long time as the presiding officers have to make rulings about findings from all the villages. They issue fines and suspensions and decide whether an auditor's version or a lower-level bureaucrat's version is accurate. I have attended mandal-level meetings that lasted more than ten hours. The hearings are organized according to village, and which village goes first is an arbitrary decision that sometimes is made at the last minute.

The structure of these meetings is fairly uniform: an auditor reads out the specific audit finding loudly, often using a microphone, and the presiding officer gives lower-level bureaucrats a chance to respond. Which lower-level bureaucrat gets summoned depends on how the social auditors classified the issue, as well as how the presiding officer chose to categorize it. In some audits, social auditors would attempt to pin a problem on all of the lower-level bureaucrats (field assistants, technical assistants, computer operators, assistant program officer, and the mandal program development officer) for every issue, arguing that they all had to be involved. Who gets called to testify ultimately depends on the discretion of the presiding officer, and the tendency I have observed is that the officer tries to find the person lowest in the hierarchy. The presiding officer makes a decision, announces it, records the decision, and calls for the next issue to be read.

What follows is a collection of things I heard at the mandal-level public hearing I attended. The issues cover a range of last-mile problems that social audits have uncovered.

Underpayment of wages

AUDITOR: *A resident of this village panchayat, Thangamma, wife of Mallayya, job card number, YYY, work ID number ZZZ, did canal channel work for four days from 12/4/2012 to 18/4/2012, for six days from 19/4/2012 to 25/4/2012, and for five days from 25/4/2012 to 2/5/2012, according to the records. She showed her account book in the gram sabha, and it shows that amount is paid. She has not received the money.*

PRESIDING OFFICER: *What happened here?*

FIELD ASSISTANT: *I don't know how this happened.*

PRESIDING OFFICER: *Recovery of the total amount. Please pay the worker right away.* [Writes his decision on the report]. *You make such mistakes, you will go home* [lose your job].

Paying the wrong person

AUDITOR: *N. Pullamma, wife of Roshanna, resident of this panchayat, job card number YYYY, and work ID number ZZZZZ, worked on channel-related works from 19/4/2012 to 25/4/2012. The record indicates that six days' work was done. She has not been paid.*

PRESIDING OFFICER: *What is the amount?*

AUDITOR: *Rs. 525.*

PRESIDING OFFICER: *Is it gone to the other person?*

AUDITOR: *Yes, it is gone to another person, who did not do the work.*

PRESIDING OFFICER (addressing the field assistant): *How did you write the name of the other person?*

AUDITOR: *The name of Roshanna is there in the muster roll, but in the pay order a different name is there.*

COMPUTER OPERATOR [lower-level bureaucrat]: *It seems to be a name mistake.*

PRESIDING OFFICER: *How can it be a name mistake? How can you put the name of the man who has died? OK, get the money and you have to pay. Otherwise, we will report to the police station. Pay within one week. You should pay in front of the MPDO.*

Taking a commission for paying a worker

AUDITOR: *In XYZ panchayat, work ID XXX, the worker Chinna son of Seshanna, the pay order mentions that he got paid Rs. 5,500 in June. When we inquired, he said that he only received Rs. 5,000. We brought this up in the gram sabha* [village social audit meeting] *too.*

PRESIDING OFFICER [addressing the field assistant]: *Was Rs. 500 a bribe? Why didn't you pay completely?*

FIELD ASSISTANT: *Initially I paid 5,000, thinking that I will pay him later.*

PRESIDING OFFICER: *So you retained Rs. 500 as bribe only, why did you do so? Never do so again.*

[Writes his decision to recover Rs. 500 from the field assistant]

Not measuring work in the presence of workers

AUDITOR: *In this village, workers have reported that the markings* [measurement of work] *are not done in their presence. The TA [technical assistant] said in the gram sabha* [village social audit meeting] *that the marking of the measurements is done in the presence of the mate.*

PRESIDING OFFICER: *It is fine to do it with the mate, but you have to take at least two or three workers with you to do the measurement.*

Absence of first aid facility

AUDITOR: *In this village, first aid facilities are not provided, according to the workers.*

PRESIDING OFFICER [looking at the mandal program development officer]: *OK, arrange first aid.*

NREGA work not given when worker requests it

AUDITOR: *A resident of this village, Panipulu, belonging to Harijana Street, reported in writing that work is offered only for 20 to 30 days, though it is supposed to be given for 100 days. He further notes that the pay is only Rs.20–30.*

ASSISTANT PROGRAM OFFICER [the supervisor of the lower-level bureaucrat in the mandal]: *This is not true. They don't come for work. They go for high-paid work elsewhere when the [NREGA] work is offered.*

Presiding officer instructs the assistant program officer to look into it and reminds him that he needs to ensure that NREGA work is provided on demand.

Wall painting of NREGA expenses not done

AUDITOR: *In this village, the details of the social audit aggregate records are supposed to be written on walls. But are not done so. We discussed it in the gram sabha [village social audit meeting]. The assistant program officer said this will be written soon.*

The presiding officer orders that this information be painted in the village walls. [The idea of painting this information on the wall is that it gives all NREGA expenses in a public place, thus providing transparency at the village level.]

Records maintained in English, not in Telugu

AUDITOR: *In this village, all the record details are written in the book in English instead of Telugu.*

PRESIDING OFFICER: *Yes, use Telugu to write the records. That is the rule.*

No NREGA job cards

AUDITOR: *In this village, wagers do not have NREGA job cards, as they have been lost in the floods.*

PRESIDING OFFICER [addressing the lower-level bureaucrats]: *Haven't you given the job cards to them?*

ASSISTANT PROGRAM OFFICER: *Sir, we have not issued them the job cards. They are not yet available. The printed cards are not ready.*

PRESIDING OFFICER: *Ok, get it done.*

Tampering with official records

AUDITOR: *We have seen extensive use of whitening markers as well as several crossings out in the muster roll and the measurement books. We brought this up in the gram sabha [village social audit meeting]. The ombudsman said that the field assistants need to be trained to not do this.*

PRESIDING OFFICER: *Why do you cross them out and edit so much?*

FIELD ASSISTANT: *We will not repeat this. The mates had made mistakes in writing the records.*

Worker not paid

AUDITOR: *Garividi, a resident of this panchayat, worked for 35 days and got paid Rs. 1680 as per the records. When we inquired with her, she said she did work but did not receive the payment.*

PRESIDING OFFICER: *Assistant program officer, get the payment done.*

Overpayment of wages

AUDITOR: *In this village, work was done by Jagan for repairing the canal. Work seemed to have been done. The muster roll said he worked for 15 days, but according to the pay order the workers were paid for 30 days. So they all got excess wages.*

PRESIDING OFFICER: *Why did you do that?*

[No answer]

The presiding officer writes down "recovery," meaning that the excess wages paid to the workers had to be recovered. As we will see, this was the type of audit findings that the workers worry about and lower-level bureaucrats exploit to pressure workers not to speak out too much.]

Work exceeding 100 days

AUDITOR: *Four residents of this village, with the following work IDs, have worked to repair the well and have received no payment. They have worked for 20 days. When we asked the assistant program officer, he said those people have received no payment because they completed 125 working days for the year already.*

ASSISTANT PROGRAM OFFICER: *They cannot be paid for excess days.*

PRESIDING OFFICER: *This is a drought mandal, so 200 days can be offered.*

ASSISTANT PROGRAM OFFICER: *But we have not got the approval yet.*

PRESIDING OFFICER: *We will make an exception, they need to be paid for the work they did.*

Workers not getting paid

AUDITOR: *In this village, we have found three workers who have not been paid, one was for Rs. 450, the other Rs. 650 and the other Rs. 750.*

PRESIDING OFFICER: *Since there are smaller amounts, why are we wasting our time bringing these small issues?*

AUDIENCE: *This may be small enough for you, but not for us.*

Presiding officer nods and writes "recovery."

Overall, the function and intent of the mandal public hearing are to create an official means by which the upper-level bureaucrats can adjudicate and finalize the findings of the first two phases of the social audit. From the perspective of the upper-level bureaucrats, these meetings, which they organize and preside over, confer legitimacy on the process. Since the meetings are held at the mandal headquarters, and not in the village, it allows the upper-level bureaucrats to blunt the local elites, whose power is stronger in their village. But the mandal public hearing loses the participation of workers, for whom the meetings are far away. From what I observed through my own attendance, the mandal-level meeting became primarily a bureaucratic settling of accounts with the presence of outside social auditors and often local media lending ostensible credibility.

Table 6.2 summarizes who participates in each level of meeting.

Putting all three phases together, it is fair to say that the household surveys and the village social audit meetings give workers the opportunity to participate in rewriting state records. Upper-level bureaucrats control the proceedings of the mandal-level public hearing and ultimately determine what gets written. This meeting is held far away from the village, where the local politicians can wield more power. However, upper-level administrators tended to agree with the social auditors at least half the time.[10] Further, a study of the perceptions of social auditors argues that there is a deterrence effect on corruption by the lower-level bureaucrats because of the audits (Pande and Dubbudu 2017).

There is one significant limitation to the decisions made after the audit process. The vigilance department responsible for the follow-up of audit decisions is not adequately staffed and, as a result, a significant percentage of determinations are not followed through. The audit decisions need to be acted upon and penalties need to be collected, and that process is not transparent (Afridi and Iversen 2014; Aiyar and Mehta 2015). Upper-level bureaucrats do not adequately check to ensure that fines have been collected, wages paid properly, or excess wages reclaimed.[11] Further, the appeal process is held in private, behind closed doors, at the district level. Not every decision is appealed in practice, but can be, which structurally allows the possibility for private settlements within the bureaucracy.

Table 6.2 Participants in the Social Audit Process at Each Stage

Meeting	Auditors	Workers	Lower-Level Administrators	Upper-Level Administrators
Household survey	✓	✓		
Village meetings	✓	✓	✓	
Mandal-level public hearing	✓	Rarely participates	✓	✓
District-level private hearing			✓	✓

There simply isn't the political will to create the administrative infrastructure adequate to ensure that rulings made during the audit process are enforced. In other words, the extent to which last-mile problems can be resolved is indeed limited by first-mile problems.

Conclusion

This chapter argues that the implementation of social audits in Andhra Pradesh has evolved to accommodate fundamentally new possibilities for state-society relations, particularly with respect to marginalized citizens. I offer the metaphor of rewriting the state records as a way of thinking about these new relations. Rewriting is the ability to contest and make accurate the content of government records, in this case NREGA records. As such, I argue that the possibility of rewriting the state itself needs to be recognized as a positive and desired outcome. At this point in time, rewriting state records is a possibility and not a secure achievement. There are limits to it. First, the intervention is firmly located in one program of the state, NREGA in Andhra Pradesh, and has not been extended to other developmental programs. Second, the social auditors serving as representatives of the poor are attempting to facilitate this rewrite; poor workers do not initiate these actions directly. Third, the openings that upper-level NREGA bureaucrats offer are limited by the resistance of lower-level bureaucrats and politicians and by the complicity of some NREGA upper-level bureaucrats to ignore the findings. With all these caveats, social audits can be seen as a way to foster contestation at the last mile and thus as a potential way to make the state accountable to its poorest citizens (Jenkins and Manor 2017). The fact that workers can read records and participate in changing them is unprecedented in India.

However, workers do not always participate in public meetings to support the social auditors. In one audit I attended, the auditor was unwilling to reveal the workers' names. It was only after several days that I understood the reason for this hesitancy. At the mandal-level public hearing, I noticed a group of workers waiting impatiently for their findings to be read out. They all stood up when their village's name was called, but the presiding officers of the audit told them to sit down. Even though their village was being discussed, their particular issue did not come up for some time. The presiding officer read out each issue and then cross-examined the individuals concerned in the complaint.

When the issue that the impatient group of workers was concerned about was finally raised, the presiding officer called the name of the villager who had made the complaint. There was laughter when he rose to stand by the field assistant. The presiding officer asked whether he had given testimony to the auditor.

The worker acknowledged that it was his thumb impression on the document but added that he did not understand the issue. He was confused. There was no problem. He had received the money. He wanted to withdraw the complaint. There was nothing anybody could do. The auditors were furious and everyone present was laughing. The issue was dropped. The presiding officer thanked the worker for showing up to the meeting. While this could be viewed as the worker being forced to withdraw the public testimony and simply record it as a failure of the audit process, the story is both more complicated and intriguing. As I will show in the next chapter, when workers are mobilized, the audit process can allow for private bargaining between workers and lower-level bureaucrats, leading to private settlements outside the sphere of public meetings. More broadly, the next chapter shifts away from literal consideration of the public meeting to a more contextual understanding of how NREGA fits in with the local political economy of a village, which opens the door to even more radical outcomes of NREGA than its originators planned or could conceive of.

7

Caste, Class, and Audits

As I trudged up the hill to the worksite, a thirty-minute walk, the workers who had come with me did not know what to make of me. They seemed nervous about the fact that I was accompanying them. The field assistant stopped by on his motorcycle and offered me a ride, promising that we would be able to see multiple worksites at the same time. I politely refused and told him I wanted to do NREGA work. He laughed and went away. The workers had probably heard that I was coming to watch them; they were surprised when I later said that I wanted to work alongside them.

As soon as we reached the worksite, everybody went to his or her work group. The task for the day was building earth bunds (earthen walls) on a hill. When I first arrived, I just watched. I was not given any work even though I had expressed an interest in working. I learned that everybody brought their own tools: a pickaxe, a grub hoe, and a basket. There were no spares. After a bit, one of the women signaled to me to join her subgroup. She said she could use some extra help. A few people shouted at her for doing this. Digging bunds involves breaking up the ground, removing stones, and carrying and depositing sand. I wanted to prove that I could do it. I hoped that working would get me closer to the workers.

I soon realized that I did not have the skill required to do what the government classifies as "unskilled" labor. The woman was patient and said she would show me how to use the tools to work properly. I poked around and narrowly escaped chopping off my leg several times, worrying all the time that flying pieces of stone from nearby digging would hit me in the eyes. I worked dutifully for a bit, but the sun was very hot and I soon felt that it had been a long session.

I also wanted to try my hand at removing the stones from the ground. Another man in the group did this task, and he hesitantly gave me the necessary tool. He was clearly worried that I would break it. He told me that you have to use the tool with care and not hit the stone directly but on the side to loosen it from the ground. He showed me how to do it a few times, but to no avail. There was a constant clacking sound from the tool hitting the stone. I realized that I might reduce his wages by taking away his tool, so I decided to try the work only when he took a break.

After some hours the field assistant came by with his muster roll. He had come to take attendance at the worksite. The worksite was not accessible by motorcycle, so he had to park and walk. He was amused to see that I was working. He said, "Okay, come on, let us go now." I told him, "I will come back with the workers." The workers exchanged glances and the field assistant left.

Soon we all took a break. A few women had brought clothes in a bucket and they wanted my permission to wash their clothes in the nearby stream. I was confused and told them they were free to do as they pleased. The conversation moved on and eventually one of the women asked me, "When should we leave?" I told them, "We can leave whenever you are done." One of them asked, "Aren't you here to supervise us?" I said, "No! I am here to do research. I have no connection with the government." Even though I had told them about my study and had obtained their consent to do research among them, a few of them still seemed skeptical about my role.

One of them said that a supervisor from elsewhere would never be willing to do manual work with them even for a day and thus I could not be a supervisor. There was some discussion of my real motivation for coming there. Opinions varied: perhaps I was a CIA agent from America, coming to discover whether the laborers in rural Andhra Pradesh were doing their jobs. Perhaps I had run away from my family. We laughed. Finally, they seemed to accept that I was a researcher. Within a few minutes, the workers knew my family history and the amount of money I had spent on airfare to get there. They did not know what to make of the fact that I had spent so much money to come to India and be with them.[1] Even after hearing that I was a harmless outsider, one of them asked, "Can we leave now?" He was unconvinced by all the discussion and still thought I was there to oversee their work. They were used to being constantly supervised by farmers in their agricultural work. But in NREGA work, workers do not have continuous supervision of the work and they like that freedom.

That day they stayed at the worksite for five hours. I continued "working" at the site for two weeks. On the second day we finished the work in three hours, which seems to be their normal working time per day. This particular worksite was up in the hills and it was clear that the workers who were landless laborers did not find the work directly useful to them. For them, the NREGA work was useful primarily because it earned them wages. However, as I will discuss in this chapter, the benefits from the NREGA extended beyond wages. It gave local workers more bargaining power with members of the Reddy caste, who owned most of the land in their village.

The chapters so far have looked at struggles to build institutions to facilitate transparency within the NREGA program. The interventions geared toward ensuring accountability and transparency played out as struggles between upper-level bureaucrats and their subordinates and between social auditors and lower-level bureaucrats and local politicians, their sometime allies.

This chapter leaves the realm of bureaucracy and examines the implementation of NREGA in a large agricultural village. How does the NREGA process unfold in a village that is deeply and historically divided by caste and class relations? The analysis focuses on how NREGA gives workers leverage in a large agricultural village that is sharply divided between those who have land and agricultural laborers who are landless. I look at how class and caste relations affect the outcomes of NREGA.[2] While the data I present in this chapter were gathered in one village, I also draw on information from other villages where I spent time during my fieldwork.

As scholarly research on NREGA develops in Andhra Pradesh, it is becoming clear that the implementation is not perfect. One study of NREGA social audits found that workers prefer to be spectators rather than participants because they believe that the audits have limited impact. The authors find that there is "limited . . . redress" for the grievances the audits uncover, largely because of the complexity of the reporting and management structure of NREGA (Aiyar and Mehta 2015, 68). Upper-level bureaucrats do not always give audit reports the attention they should have. And as I showed in Chapter 6, there are indeed limits on how far upper-level bureaucrats can go to take actions on the findings. The decisions they make during the appeal process, which is private, often undermine the decisions taken in public audit meetings. It is likely that if the bureaucrats were to take more effective action, workers would participate more fully in the audit process.

However, in order to understand the range of effects the program has, we cannot simply look at government documents, examine testimonies of workers in public meetings, or look at what actions officials take in response to their grievances. It is also important to look at the broader economic spillover effects of NREGA on workers and how it affects their social relations with Reddies and local authorities. Also, using information to solve problems is not as straightforward as it seems. The ability of citizens to take advantage of the information depends on their social location. Recent critical work on government transparency argues that we can gain an understanding of the significance of information in any given social context only by examining power relations and public action (Benjamin et al. 2007; Fung et al. 2007; Hetherington 2012; Srinivasan 2011). In certain contexts, it is possible that the workers are afraid to speak out during social audits because of well-founded fears of reprisals (Pande 2015; Fox 2015).

The remainder of this chapter is divided into two sections. The first section describes the sociopolitical context of the village, with a focus on how Dalits have been mobilizing to gain power that predated the introduction of NREGA, a phenomenon that was not just local to the village. The second section discusses how the implementation of NREGA further affects power relations in the village. It then shows how, even in the context of entrenched social and economic boundaries, effective implementation of NREGA can improve circumstances for workers, extending beyond outcomes in NREGA to improving their bargaining power in relation to the dominant landowners and resulting in an overall increase in agricultural wages.

The Political Economy of a Village

With a population of about 5,200, the study site for this chapter was one of the biggest villages in the Kurnool district in the Rayala Seema region. I traveled there from the mandal administrative office by bus. The village had paved, well-connected roads where buses and motorcycles operated easily. It is internally segregated based on caste, similar to all the non-tribal villages I visited. Dalits, who identified as Malas or Madigas, account for about 34 percent of the population.

In the state of Andhra Pradesh, the two dominant land-owning castes, the Reddies and the Kammas, generally live in different regions. The leaders from these castes typically hold political positions. Reddies are typically members of the Congress Party and Kammas generally belong to the Telugu Desam Party (TDP). The Reddy caste is dominant in the Kurnool district. In local usage, "Reddy" is used to refer to any male member of the landed class, while "Dalit" refers to a member of the former "untouchable" caste. Large numbers of landless laborers are Dalits. However, it is important to note that not all Dalits are landless; some do own land.

Everywhere I went in Andhra Pradesh, villages were completely segregated based on caste.[3] The village I chose to live in had one of the largest landholdings in the district as measured by the number of acres under cultivation. I chose a large village because I hoped to witness as marked an interaction as possible between landed and landless residents. The landed farmers were also divided into small and large farmers, and these two groups have different interests.

Because I wanted to understand the history of the village and the evolution of the relationship between these players over time, a friend advised me to inquire in an unlikely place: the local police station.[4] The police in Andhra Pradesh have kept detailed records of their surveillance in the village that date back to the colonial era. These records helped me see the evolution of village conflicts over the course of decades. They showed the power of the Reddies, who were almost never formally charged with crimes, and the slow process by which Dalits have empowered themselves by reclaiming public spaces, blocking roads, and filing formal petitions. These records gave me an understanding of the social context in this village: the gradual transformation from a feudal society that the landed Reddies dominated to a more open system in which Dalits were able to occupy public spaces and attend schools.

I spent a few days sitting on the floor in the police station and took notes, as I was not allowed to photocopy them. They were bound in thick notebooks, each dedicated to one village in the mandal. I saw jottings that extended back thirty years, usually written in English and reading almost like the diary of a journalist or a field researcher.[5] The records indicated that the police were often aware of crimes even when no formal cases were reported. These were not legal documents or formal charge sheets; they were informal and meticulous notes the police kept so they could understand the activities in the village.

The police also had kept detailed records about the landed class: who owned how much land, who were the "troublemakers," how and where violence had erupted, how many deaths were due to preexisting conflicts, the size of the "army" that each leader commanded. They also recorded instances of Dalit resistance to elites. Several petitions had been filed over the last three decades in which Dalits asked for permission to celebrate their own events. One of the letters asked for permission and police protection for Christmas celebrations for a two-hour period. A few others reported harassment by Reddies. They asked the police for protection during weddings. These signed documents were the Dalits' attempts to reclaim the public spaces of the village and were evidence of a changing social system.[6] The police records showed me that the level of police surveillance of the local population, particularly the Dalit groups, is extraordinary.[7]

This contrasts with a dominant understanding that local Indian governments are weak or nonexistent. Lant Pritchett, a development economist, powerfully characterized India as a "flailing state . . . a nation-state in which the head, that is the elite institutions at the national (and in some states) level remain sound and functional but . . . this head is no longer reliably connected via nerves and sinews to its limbs" (Pritchett 2009, 4). The implication is that the state at the local level is disconnected from upper-level bureaucrats. However, the police records made it clear to me that the coercive state apparatus (the police) was present in this village and was happy to reproduce long-entrenched local structures. While the police kept detailed accounts of the law-and-order situation, I could not find historical records created by representatives of the state in the village about issues such as who had access to water, whether Dalit children were going to school, or whether people were getting work. Historically, state institutions at the local level have been concerned with preserving power relations; hence the focus on law and order over development.

However, Dalit groups have been mobilizing and demanding change. Today, Dalits in the village are not afraid of the landed class and don't have to seek permission from the police when they use public spaces. A few days after I entered the village, I observed evidence of this change. A group of youths was erecting a huge banner on the central pathway of the village that announced a celebration in the Dalit church. In this village, the Dalits have embraced Christianity, as is the case in most other villages in Andhra Pradesh. The symbolic gesture of placing a banner in a public space, where Reddies would see it, was an act of self-affirmation and defiance. This level of assertion did not arise overnight. As I watched the young men put up the banner, an older Dalit man told me such an act could not have happened even a decade earlier. The strength of these decentralized collective actions by marginalized groups determined the extent to which political parties took development programs seriously (Srinivasan 2015; Maiorano 2014).

The introduction of development programs such as NREGA in the village meant that upper-level administrators could force local bureaucrats to maintain proper documentation about development expenditures and who gets work. What was new and radical in the social audit process was that for the first time, Dalits and other ordinary citizens were able to inspect these records and question their veracity. The implementation of NREGA has led to more willingness among upper-level NREGA bureaucrats to control lower-level bureaucrats and to thwart the influence of local politicians to ensure that the program is implemented properly.

The determination of Dalits to occupy public spaces without fear created the space for a viable social audit process in Andhra Pradesh. Rao and Sanyal (2010) have studied the ability of marginalized people to speak out in state-sponsored public meetings. They analyzed 290 randomly selected gram sabhas (village public meetings) and found that marginalized citizens in the southern states, which includes Andhra Pradesh, were able to use these meetings to contest the decisions of village councils and other government institutions and to ensure that they receive entitlements from the state. They found that through participation in these meetings, citizens can present their opinions and grievances effectively and forcefully. Most important, they find that marginalized citizens were generally not afraid to speak out in public meetings. I found that Dalits in Andhra Pradesh, where they had a long history of mobilization to secure basic rights, were not afraid to participate in social audits and to contest NREGA records.

Despite the gains that Dalits have made, there is still a long way to go to dismantle the oppression of caste dominance in India (Balagopal 2011; Harriss 2012). The geographical separation of castes in the village where I stayed seemed to be frozen in time, as was the case in every village I visited. Dalits are forced to traverse Reddy areas when they leave the village, and thus Reddies see who comes and goes. There are also caste divisions among Dalits, who are subdivided into Malas and Madigas.[8] I stayed in the Mala portion of the Dalit area, and I experienced the sensation of being watched by the Reddies who sat and chatted outside their houses as I made my way to the bus stop. I was told that only a few decades ago, Dalits in this village had to carry their slippers in their hands when they walked through these streets. This was a blatant form of discrimination to force Dalits to show respect to members of the Hindu caste.

The Reddies' Opposition to NREGA

I did not have to try to get Reddies to talk about NREGA: they hated it and were glad to say so. The dominant reaction was the claim that NREGA made workers lazy. I heard this comment from every Reddy I questioned. According to one Reddy, the workers' laziness affected Reddies directly: "After NREGA the workers are not interested in working on our lands. They tell us, 'In your land, we have to work the whole day, but in NREGA we only work for two hours, so we cannot work for the same amount.'" One farmer tried to offer a solution: "NREGA is a waste. It does not benefit farmers. The wage has increased. They come whenever they want to. They should move the NREGA work to start from March instead of starting it from February." I heard other farmers push the date even further, to April, which would have made NREGA work available only in the summer months.

Some farmers claimed that NREGA made workers incapable of sustained work. They said that the bodies of the workers became used to not working, thus damaging their capacity for prolonged agricultural work. As a result, Reddy farmers were forced to hire more workers.[9] One farmer complained, "Nobody wants to work [in my farm] now. They just want money. The NREGA routine was just go, sit, and come back. The management needs to supervise. There is a percentage scheme: you get some, I get some. Who will speak out? There is a commission. There is no use of NREGA to the village. NREGA workers should be redirected to work on farmers' land." This farmer saw NREGA work as easy money for workers. He was also pointing out a favorite trope: discredit NREGA as a corrupt program that gave some workers an advantage. He was complaining that NREGA work had no supervisors to ensure that the workers were doing their job. He (and every other Reddy farmer I spoke to) felt that NREGA is easy money and that workers are getting a huge subsidy from the government to do nothing. Farmers saw NREGA as a threat to their dominance in the village.

I heard many farmers insist that the NREGA should include agricultural land in its list of work projects. They told me that they were not against NREGA, perhaps coming to terms with their inability to change the situation. "NREGA is good," one remarked, "if we are able to get the government to get the laborers to work on our lands." In effect they were asking for a state subsidy to regain their control of the laborers. However, if NREGA diverted projects to private Reddy-owned lands, it might lose its radical potential as a rights-based program. Keeping NREGA work as an alternative to working for local farmers enables workers to bargain for a better wage for agricultural work because farmers are no longer the only potential employers. Workers can choose to demand NREGA work whenever they need it and are freed from their former relationship with the landed Reddies.

One farmer spoke in a low voice and asked me not to identify him, a rare occurrence. He said:

> The people who are behind this are the leaders. They don't do any work but just show that there was work done for the audits. There is no use for the NREGA work. They don't do roads. They don't build useful assets. If we ask them we don't get anything. They tell us we don't have rules to get the NREGA money to redirect it on our lands. There is no place worse than this place in the whole earth. It is happening elsewhere. Only in my village there is nothing. The big farmers are big thieves. It is all done with the politicians. The workers are spoilt by the supervisors giving them a drink. I would also be corrupted by a drink.

The "leaders" the farmer referred to are the lower-level NREGA bureaucrats. He had tried to pressure them to redirect NREGA work to his lands without success and was surprised to find that the local NREGA bureaucrats could not comply with his request. They had told him that the decisions about work projects are not in their hands because upper-level bureaucrats control what works is allowed. The farmer rejected this explanation and saw this as a conspiracy involving workers, lower-level bureaucrats, politicians, and big farmers. From his point of view, NREGA benefits the workers at his expense. He was frustrated about the fact that the farmers who owned large landholdings and had connections to local politicians could not influence the local implementation of NREGA. This is evidence that the strategies upper-level NREGA bureaucrats have implemented are working to ensure that the program is implemented effectively. Even if lower-level bureaucrats wanted to collude with farmers to direct workers to privately owned land rather than to public works, they know that the social auditors will come and verify the worksite and talk to workers to learn where work was done. They do not have the discretionary powers to open up work wherever they want to. This farmer did not understand all of this and was upset.

Revealingly, the farmers who owned many acres of land tended to speak about abstract issues. They were not threatened personally by NREGA because most of them had leased their land to tenant farmers. Many of them were absentee landlords who had moved to the city. The large-scale farmers I interviewed typically told me that NREGA concerned bureaucrats and laborers and that I should go speak with them. Large farmers are very powerful and have strong ties to local politicians. If their economic interests were significantly affected by NREGA, they would have intervened aggressively in the program to stop its effects. They could have tried to force the field assistants to redirect NREGA work on their own lands or to control lower-level bureaucrats. Almost certainly they would have tried to thwart the social auditors when they entered the village. However, none of the owners of large farms I spoke to seemed concerned about the program or about the social audits. This was one of the reasons that the upper-level bureaucrats could control the last-mile problems: the most powerful actors in the village did not feel threatened by NREGA.

The smaller farmers I spoke with were explicit about why the big farmers did not align with them:

> We tried to tell the MPDO [mandal program development officer] to stop NREGA work. We got the collector [district head of administration and revenue] involved as well. But they just nodded. They said, "Take the labor after they finish NREGA work." But the reality is that the laborers are tired just walking back and forth in the sun. It is far away for them. We could be strong if we act together, but nobody is listening to us. The big landlords are not interested in fighting with us, because they do not care. They give their lands for lease. They don't need labor. They are not coming to support us. We need to give the worker food. We need to give them drinks and lure them to come to work.

The disadvantages of NREGA thus fall most heavily on the small farmers who own land that must be tended but do not have the ability to lease their fields when workers are unavailable and do not want to pay the higher wages that the workers now demand. Some who have leased land from large landowners are paying non-negotiable rents, which burdens them further. The concerns smaller farmers expressed about losing some power because of NREGA is a testament to the fact that in this village, the program is being implemented to benefit the most marginalized citizens, as the law that created the program intended.

One farmer in Andhra Pradesh told me:

> The farmers are not doing well. That's why we have farmers' suicide. We need a farmers' union. We need to stop planting and call for farmer strikes. Then they will all come running. Everybody is striking. Collectors are striking. Farm workers are striking. The factory workers are striking. The government employees are striking. We need to be striking. Nobody is representing us. We need to unionize. We need to declare a crop holiday here.

It was clear to me that small farmers felt so helpless in the face of NREGA and the increasing wage demands from workers that striking often seemed like the only avenue left to them.

Several of the farmers I spoke with wistfully remembered the "good old days" when laborers could be put to work on their private lands. They discussed several possible strategies for coping with NREGA, including negotiating with NREGA administrators for a farmer-friendly schedule and stopping NREGA work in their village.[10] They frequently mentioned their desire that NREGA redirect work projects to private lands. This idea was even being repeated in policy circles at the state level in 2012.[11] The farmers were quite optimistic about the possibility that this would happen. The way they saw it, either the NREGA program should be dismantled or it should direct workers to work on their own lands. They strongly preferred the latter.

One of my interviews was with a former faction leader, a Reddy whose name I had seen several times in the police ledger but who had mellowed over the years. He made the following remarks about Dalits:

> There used to be a fear before. They used to be afraid. Now they have learnt to question. The state is also giving them rice. They are getting aware of their rights. We used to control the laborers. We would not give enough money to workers. We would not give payment on time. Everybody was like this. . . . The problem with the caste system was not that the system was wrong, it was the implementation. The caste system was a good division of labor, but over time things went bad. We started looking at [the Dalits] as subhuman. This is how the feelings became bad. There used to be killing. Now the "moorkham" [animal] feeling has gone. The change has come. They are doing well. . . . These people did not even have proper food to eat. Now they have enough money.

I was surprised to hear this clear acknowledgment of how badly Reddies had treated Dalits in the village. This man suggested that the present-day resistance on the part of Dalits is a consequence of past acts of domination. He had witnessed the Dalits' struggles over time that had forced him and other elites in the village to recognize them as part of society. The implementation of NREGA and the audits need to be seen in this context. A different way to view these struggles is through understanding that a program like NREGA, with its transparency and audits, would not have worked as well as it did if Dalits had not struggled over many years and insisted on better treatment.

The relationship between Reddies and Dalits cannot be examined purely in economic terms.[12] There is also the ubiquitous abuse and contempt of Dalits' experience, the overwhelming social power of the Reddies, and the helplessness with which the Dalits faced the demands of the landed caste until very recently.

Workers' Support of NREGA

Dalit workers unanimously liked NREGA and wanted it to continue. While many of them did not know about the on-demand element of the program, they felt that the state had implemented the program well. They noted that NREGA gave them work in their own village and was a good substitute for earning income from agricultural work. They told me that agricultural work is not available continuously and that most of the Dalit workers had come to rely on NREGA income. For the first time, they felt some freedom to work without supervision, in contrast to agricultural work, where they were continuously surveilled by a Reddy landlord. They knew that I was talking to the Reddy farmers and told me not to believe them. They knew Reddies were not happy that they were working on NREGA projects, and they were happy that Reddy farmers could not stop them from doing so. NREGA has given workers some respite from economic dependence on farmers and a sense of control over their work. It is important to understand that for workers, NREGA represents a shift from the quasi-feudal clientelism that characterized their work with the Reddy landlords.[13]

My conversations with Dalits would start with a discussion of work and invariably end in an analysis of their relations with the Reddies. One worker observed, "We used to just go and work continuously for the Reddy. Even in the night we had to be available for work. Then we [would] have to start early in the morning. We did not get any wage. We used to get food and country liquor. It was like that." The landed caste's oppression of the Dalits has a painful history that is sometimes hard to bring out. In one discussion, a Dalit referred to caste-related discrimination as having "caste feelings." He was initially hesitant to talk to me about the issue, but when pressed he spoke as follows:

> I will tell you a story that happened in this village. It was a story about my uncle. It was natural for the workers to get kanji [porridge, usually made of rice soaked in water] from the Reddy. The kanji used to be served by the women in the household in a glass, a special container reserved for distribution purposes. But here the practice was that they would serve only the water to the workers, leaving the rice at the bottom of the container. One day, when the kanji was transferred, my uncle noticed exactly one morsel of rice that had slipped in by mistake to his cup. He immediately took hold of the grain of rice, tied it to a rope, and ran around the village. He was talking to the rice, it seems. "Why are you here? Why do I need this morsel of rice from the house of those bastards? Why do you come into my life and affect my peace?" He made such a scene that people from the village gathered around him. He then resolved not to go to that house to work anymore. That is our story.

The story is an ironic indictment of the cruelty Reddy employers too often showed the Dalits. The impact of NREGA cannot be separated from the history of caste oppression.

Discussing caste is a tricky issue. It is always present in the way the villagers live their lives. For example, it determines where their homes can be built and which part of the village they will inhabit. But it is not something one can easily bring up in conversation. I was eager to learn how and why the role of caste might have changed over the years.[14]

Traditionally, Dalits were not paid wages for their work. Instead there was a system called *vetti chakri*, in which workers received food in exchange for their labor. Being paid in cash is a recent phenomenon for the Dalits. One of them recalled,

> We started getting cash twenty years back. We used to get INR 1 for our work. Now we get INR 200. We got change. We got it because we have become aware in our society. Kids are learning slowly through schools. When we don't have anything, we go to the Reddy, and then we started having Ma Reddy Ma Reddy sentiment [My Reddy, indicating loyalty to their landlord]. We still offer respect, but things have been slowly changing over generations.

Traditionally, when workers did agricultural work, Reddies would accompany them to the fields. The workers would leave in the morning with their lunches packed and return after sunset. The Reddies constantly supervised them to ensure that they were working. I was curious to see how the workers were supervised in the NREGA system. Some of the Reddies had suggested that part of the problem with NREGA was that there was no supervision of the work, but the workers told me not to believe them. They readily accepted that they worked far less on NREGA projects than they do when they work on the agricultural land. They told me that they were paid based on the amount of work they did and explained the role of the NREGA technical assistant, whose job was to go to the worksite and measure the work completed.[15] They showed me their job cards and pointed to the variation in the amounts of money they had received. They were unwilling to be characterized as "lazy workers." Most important, they can stay in the same village and refuse to work unless they get paid wages that are comparable to what they got under NREGA. NREGA also gives them an alternative to migrating to cities for work. Many workers managed to finish NREGA work and then do agricultural work on the same day. NREGA gave workers more options.

It was clear that workers wanted the NREGA program to stay because it gave them the possibility of changing their relationship with the Reddies. When I asked them whether they believed the Reddies were responsible for the implementation of the program, one of the laborers said, "If it was the Reddy, we wouldn't get a single rupee. They would say that if we go to NREGA we cannot come to their land. They would have stopped the NREGA work if they have work in their land." It was clear that Reddies were not able to stop the work. That is also because the number of days were restricted. As one worker said, "We don't even have one hundred days of work [the minimum guarantee of NREGA]. But we are happy to get half that in a year per household. Imagine if we got one hundred days per person: the Reddies would be up in arms." Clearly he and his fellow workers viewed NREGA as something to be preserved.

Workers valued the system not only because of better wages but also because it gave them the autonomy to decide where they would work and a sense of self-respect. An incident that happened while I was staying in the village illustrates the strength of the Dalits' desire to be free from the control of the landed class. I was talking to a young Dalit man who was wearing a white-collared shirt. He told me that the Reddies had not welcomed his wearing such a good shirt. He said that the day before, he had been walking on the street past "his" Reddy's house. The Reddy, seeing his shirt, seemed visibly upset but did not ask him to remove the shirt, as would have been the norm in earlier times. Instead, he told the youth to move a heap of cow dung from area to another. The young man claimed that this was pointless work that the Reddy thought up just to ensure that his shirt would be soiled. Seeing my surprised reaction, the youth offered to walk with me down the street, confident that the interaction would repeat itself. The incident proved to me that although caste relations have changed, they are still a major and disturbing force in the village. Many Dalits still depend on Reddies economically. The young man told me, "This is the reason we like to have more work options." Many men and women from the village who have migrated to cities in order to escape the caste-based constraints of the village live in worse conditions, so preserving NREGA was very important to workers who chose to stay.

Changing the Balance of Power

YSR, the late chief minister, had the political acumen to appoint Raju, a Dalit, as the head of the Andhra Pradesh's rural development department, which ran NREGA. Raju was acutely aware of the corruption at the last mile and sought to control local politicians and limit the autonomy of the lower-level bureaucrats. Raju knew the power of landed Reddies from personal experience and was aware of the power they have with lower-level officials. He and his fellow upper-level bureaucrats created a system that took control away from Reddies. For example, Raju sought to ensure that workers are hired directly by NREGA lower-level bureaucrats rather than by local contractors.

Given that very few villages in India have bank branches, paying NREGA workers directly was one of the central last-mile challenges that occupied the upper-level bureaucrats. The upper-level bureaucrats experimented with different mechanisms to use technology to ensure timely payments to workers (Mukhopadhyay et al. 2013). To ensure that the payments went directly to workers and were not siphoned off by local intermediaries, workers had to be present to receive the money. The upper-level bureaucrats used biometric authentication of workers, secured through a combination of thumb impressions and iris scans, to ensure that cash was paid directly to workers. However, using technology like biometric authentication did not eliminate the need for the intermediary who had to be recruited to distribute cash (Srinivasan et al. 2018). The upper-level bureaucrats experimented with post offices, hiring different local private companies (Mukhopadhyay et al. 2013) to handle the payments as they found problems of corruption. Ultimately, the process of hiring these intermediaries at the mandal level was a political process that was another instance of governance through patching.

Another example is the innovation that was fought for by civil groups that eventually became part of the NREGA specification of having a worker called a mate at each worksite. This was a way to give power to the workers and involve them in monitoring the field assistants. Mates are hired to be representatives of the workers and are responsible for filling out official documents and keeping the muster rolls. Each mate is a worker who is the leader of their work group, which has about twenty people. In addition to doing the same work the other members of their group do every day, mates record attendance by entering names on the muster roll and taking thumb impressions from the workers toward the end of the workday. They are paid slightly more than the other workers in their group.[16] This is because, in theory, mates will operate to promote the interests of the workers. However, as I describe later, mates in Dalit villages have a complicated relationship with other workers and field assistants.

To fully understand how the outcomes of patching works in a village, let us consider how NREGA work is decided and assigned to a work group. The process starts with the upper-level bureaucrats in Hyderabad, who prepare a list of permitted work called the "shelf of works."[17] It determines what type of work will be done in that particular mandal for a particular NREGA season. To ensure that workers can be part of the decision-making process so they can choose the work that benefits them, the NREGA law mandates that a village meeting be held to decide which work projects will be done.

In the village where I stayed, the NREGA program officer in the mandal office showed me documentation with pictures to prove that there had indeed been such a village meeting to decide work. He kept a notebook that meticulously documented all meetings. The pictures showed people from the village attending the most recent meeting and approving the work schedule. I remarked that all the gram sabhas for the entire mandal (about twenty villages) were recorded as being completed in just couple of days. He nodded and said, "We work hard." But it was clear to me that the process had been carried out as a mere formality. This clearly violated NREGA principles, which dictate that the workers themselves will decide the nature of the work they will do. In reality, the workers were never consulted. The gram sabha was assembled only for the sake of proving later that there had been a meeting. The workers did not know what kind of work they would be doing until very late, often the day a project began.

Works that were allowed in NREGA mainly took place on government lands. At these sites, workers repaired canals; built contour trenches, bunds, and earthen dams; deepened and repaired flood channels; built mud roads; and cleared bushes. In some cases, a patch was issued through software changes that would make it possible for NREGA work to be allowed on private lands, particularly on lands Dalits and Tribals owned, to make it suitable for cultivation.

Each worker was paid based on a measurement of what his or her work group accomplished each day. For example, if the work involved digging a vermicomposting pit, the measurement verifies the dimensions (height, width, and depth) of the pit. In theory, payments are governed by an elaborate piece-rate system that has been established through a series of time-and-motion studies.[18] Pay rates are determined by measuring the collective output of each work group, instead of by tracking individual output. This is an attempt to incentivize the workers to work collaboratively.

Similarly, the measurement system also went through a series of patches. Work measurement was not enforced in the early days of the NREGA program. One of the state bureaucrats told me candidly that when NREGA was first introduced in the state, government officials just wanted workers to become aware of NREGA as a possibility: "Measurement would have put excessive pressure on the lower-level bureaucrats to maintain records, not to mention the workers complaining about the workload. We just left it loose for a year; there were no shackles to prevent deviations of any kind, and it was a free for all."[19]

Ignoring the measurement requirements was a way to gain consent from lower-level bureaucrats and workers to implement the NREGA program. A media person in the mandal corroborated this story; he told me that there was no measurement and that the workers did what they pleased in the early days of the program. This strategy had a negative consequence: the journalist added that "the lower-level bureaucrats and the mates started forging attendance registers and making money." In the early years of the program, administrators calculated that the most important thing was to ensure that the NREGA was implemented, that work was created, and that workers were paid. These upper-level bureaucrats were keenly aware of the importance of not being too meticulous too soon.

During my time in Andhra Pradesh, the work was only intermittent when NREGA work was on the calendar, even during the summer months. At a state-level meeting where I was asked to give my feedback, I mentioned that the policy of allowing work to be stopped and started according to the whims of bureaucrats significantly affected the "on-demand" nature of work.[20] I learned that some of the unexpected stoppages are attributable to the concerns of upper-level bureaucrats about corruption. For example, when upper-level bureaucrats discover that lower-level NREGA bureaucrats or other local people are engaging in fraud involving worksite materials in a certain type of work, they issue a patch to ban that type of work in all villages across the state. If the only type of work that is sanctioned in the village is the banned work, that effectively means stopping NREGA work in that village.

Because the process is centralized, and controlled by a software patch, even district-level bureaucrats cannot open new types of work that has not been approved at the state level. Lower-level bureaucrats often resented this centralization. I heard many district-level bureaucrats complain that there were no easy ways to add work. New categories of NREGA work are created through paper-based protocols; new categories cannot be added online. Farmers also tried to force local NREGA bureaucrats to assign work projects on their private agricultural lands. The centralized power that the program's upper-level bureaucrats have gained in allocating work protects lower-level bureaucrats when they encounter such requests; it is simply not in their power to make decisions about where NREGA work is done. While some lower-level bureaucrats complained to me about their lack of discretion in this matter, they also noted the benefits of not having to deal with pressure from local elites. While centralization has taken some autonomy away from lower-level officials, the advantage is that it prevents local bureaucrats and farmers from taking control of the system.

The guaranteed wage had a ripple effect and proved to be transformative. The journalist I spoke with told me that as a consequence of having "guaranteed money" from NREGA, workers started demanding higher wages from the Reddies for their agricultural work. Before NREGA, the daily wage for agriculture work was INR (Indian rupees) 50 for men and INR 30 for women. For that wage, they worked for eight hours, from 9:00 a.m. to 6:00 p.m., with a one-hour lunch break. But with the advent of NREGA, the daily wages in this village increased to INR 125 for both men and women, and they continue to increase whenever the minimum wage is increased in Andhra Pradesh.[21]

The journalist said that local farmers "suffered" as a result of this jump in wages.[22] When workers refused to work for less than the NREGA wage, the Reddies approached local mandal-level NREGA bureaucrats and politicians about the issue. The Reddies pressured the local mandal-level NREGA bureaucrats to stop work, claiming that they needed people to work their land. The law mandates that NREGA work should be given to workers whenever they request it. Yet in practice NREGA work is often stopped in the peak agricultural season to ensure that farmers will have laborers available to work. The journalist recalled that "the [NREGA program officer for the mandal] prepared it. They [lower-level NREGA bureaucrats] called for a meeting for all farmers and asked them when they wanted the laborers and the schedule was prepared based on their input. The farmers were satisfied." In my conversations with workers, it was clear that they were not happy about this and felt that this compromise worked against their interests. NREGA work peaked in this village in the summer when there is no agricultural work. If the work is available throughout and with no limit on the number of days of work, it would give workers an option to choose NREGA work over agricultural work. But that would also mean a greater resistance to the NREGA program from farmers. Studies looking at patterns of employment confirm this observation across all villages in the country (Sukhtankar 2016). But other than that, I could not find a "schedule" for opening NREGA work that was adhered to systematically. A national survey in 2010 estimated that about 19 percent of households reported attempting to get work under the act without success (Imbert and Papp 2015).

NREGA rules do not officially allow these compromises. Indeed, the intention in the founding legislation was that workers would be able to demand work at any time. Many activists claim that the limited schedule violates a key tenet of the program that sets it apart from previous development schemes. When I asked NREGA officials about the schedule, they initially denied its existence, then argued that it was necessary to take local conditions into account. The local member of the Legislative Assembly was explicit about this compromise. He was a Dalit and understood the workers' interests, but said, "We have to take care of the Reddies as well, otherwise they will create a scene."

Political Economy of Monitoring at the Last Mile

I arrived in the village one month before the NREGA social audits were scheduled to take place and went to the mandal office to familiarize myself with the preparations there. I had seen lower-level bureaucrats make such preparations in other locations, so I had some idea of what to expect in the office.[23]

Although I did not see those preparations up close in this mandal, I had observed them in a different mandal, where field assistants worked frenetically to create the necessary documentation. The process started with a meeting at which the NREGA program officer from the mandal announced that the auditors were coming in a few days. He instructed the field assistants to ensure that their documents were properly filled out and organized. The audits require that the documents be organized by village. This is one of the reasons auditors inform the mandal beforehand that they are going to perform an audit, even giving out schedules, despite the fact that such advance notice violates the purpose of an auditing procedure. If no warning were given, none of the documentation would be prepared and there would be avoidable delays. Giving advance notice of audits has thus become the standard practice. I have seen circulars sent through the government hierarchy that inform bureaucrats of an upcoming audit.[24]

By 2011 and 2012, lower-level bureaucrats had learned what the auditors typically look for, since the audits had been repeated several times. They had learned to make sure that supporting documents are in order and to reproduce any missing documents for the occasion. This requires detailed work. In the village where I witnessed preparations for an audit, some of the field assistants showed genuine fear about the audit because they believed their jobs would be in danger if all of the documents weren't in order. The more politically connected field assistants, however, were not worried. One of them played funny dialogues from popular movies that mirrored their helplessness. Nonetheless, in general a tense atmosphere prevailed in mandal offices before social audits. The auditors constantly find new ways to examine the data or to change what they look for. Most important, they talk directly to the workers. So even though they have advance warning, lower-level bureaucrats feel threatened by the audits. The deterrence effects of social audits on last-mile corruption are harder to measure, but this can be seen as an indication that the audits were consequential. A study looking at the perception of social auditors documented that the auditors felt that audits put pressure on lower-level bureaucrats to follow the rules, pay workers, and measure worksites, arguing that audits had a deterrence effect on lower-level bureaucrats (Pande and Dubbudu 2017).

The bureaucrats in the mandal associated with the village where I stayed did not let me observe their initial preparations. I protested that it was a government office and that I had the right to stay, but they replied, "Please, sir, we are busy. Try to understand, this is what the MPDO wants us to do. We are helpless. This is torture, sir. They are only paying us 2,200, and we have to do all this work." I left the building, not wanting to make their situation worse.

Preparation for the audits had ripple effects in the village. Even though I had spent a month in the village already, up to this moment I had not realized the full nature of the role of the mates. Prior to this point, my conception of the mate's role stemmed from the state's expectation that mates were representatives of the workers. As far as I could see, they acted like workers, too.

But with the audit looming, I stumbled upon a group of mates sitting and chatting and discovered another facet of their position. The assumption is that since the workers select the mate from among themselves, he has their interest in mind. While this was largely true in the Adivasi areas, it wasn't the case in the Dalit village.[25] There, it is difficult for auditors to get accurate testimony from workers because they can speak only through the mates. Before the audit, the field assistants in the mandal tell all the mates to warn the workers not to talk to the audit team. The mates are the only workers who attend the audit meetings. If a mate confesses to his "corruption" during the meeting, he is "fired" and the state notes that it has taken action. But firing a mate does not mean much because he never had an official government post in the first place. When I asked one mate about the auditors, he said, "We are the easiest to go after, but what are they going to do? All they can do is remove us from being mates so we become workers [again]."

When I fell into conversation with the group of mates during the village's preparations for the audit, we began chatting about how money is made in the village. The mates explained a scheme in which everybody—workers, mates, and lower-level bureaucrats—are paid off. One gave an example:

> The worker puts in only a half meter, but we exaggerate the depth of the [ditch]. When the technical assistant comes to check, he gets a cut, as he can see that the work is not completed. The worker gets the whole amount whether he worked or not—if we don't give the money to the worker, then he is going to upset the whole thing. So we take care of them. We make money by writing extra names in the muster.

The mates were describing in some detail how workers are sometimes included in the overall scheme. Workers are supposed to get paid based on the amount of work their work group completes; in other words, they are paid by the job, rather than by the hour. The technical assistant measures the work at the worksite every week to calculate the amount of work done. As was evident in this interview, technical assistants sometimes exaggerate the actual work done. In this case, the workers were fully compensated for their work even though they did not complete the job. Technical assistants collude with the mates to add names of workers who did not work to the muster roll. Both use the illicit money that the padded muster roll generates to pay themselves and the workers whose names were there on the musters. This is a risky move, as there is a possibility that the auditors will discover this scheme. The specter of the audits ensured that the workers had to be part of the scheme. Mates were the conduit between the workers and the field assistants and helped secure their consent. While, at one level, the act of workers colluding with the field assistants to cheat NREGA funds can be seen as a failure to root out corruption, this act needs to be seen as evidence of how relations between the workers and the local state are changing.

The mates, who start out as workers, thus became middlemen who sometimes were willing to act against the interests of the workers. When I asked whether they were middlemen, they laughed and said, "We are Dalits too. We do not have money. We just skim some money. There are bigger things that are going on, and nobody is going after them [the local elites]." One mate bemoaned the fact that the workers do not understand the dynamics of the system and blame the mates for its shortcomings:

> Everybody says a mate is a *donga* [thief], but nowhere does it come out that the worker is a *donga*. The worker does not seem to realize the equilibrium. The workers want everything. They don't realize that there are others in the game. Everybody needs money. Money is made through fake names. The worker says why shouldn't he be paid when others are paid. If workers work, then it would be a different matter. Why do you think the workers are coming to the gram sabha and speaking with confidence? "Ten acres of removing thorns shown in the record." In practice they do it for two acres. Everybody benefits.

This mate said that while the workers do get a cut, they sometimes don't get the full amount because others are involved. He was upset that workers want more. The mates explaining the situation to me said that "the whole logic is worked out. The money trickles up." They mentioned all the actors involved—the field assistant, the technical assistant, the intermediaries involved in payments, the engineering consultant, the mandal program development officer. Although they were not aware of the NREGA bureaucracy beyond the mandal level, their understanding of the digressive practices of lower-level bureaucrats was comprehensive.

While this mate was admitting to participation in corruption, the presence of outside auditors is a check on such behavior. During the social audit, the auditors verify every worksite to see whether work is done. They also talk with the workers to corroborate the data they see in reports and documents. The audits had a deterrence effect on the frauds that were committed.

The mate interpreted what could be officially labeled as "corruption" as a form of redistribution, one that he had a share in. To the extent that the auditors dampen this possibility, mates are at loggerheads with the auditors. This complicates the story that the workers will all benefit from the presence of the auditors, as it depends on the local social relations which requires a nuanced understanding of the political economy at work.

Lower-level NREGA bureaucrats have learned not to cheat workers because workers won't be afraid to speak to the auditors and create trouble for them. This seemed to ring true not just in this village, but across Andhra Pradesh. However, field assistants have not stopped skimming funds from NREGA; they have simply changed how they do it, as I learned in a conversation with one of the state-level leaders of the field assistants' union.[26] He told me about the percentage scheme, which mirrored what I had heard from the mates in the village where I stayed. He said, "We don't touch the labor [wages] side of things. We used to before, but we have decided to change, to focus on the material side and to exaggerate and fudge the cost of materials prepared for the work." I heard similar remarks from auditors. It seems clear that NREGA bureaucrats siphon program funds into their pockets through the mechanism of documents that report inflated material costs. They no longer skim money from funds allocated for workers' wages. However, the field assistants deliberately allowed mates to steal money from workers to gain their support.

Another riskier form of fraud is the bribes some mates attempt to give auditors to look the other way when they identify discrepancies in the NREGA documents. The auditors use measuring tapes to calculate the work that has been done. If they find discrepancies between their numbers and what they see in the documents the technical assistants generate, they note it in their reports. I attended several audits and went to the field sites to measure the amount of work that was done alongside the auditors, and I can corroborate discrepancies like the ones the mates had mentioned to me. I asked the mates about the audit team that would soon be arriving. "If the auditors do a good job, we will also settle them under the covers," one said. "All of this is taken care of before the gram sabha. The last time the auditors came, we gave them some chicken and liquor and settled the matter. But we try to avoid going to that level. Our workers won't talk. We will instruct them what to say." Another mate told me more cautiously, "The auditors cannot be captured all the time. They cannot be reliably captured. We don't know who comes as auditors this time." The social audit leadership had anticipated this and works to ensure that the auditors are carefully assigned. Because auditors do not visit the same village twice, there is no possibility of sustained collusion between the auditors and the bureaucrats.

As a result, the deterrence effect of the audit I observed was real. The field assistants did not want to be targeted as perpetrators of fraud. They were visibly tense throughout the audit. It was clear to me that audits had the effect of ensuring that lower-level NREGA bureaucrats did not cheat the workers and the state.

When the topic of mates arose in my discussions with audit supervisors and upper-level bureaucrats, the supervisors revealed that they knew about the role of the mates in the chain of corruption. The upper-level bureaucrats insisted that mates are NREGA workers; they had created a role for a worker to be chosen as a mate to give one more role to NREGA workers in the day-to-day operations of NREGA. The idea was to give workers (via the mates) direct access to a key document that determined how workers got paid. However, when I suggested that the state's view of mates as supporters of the workers was too optimistic, one senior bureaucrat replied, "That is the extent of what we can do as a state. If the mates want to cheat their own workers, what can the state do?" It was an admission that the last-mile problems are not that easily wished away by clever design. Further, it also shows that marginalized citizens (in this case mates) have agency and they work through complex means, not necessarily upholding what the upper-level bureaucrats desires.

What constitutes success is complex, as are the political and economic divisions at the local level. Mates play a complex role. On the one hand, they represent the workers. On the other hand, they find ways to benefit from the program and strike deals with field assistants. The ability of marginalized citizens to strike deals with members of the state is a significant achievement that needs to be recognized. While the audits gave the information to the workers to strike such bargains with the state, the historical processes of social mobilization by Dalits was a prerequisite that began long before NREGA was implemented. Finally, outcomes are not just the result of contestations in public meetings. They are also reached through private settlements away from the glare of these meetings. But one can only see this by understanding both the history as well as the political economy of the village, as I analyze in what follows in this chapter.

I was in the house where I was staying when the auditors came by to ask their routine questions of the house owner. My landlady told me, "Look at these auditors—they are dressed so badly. They are not officers. They cannot do anything. All their findings will be dropped." I was surprised by her quick condemnation. She had gone from looking at their clothes and commenting on their appearance to determining whether they had any strength in the bureaucracy. Then I remembered that I had heard discussions about such observations during training sessions for the auditors.[27] But when the auditors requested uniforms and state-issued ID cards establishing them as state employees, their supervisors had rejected the idea, claiming that the auditors should be seen as fellow workers because that would give the workers confidence about answering their questions. In practice, this decision occasionally had the opposite effect: a few workers did not think that the auditors were important because of their lack of official dress and thus dismissed their questions. Auditors learned to cope with this and began dressing more formally. The biggest reason that workers trusted the auditors was that they took great efforts to be separate from local bureaucrats and politicians. The adversarial relationship social auditors had with lower-level NREGA bureaucrats sent strong signals to the workers and generated trust.

The auditors were determined to do a thorough job. They told me that they had received many statements from workers: the word had gone out that other people had spoken to the auditors. The mates and the field assistant were putting pressure on the auditors to reveal the names of the workers who had made statements. Although the auditors initially refused to reveal that information, they later yielded to the pressure and read out the audit findings along with the names of who testified before the village-level audit meeting. I asked the auditors why they had given out the list. One senior auditor replied, "If we did not, then it would be hard for us to prove our case in the meeting and they would dismiss the evidence." Audits had started to require reading out the findings at the village social audit meeting. Every finding had to be signed by an ombudsman in front of the village meeting. The public reading served a dual process. It was to inform workers of the audit process, but it also was a way for the field assistants to discover the details of the audit process.[28]

The village social audit meeting was held in the village square. At first glance, it seemed to be well attended. It even appeared that workers were participating in the event. But on closer examination, it became clear that only three groups were present: the mates, the lower-level NREGA bureaucrats (field assistants, technical assistants, engineering consultants, and computer operators), and the auditors. Workers would often be brought in from their houses to the meeting if they were willing to change their testimony. Almost at once a fierce argument broke out between the mates and the auditors. The mates disputed all of the auditors' findings. The person who was supervising the meeting, a mid-level bureaucrat who worked in a different program, sided with the NREGA bureaucrats. There was vigorous dispute and confusion about what exactly his role was. The senior auditors stated that he was there merely to record the proceedings in order to maintain some appearance of objectivity. But he insisted that he had to evaluate the decision on each claim that was brought up and decide whether to accept that evidence or not.

As I discussed in Chapter 6, upper-level bureaucrats and the SSAAT leadership sought to use the mandal public hearing as the venue where decisions about how to resolve workers' grievances were made. At the village level, the lower-level bureaucrats and politicians wield a lot of power, but they diminish at the mandal level. In addition, the auditors explicitly sought to keep the politicians off the dais. The politicians largely keep out of the mandal public hearings. The upper-level NREGA bureaucrats allowed the auditors to present their evidence and then gave the lower-level bureaucrats a chance to respond. Reddies did not attend the village social audit meeting.

The Reddies I spoke to did not think much about the auditors. They had trouble recalling the last time the auditors had been in the village and did not seem to particularly notice that the auditors were in the village for another audit. They reported to me that the entire audit unit was a sham. They wanted the auditors to find more examples of fraud among NREGA employees. From their point of view, the audit unit was part of the state. I tried challenging them with the fact that the audit unit includes youth from the nearby mandal, but they dismissed them as pawns of the bureaucrats, who would do what they were told to do and thus lacked any agency. The auditors are trained to avoid speaking to Reddies because of the worry that they will unduly influence the process. As a result, they have avoided one source of corruption: elite capture of the auditors.

When the auditors were going door to door, double-checking the official records by talking to workers, I saw how the audit process enabled workers to settle these accounts in private settings. I noticed that a worker in the house across from where I was staying gave a statement about her delayed payments in addition to answering the auditors' questions. I did not think much of it, but later that evening, I saw a mate stop by the house. He asked for the woman who had given statements to the auditors and gently asked her why she had made that statement to the auditor and not to him. She said she had done that in the past but had received no response. After some deliberation, the mates promised to arrange to have the worker paid, if she withdrew her complaint in the public hearing. She agreed to go. The presence of auditors provides workers with information and a channel to express their grievances, ultimately giving them a leverage they did not have before. If there were no audits, workers would not have found out about the precise details of the payment as well as an opportunity to contest that record. In this case, the mates try to settle them privately.

In my conversations with the mate, it was clear that he was doing the bidding of the field assistant. The mate had worked with the field assistant to cheat other workers in his group. But when the worker found out from the social auditor that she had been cheated, she chose to report to the auditor.

In this instance, the mate intervened to protect the field assistant by asking the worker to take back her complaint and promising her that he would give her all of the wages she was owed. This mate is part of the same work group as the worker and lives on the same street as she does. I have seen him go to the same church as her and attend the same birthday celebrations. They are part of the same social group. While there is no guarantee that the mate would do what he promised, it seems extremely unlikely that he could get away with not paying her the wages she was owed.

That conversation points to how the equilibrium between the workers and the lower-level bureaucrats had changed. The strategy that upper-level bureaucrats used to minimize the distance between state officials and workers has worked, but not in the way the bureaucrats originally imagined. Workers are able to use the mates to get the back wages they are owed. The incident I observed was extraordinary: an ordinary worker negotiated for her rights directly with a state surrogate. The negotiation she engaged in was facilitated by the social audit. The fact that marginalized workers can speak out and protect their interests points to a shift in the balance of power between workers and lower-level bureaucrats. The social audit process makes it harder for field assistants to directly steal workers' wages. It is no surprise that workers wanted to preserve NREGA. They valued the program not just because of the better wages they earned, but because it gave them a chance to question the accounts of a state program. Their leverage stems from presence of auditors and a shared interest among mates and workers in maintaining NREGA.

I witnessed this scene outside the formal spaces the state has set up for settling worker grievances. It is an example of the type of informal negotiations that happen because of the opportunities the audit process gives to workers. Part of the reason lower-level NREGA bureaucrats fear the social audit is that the process informs the workers about their rights and sometimes leads the workers to ask for all of the wages they are owed. Audits provide opportunities for workers to settle their accounts with local bureaucrats, even if the settlement does not happen in the full glare of the public meetings.

Conclusion

This chapter has looked at how NREGA gives workers in a large, socially divided agricultural village leverage and how that influences their willingness to participate in social audits. The implementation of NREGA must be understood in the context of the historic power relationship between Dalits and Reddies. It is an example of the state's shift toward recognizing the rights of Dalits. Even ineffective implementation of the program undermines the Reddies' monopoly on employment and gives workers leverage to demand higher wages and exercise their rights more broadly. I have argued that Dalits are able to participate in social audits because of the decades of progress they have made through social mobilization and the economic incentives they have to participate in NREGA.

However, analyzing what constitutes success in the NREGA program is a complex question. The implementation of NREGA has reduced the ability of lower-level bureaucrats to engage in corruption at the last mile, has delivered wages to workers, and has improved the power of workers to bargain with farmers when they do agricultural work. Thus, it can be said that social audits work and that the participation of Dalits matters to the success of NREGA. Yet the implementation has flaws. Most noticeably, Dalit workers do not fully participate in public meetings. In their analysis of social audits, Aiyar and Mehta (2015) point to one central flaw: the lack of appropriate follow-up actions from upper-level bureaucrats disincentivizes workers to participate at a deeper level in the social audit process. If bureaucrats followed up on social audit findings, workers will participate more in that process.

In this chapter, I have offered two other reasons why workers do not participate more in social audits. First, even though NREGA is implemented imperfectly, it still benefits workers. The freedom they have to choose NREGA work has given workers leverage to negotiate with Reddies for higher agricultural wages. They wouldn't have this leverage if NREGA were to disappear, and this may be a reason why they are reluctant to speak out more during social audits: they fear that if they were to speak out more, NREGA would be shut down. Second, public meetings are not the only channel through which settlements are made. They are sometimes made in private negotiations. The audit creates the framework for such private resolutions of grievances. Thus, I argue that looking at levels of workers' participation in public meetings is not the only measure of the effectiveness of social audits. Ultimately, I have shown how the NREGA administrators, through patching, have worked to tip the balance of power in favor of workers.

8
Conclusion
Patching the Balance of Power at the Last Mile

Shedding new light on the challenges and benefits of using information and technology to implement development programs has been the goal of the evidence and theoretical analysis that I have offered in this book. I have drawn my evidence from one of the largest development programs in the world, the Indian National Rural Employment Guarantee Act (NREGA), examining in detail NREGA's implementation in the South Indian state of Andhra Pradesh.[1] My analysis raises and explores two fundamental questions. First, how can such programs effectively deliver benefits to marginalized citizens in ways that enhance the rights and freedoms of these citizens? Second, what should such programs do to avoid being captured by either state or local power systems?

While the case is complex, I have tried throughout to keep my argument straightforward. I started the book with a discussion of a social audit of NREGA conducted by a landless labor union (Jan Jagaran Shakti Sanghatan) in Bihar. The social audit process revealed that attendance registers (muster rolls) had been tampered with by local elites at the village level. The vignette revealed how state and local power systems often siphon off money from development programs. The ability for activists and workers to not only publicly examine state documents, but also challenge local elite power, was a radical moment in and of itself. In the Bihar case, this was achieved through the social audit process, which was possible because of the Right to Information Act (RTI) of 2005. In Andhra Pradesh, through willing bureaucratic support, the social audit process created a better implementation of NREGA.

NREGA was a result of campaigns by social movements and civil society to ensure that every rural citizen has the right to work and the right to income resulting from that work. However, in highly unequal societies—with lack of literacy and deep asymmetries of power—marginalized citizens may not be in a position to exercise such rights (Walle et al. 2012). Public questioning of state actions requires constant vigilance by civil society or unions, which are not uniformly present. Moreover, often with no countervailing power, even the best-intentioned development projects suffer from "last-mile" problems in implementation.

It is well acknowledged in the literature that in order to succeed, development programs need to confront power (Li 2007; Harriss 2001). The neglect of questions of power is not exclusively a last-mile problem (Rajadhyaksha 2011). Most problems occur at the first mile because of politics, corruption, apathy, and structural violence committed on the poor by state bureaucrats, irrespective of where they are located in the hierarchy (Gupta 2012). Moreover, lower-level bureaucrats and politicians are not all rent seekers, corrupt to the point of necessitating the elimination of local discretion (Tendler 1998).

However, the point of departure of *Patching Development* is the assumption that good design and political will are necessary but not sufficient conditions for dealing with last-mile problems. Indeed, it is possible to address and effectively mitigate last-mile problems with the right implementation of the appropriate socio-technical infrastructure. I chose to study the NREGA implementation in Andhra Pradesh, where there was political will to implement an apparently well-designed program (Maiorano 2014), but, nonetheless, as I have shown, challenges at the last mile still needed to be confronted to ensure the program works for its intended beneficiaries.

The capacity of local actors to capture state programs and resources is based on their local social power, the alliances they build, and their ability to exploit information asymmetries. The bureaucratic systems that link higher levels of government to the local government (in the Indian context: districts, blocks, mandals, and panchayats) are opaque. To ensure that welfare programs deliver intended benefits to the poor, accountability systems must enable citizens to hold the state answerable at the last mile (Fox 2020). Most importantly, holding the state accountable requires understanding the intricate politics involved in the local implementation of these programs. This is what I set out to do.

In particular, I focused on the evolution of policy mechanisms that were necessary to deal with resistance from the local power system.[2] I showed how state bureaucrats leveraged local information to deal with implementation failures by building participatory bureaucratic institutions to gain support through the engagement of the very marginalized citizens that the program sought to help. As I have shown, the local system of power is hard to transform, not because of inertia, but because of counter-strategy from actors at the last mile whose power was threatened by the program. Yet, as I have argued, bureaucrats do not possess the capacity to fundamentally change this power axis through direct confrontation with local elites, but instead have to rely on a continuous series of responses that react to local implementation and information, a process I call "patching development." The particular practices through which NREGA was managed in Andhra Pradesh were the result of a process of contestation within the NREGA bureaucracy, as well as a combination of pressure and cooperation between social activists and bureaucrats.

Patching alters power equations by directing attention to the mundane minutiae of processes. These include changes in institutions and technology, changes in documents, and changes in other implementation practices and procedures. Political will is an important precondition for the process of patching. The need for patching points to the fallibility of state institutions and their information systems. Patching highlights the ability of upper-level bureaucrats to access local information about implementation details to address the counter-strategy from powerful actors at the local last mile.

The process of patching development has three key features. First, patching is top down, where the patch sender is at a higher level than (i.e., has jurisdiction over) the patch receiver. Second, patching is about fine-grained changes, where patches are extremely specific and make focused alterations to policy. Third, patching is iterative, where patches are repeatedly authored, are sent based on new information, and become part of a continuous cycle of small, detailed changes to overall program implementation. Patches, then, are a series of incremental remedies rather than a one-time overhaul. By patching, states can repeatedly change their practices and plans based on information and challenges as they arise during the implementation process.

I have attempted to avoid both the uncritical exuberance of some information- and digital technology–based policy solutions to last-mile problems, as well as the exclusively critical view of state bureaucrats often assumed in the literature on the state. Instead, given the deep-rooted strength and tenacity of local power systems, it is critical to consider how state action is able to confront the sober reality of extremely poor conditions of education, health, and employment, as well as gender- and caste-based inequalities that persist in most parts of the world. This approach has revealed both what is required for citizens to make claims on the state and how upper-level bureaucrats can create mechanisms that enhance and reinforce accountability. Usually, these processes are neither neat nor orderly. In particular, I have shown that struggles over the use of technology and transparency of information, as well as control over documents and public meetings in Andhra Pradesh, have led to a much more contentious sphere where the exercise of power over documents is both fluid and highly situated. Consequently, the resulting information must be examined in relation to specific contexts. My analysis has focused on the politics of implementation at three levels: relations within the bureaucracy, relations between state and society, and relations within society at the last mile.

My intention in this conclusion is to revisit the process of patching development that I have analyzed in the preceding chapters, underlining how my analysis has challenged the way in which the development literature has traditionally interpreted the use of digital technology, citizen participation, and government transparency. It ends with summarizing my vision of the process of patching as well as its limitations.

While my evidence is drawn from a specific case study, the analytical arguments can be applied in a range of developmental contexts. Future applications of the idea of "patching development" will no doubt refine and improve my formulations, hopefully incorporating them into a continually evolving debate. Nonetheless, I hope that the basic architecture of my argument will serve as a useful tool in confronting a diversity of challenging developmental cases.

Outcomes and Mechanisms of Patching in Andhra Pradesh

NREGA's impact in Andhra Pradesh was substantial. First, NREGA workers got to work in their own village and got paid, delivering wages to marginalized citizens as promised. Men and women were paid equally, a departure from the norm. Second, as I discuss in Chapter 7, NREGA's impact extended beyond the program itself to improve more broadly the marginalized workers' bargaining power in relation to the dominant landowners. As a result, agricultural wages increased. A recent study found that in Andhra Pradesh, NREGA increased mean income of NREGA workers by 12.7 percent, with 90 percent of that increase coming from an increase in agricultural wages (Muralidharan et al. 2017). By reaching poor citizens, NREGA targeted and meaningfully improved their lives, accomplishing something few other programs had been able to do. This was no small feat; in fact, it required fundamentally rewriting relationships across the state and society. In earlier development programs in Andhra Pradesh, the relationship between upper-level bureaucrats and marginalized citizens had been routed through local stakeholders, which contributed to last-mile problems. Upper-level bureaucrats in Andhra Pradesh worked to shift that (Reddy 2013; Maiorano 2014). They governed NREGA by attempting to limit the "local power system nexus."

Table 8.1 schematically shows the shift in relationships between high-level bureaucrats, low-level bureaucrats, marginalized citizens, local politicians, and local elites after the implementation of NREGA. It points to shifts in social and bureaucratic relations that were enabled by the mechanisms that were put in place and which I observed in NREGA during my fieldwork. The outcomes are by no means a secure achievement across the state. I have not seen this approach being applied across all state programs, which shows the criticality of social mobilization and political will in creating the enabling conditions for patching development. Yet, I hope that there are lessons to be learned from such modest achievements. Much of this book has been devoted to examining how these relational shifts occurred.

Table 8.1 Outcomes in Andhra Pradesh

Relations with Constituents	Lower-Level Bureaucrats	Local Politicians	Marginalized Citizens
Upper-Level Bureaucrats	Upper-level bureaucratic control ↑	Bureaucratic autonomy ↑	Create grievance redressal opening
Lower-Level Bureaucrats	N/A	Bureaucratic autonomy ↑	Voice of citizens in contesting lower-level bureaucrats ↑
Local Elites	Bureaucratic autonomy from elite demands ↑	N/A	Citizens' bargaining power ↑

Table 8.2 lays out the mechanisms—such as technology, social audits, or the public disclosure of documents—through which NREGA was able to effect change and how this change solved problems in the last mile. By breaking down the mechanisms through which upper-level bureaucrats and citizens were able to hold lower-level bureaucrats accountable, this analysis highlights the components of an institutional strategy required to effectively patch development. Three features of NREGA were critical to overcoming the last mile problems in implementation. First, upper-level bureaucrats used digital technology to control lower-level bureaucrats through a form of intra-bureaucratic monitoring to eliminate misappropriation within the bureaucracy. The technology was constantly updated to cope with the ongoing resistance from the lower-level bureaucrats and to ensure that the intentions of the bureaucracy were followed through at the last mile. Second, an effective participatory bureaucratic institution needed to be built that went beyond providing information to citizens, but was also able to mediate the struggle for accountability at the last mile. The social audit institution allows for an independent audit of the program and is able to publicly contest the official record. Third, providing marginalized citizens access to official documents is a needed step forward but, still, only half the equation; more importantly, the state should be willing—and have the capacity—to act on citizens' findings. In software parlance, citizens need not only "read access" to documents, but also "write or edit access," i.e., the ability to enforce a rewrite of state records.

The main function of public meetings within the NREGA auditing process is to communicate the findings of the auditors and to make decisions on the petitions and complaints lodged by citizens. Social auditors were motivated to take the NREGA records and read them out to NREGA workers, and the auditors' participation was a given. Historically, Dalits were politicized through their involvement in social movements fighting for dignity, rights, and equality.

Table 8.2 Mechanisms for Overcoming Last-Mile Problems in Implementation

State-Society Actors	Outcomes		
Implementing Mechanisms	Lower-Level Bureaucrats	Local Elites	Marginalized Citizens
Upper-Level Bureaucrats	Devised ability to monitor through technology Shifted certain decisions based on local reactions Presided over social audit meetings and took decisions	Centralized hiring of lower-level bureaucrats and removed local elite power Controlled when to open up work using a schedule Regulated the type of work allowed under NREGA	Established workgroups and made it fixed Created possibilities for citizens to access government records Increased direct interaction with citizens in social audits
Social Auditors	Verified records created by lower-level bureaucrats Visited field sites to measure NREGA work Generated social audit reports	Social auditors avoided local elites	Hired village social auditors from the family of marginalized citizens Read out state records in public and private meetings Supported citizens' voices against lower-level bureaucrats
Lower-Level Bureaucrats	N/A	Hid behind the computer against demands from local elites	Settled accounts privately outside of public meetings

When auditors visited their homes and asked them to testify in meetings, they were able to. Yet, having the ability does not mean they will actually engage in the manner and on the terms that the upper-level bureaucrats desire them to participate.

The upper-level bureaucrats focus on the auditors' monitoring of the local state with support from the workers. The auditors attempt to engage only with workers, rather than other actors in the village. Yet other actors are often deeply influential in the social structure of the village and in the tensions and conflicts that are present in the community. Auditors try to dampen the influence of the landed class and the political parties, particularly the opposing political party, by leaving them out of the audits. But the lower-level bureaucrats insist on fully open local village meetings.

One of the innovations of the social audit process was the prevention of secret audits controlled by the powerful. In theory, public hearings ensure that the findings cannot be suppressed because of the number of citizens present to witness and question the proceedings. In practice, however, I found that these public meetings also allowed lower-level bureaucrats to seek to influence the auditors and put pressure on the workers to change their testimonies.

To the extent to which social audits were effective, the resulting shifts in state-society relations ran counter to powerful and historically entrenched hierarchies and interests (Sainath 1996). For the implementation of NREGA to facilitate this reordering required a political commitment by the state to rewrite its relationship with the poor. Given the strength of the historical hierarchies between Dalits and landowners in villages, as well as the way the interests of these hierarchies are generally safeguarded by local politicians and low-level bureaucrats, the outcomes in NREGA required significant political will to enable upper-level bureaucrats to act in the interest of the marginalized citizens. However, while this commitment was necessary, it was only the starting point. The progress made under NREGA did not unfold in a vacuum and must be viewed in the context of the historical struggle for equality by marginalized peoples and as yet another step toward empowerment, as discussed in Chapters 2 and 7.

The social auditors attempted to work around the problem of local elite capture by implementing a number of strategies ranging from not conducting the meetings to revealing very little in them. As a result, the auditors in general try to not air their findings publicly in order to prevent lower-level bureaucrats from manipulating the workers. Ironically, the lower-level bureaucrats often want the testimonies to be read out only so that they can pressure the workers to withdraw their complaints. Openness, therefore, can be a double-edged sword, and its desirability depends on the context and on how and why it is been put to use. What is openness to auditors manifests itself as monitoring to the lower-level bureaucrats. Not surprisingly, the lower-level bureaucrats resisted.

Dealing with contestation over public records cannot be resolved by simply providing new social audit records (Sharma 2013). As I show, these audit reports are challenged by lower-level bureaucrats, and this contestation, as with information problems more generally, cannot be resolved by more information, even if it is digitized (Srinivasan et al. 2017; Tsoukas 1997). Social auditors found discrepancies in the measurements of NREGA done by lower-level bureaucrats as recorded in the measurement books and produced new audit reports (Marathe and Chandra 2020). But recording this information alone was not enough to change the records; the auditors had to present their case in the public meetings and argue against the interpretation of lower-level bureaucrats. A similar phenomenon has been documented more widely. For instance, a study that examined Paraguayan state efforts to resolve land disputes by digitizing them and making the information public found that such disagreements could not be solved simply by digitizing records, but rather required addressing the interpretation of those records (Hetherington 2011). Anthropologist Kregg Hetherington writes, "The problem was not in the papers themselves—the problem emerges only as people fight over the interpretation of the documents, when they go to court and swarm the archives and set their notaries against each other" (Hetherington 2011, 145).[3]

The fight over documents is messy and doesn't always lead to outcomes that are expected. In order to give the workers more stature and representation, upper-level bureaucrats created the role of "mates"—workers elected as representatives of the larger worker population. As I show in Chapter 7, however, the mates strive to block the monitoring of the state. Far from having the interests of the average worker at heart, they collude with lower-level bureaucrats. In one respect, the mate system points to a shift in social relations with the state. But as we saw, the ability of workers to negotiate effectively with the state depends on prior mobilization. The point is that social audits need to be evaluated not just in terms of the outcomes of NREGA, but also in terms of how they change relations between the Indian state and society and their potential to further democratize the state (Chauchard 2017).[4]

Social audits exemplify economist Amartya Sen's notion of development as freedom by extending to marginalized workers the freedom to read, circulate, and write government documents (Sen 2000). Kanchi, in the opening vignette, declared he was "feeling good" when he used the audit process to publicly confront power; this needs to be seen as a shift in development outcomes from a "weapons of the weak" perspective to one that acknowledges a new position of power, even if public confrontation doesn't always result in the state taking action on the audit findings (Scott 1985). The workers themselves are happy with NREGA and do not want to lose the program. But, because they value the work and the wages it offers them, they are afraid to testify to the auditors about the mates' corruption, believing that if they complain, the auditors will take away the program completely. Moreover, the mates are often relatives of the workers, meaning that the workers feel unable to act against them; instead, they bargain with the mates informally. Workers would rather settle for improvement than demand perfection. This preference is another reason why a political understanding of implementation processes is critical.

Progress Is Not a Constant

The changes in institutions and technologies of control resulted in a constant cat-and-mouse game in an evolving system of patching development. NREGA's implementation in Andhra Pradesh was a constant struggle at the last mile between social auditors, bureaucrats, and workers. Upper-level counterparts built new monitoring technologies and processes to address flaws discovered in the system, particularly seeking to hold lower-level bureaucrats accountable. Lower-level bureaucrats then resisted such increased monitoring, sabotaging or bypassing technologies. In turn, their upper-level counterparts built yet newer technologies and processes to deal with this resistance.

Though the oversight mechanisms and technologies were obstructed by the lower-level bureaucrats, they nonetheless enabled upper-level bureaucrats to monitor the lower-level bureaucrats in a way previously impossible. Even for the lower-level bureaucrats, technology was not exclusively a hindrance. It allowed lower-level bureaucrats to deflect pressures from local politicians by claiming that much of their decision-making power had been co-opted by "technology" and was thus out of their hands. The bureaucrats in Andhra Pradesh also have instituted the social audit process as a key element of implementing a development program, which shows how marginalized citizens can be part of the implementation.

The Andhra Pradesh model of governance has survived multiple changes of administrations—both political and bureaucratic—and continues to exhibit one of the best-performing implementations of NREGA in the country. Moreover, NREGA has become very popular among the workers, particularly the Dalits. Despite these successes, there are signs of a political weakening at the top, both at the national level and the state level, in support for these institutions. There has also been increasing pressure from farmer groups to convince political parties to link NREGA projects with agricultural work. A high-level committee consisting of the chief ministers of many states, including Andhra Pradesh, has been set up at the national level to decide how to link NREGA to agriculture. This committee was established to fulfill the election promise of the BJP government to double the income of farmers by 2022.[5] Attaching NREGA to agriculture would be disastrous for the agricultural laborers, who find NREGA work to be meaningful not merely because of the wages it pays, but also because the work increases their bargaining power with farmers and gives them freedom to work with dignity.[6] If NREGA work becomes a subsidy to the farmers from the state to pay for agricultural work, then the autonomy that the landless laborers currently enjoy—which allows them this bargaining ability and has driven agricultural wages up—will disappear. Further, the availability of alternative NREGA work ensures that Dalits have the autonomy to simply reject work on Reddy lands, which goes beyond the economic realm to give an aspect to development that economist and public intellectual Amartya Sen calls "development as freedom" (Sen 2000).

There have been attempts to institutionalize social audits using the Andhra model in Bihar, Telangana, and Meghalaya. The Bihar implementation was originally stalled because of lack of political will from the top but now has resumed and is at early stages. The Telangana implementation, which is firmly in place, is an exact replica of the Andhra Pradesh model, as the new state adopted those processes when it came to be. The Telangana implementation has actually gone beyond NREGA to cover other public services like pensions, schools, and public health clinics, as well as public distribution services such as ration shops. The Meghalaya implementation is at the nascent stage. It remains to be seen how these systems will evolve.

Limitations of Patching

While the book has focused on the struggles that necessitate patching development, I now want to foreground the limits of such maneuvers and mechanisms and then end with some observations on how, taking all these factors into consideration, the field can move forward.

In NREGA's case, the limitations were not insurmountable, as my analysis in the book of the struggles with patching showed. Here, I focus on extending these ideas beyond the Andhra context.

Politics of the patching process: If patching is coordinated by a handful of bureaucrats, it may be misguided and create more problems with transparency, even if it is well-intentioned. This problem with transparency brings to light questions such as: Who has the authority to patch? What is the process through which the content of the patches is decided? Are there suitable mechanisms through which to deliberate and judge the desirability of the appropriate patch?

Weakening local discretion: The informational infrastructure—once centralized for a system of patching—could be a bottleneck to changes in local realities that need a faster response. Navigating the right balance of control between local level discretion and centralized patching is hard in practice.

Mission creep toward solutionism: Patching is analytically different from experimentalism and solutionism. Solutionism is the tendency to reduce complex development issues to a problem that can be fixed with an apolitical technical application (Morozov 2014). Yet, in practice, patching could devolve into a form of solutionism with experimental tendencies that sees problems as one fix away and therefore does not grapple with political realities. This problem, rooted in reality, may emerge because the informational infrastructure relies on constantly fixing problems in the implementation stage. In other words, this tendency to fix could cause a "mission creep" that may embolden experimental fixes and lead to bad outcomes. In the case of freezing work groups that were intended to fix problems of manipulation of bogus work entries, the "fix" instead led to the problem of workers being unable to change groups.

Sustainability of the cat-and-mouse game needs political will: Patching as a process is an attempt to deal with resistance to implementation. This requires constant top-down vigilance and attention to small details and the process of iteration, which in turn requires power and political support. Civil society actions have the power to raise awareness and change policies and open up the workings of the state. Democratizing information about the performance of public programs does allow citizens to "see the state" (Corbridge et al. 2005). Yet exposure alone is not enough. Such movements still require sustained activity that citizen groups on their own commonly are unable to muster. State support is needed, but that depends on political will. For example, in the Rajasthan and Bihar cases, workers found the state and the political machinery uncooperative, and as a result their resistance was squashed (Pande 2014). Relying on a system of continuous support from the top, without strengthening local accountability processes, may lead to failure when the political support withers away.

Hiding behind patches: Stemming partially from the opacity of the system, constant changes by the bureaucrats using institutional fixes and technologies of governance often puts the workers at the disadvantage of having to endure systems of constant change. Ironically, these changes could also lead to local elites using the imperative of constant change to hide behind a patch, distorting outcomes and further disempowering workers. For example, in the context of NREGA, they can blame the system for lack of payment, or stop the work, arguing that there has been a new patch which necessitates this action. For their part, workers may not know whether a real patch necessitated the change, or if this was merely a story of change that was smuggled in by the local powers to marginalize them.

The Way Forward

As this book has amply demonstrated, NREGA's implementation in Andhra Pradesh was an ongoing contest between social auditors, bureaucrats, and workers at the last mile.[7] Lower-level bureaucrats resisted increased monitoring, sabotaging or bypassing technologies designed to allow upper-level bureaucrats to hold them accountable. In turn, their upper-level counterparts built new technologies and processes to deal with this resistance. The constant back-and-forth resulted in an evolving system of patching development. Yet the fluidity of the never-ending iterations employed in Andhra Pradesh also leads us to another, larger question: How does patching development speak to the broader, present-time discourse on the use of data, information, and technology?

Beyond Technocracy: Patching, Politics, and Participation

The use of data and technology is increasingly becoming central to solving last-mile problems in development, but debates on the subject are polarized (Bussell 2010). On the one hand, advocates push for the use of technology; on the other hand, critics argue against employing technocratic rationality to address problems of development.

The techno-utopians look to technology to "leap frog" societal problems, and they fundamentally believe in digital solutions to a wide variety of issues (Chadwick 2003; Peixoto 2013). In their view, technology is the magic elixir that will inevitably solve problems of corruption, bring accountability to the state, and help in targeting public works programs to the poor. For example, this technology-determinism among the elites has resulted in developmental projects like Aadhaar (India's biometrics-based national identification infrastructure) to track beneficiaries, geospatial technologies to automatically detect who is poor and to access market prices, and tech-enabled telemedicine (Singh and Jackson 2017; Madon 2011; Wyche and Steinfield 2015; Chaudhuri 2014; Veeraraghavan et al. 2009). But these programs have not always succeeded as hoped (Heeks 2003; Cohen 2019; Khera 2011a; Khera 2018a; Khera 2018b). Instead, they have created new problems (Dada 2006; Khera and Patibandla 2020; Keniston and Kumar 2004). Understandably, these unintended, problematic consequences have resulted in a reaction against technology utopianism and a rejection of impositions of technology in addressing problems (Srinivasan et al. 2017; Harari 2018; Khera 2018a).

The opposition has been based on various strands of reasoning. Many have been disillusioned by the fact that digitization creates new inefficiencies without creating promised efficiencies (Prakash et al. 2015; Masiero 2020). For example, some are opposed to the fact that technology centralizes power and removes agency from actors at the grassroots (Masiero and Das 2019; Benjamin 2007; Chaudhuri 2021). Further, communities that are traditionally marginalized rarely have the technical competencies needed to harness digitization for their own ends. Instead, technology usually strengthens elite power.

The concerns expressed by critics are important and, in many cases, the appropriate response to technology may be to resist its introduction altogether (Agre and Rosenberg 1998). In some cases, it may be useful to ask how such technologies may be developed in ways that are more democratic and supportive of democratic engagement. In other cases, the support—or the lobby—for the use of digital technology may be strong enough that resistance to technology may fail. For example, in the case of Aadhaar, a completely oppositional stand is unlikely to lead to its demise. Further, "Aadhaar is not the unified coherent infrastructure imagined in both utopian and dystopian narratives" (Rao 2019, 3). In such cases, it may be politically wiser to think of reshaping the platform (Rao and Nair 2019). Overall, there is a strong positive case for believing that well-designed technologies could indeed improve the well-being of marginalized communities.

To some extent, the technology-design community has found ways to move past this impasse by arguing for contextual engagement, collaboration, and participation that are sensitive to local dynamics to design solutions (Toyama 2015; Gandhi et al. 2009). In order to ensure fairness in outcomes, the post-colonial computing paradigm has gone further to imbue the designer with a political sensibility that is mindful of the colonial histories of these interventions (Irani et al. 2010). Toward this end, each design approach has created tools and guidelines for designers, as well as techniques to reorient them for better engagement.

Yet, given the power over design and expertise that rests with the designers, even if they are politically sensitive and culturally engaged, I believe there is a need to move beyond design solutions that rely purely on expertise. What is really at stake is the monopoly of expertise held by designers. Thus, one way forward is to wrest power away from the designer (Mitchell 2002). Technology (like an institution) is malleable, and democratic engagement is critical in order to shape technology platforms and their consequences on human lives. We need to engage with the minutiae of technology, akin to the Gramscian "war of position," that leverages technologies in the struggle. This tactic would require focusing on iteration, raising questions of accessibility and transparency, ensuring that outcomes are fair, and designing simpler solutions where the technology use is transparent for all.

Circling back to the role of technology in solving last-mile problems, I argue for a position where we neither throw out technology nor have deterministic faith in technology; instead, we should expect that the use of technology requires continuous adjustment and reappraisal. Technology use does not need to come from a technocratic vision, but instead allows for political imaginations that are subject to democratic control.[8] As I show in this book, digital technology was used to deal with local power system. It was not a one-time fix, but rather adapted to changes in order to deal with resistance to technological forms of rule.

Patching Transparency: Sunlight to Flashlight

Social audits as practiced in Andhra Pradesh complicate our common-sense assumptions about the link between transparency and public participation.

Notions of transparency often assume unproblematic participation from "informed citizens" and democratic decision-making (Weinstein and Goldstein 2012; Strathern 2000; Hetherington 2011). Yet government-mandated openness is an insufficient criterion for determining whether information will lead to citizens holding the state accountable.

Information must be understandable to those seeking to use it, socially constructed in a way that conveys its intended meaning, and targeted and actionable for those in a position to act upon it (Weil et al. 2013). Too often, government openness projects simply disclose information and make it available on websites or a notice board near the worksite. This form of transparency succeeds only in opening up information for the producers of the information—often state bureaucrats—but not for the citizens who are (or could be) the consumers of it. The idea of the state putting out information and expecting participation by marginalized citizens as *individuals* does not always work (Joshi and Houtzager 2012; Fox 2007; Janssen 2012).[9]

Real accountability requires not just transparency, but also the capacity to monitor the state by citizens.[10] In this context, the notion of the public sphere is invoked as a social process and a place for ideas to be shared and discussed openly. In theory, public meetings are a way to democratize monitoring by relying on openness to facilitate public reasoning. Yet Mansuri and Rao assembled almost 500 studies examining various top-down projects to induce participation from below to show that these efforts are most often captured by local elites (Mansuri and Rao 2013). Without the power to take on local politics, the public sphere is Ferguson's anti-politics machine: nobody shows up or is even expected to show up (Ferguson 1990). Yet, as Sanyal and Rao demonstrate citizens oral participation in development and governance can be improved by strengthening deliberative spaces through policy (Sanyal and Rao 2018).

However, much like the political will for transparency, the capacity to monitor needs also to contend with power. Even when the muster roll is in the hands of a politicized individual who knows how to find meaning in that document (as in the case of the Rajasthan worker or the JJSS worker in Bihar), that individual has to contend with the reality of the power situation. In both the Rajasthan and the Bihar cases, the workers found the state and the political machinery uncooperative, squashing their resistance. This is because marginalized citizens are not always in a position to challenge the state, regardless of the information available to them, because they are simply not powerful enough to use information for that purpose (Fox 2015). Just as programs must ensure that information is meaningful for those who need to access it, they must also create mechanisms through which citizens can make demands on the state so that upper-level bureaucrats can hold lower-level bureaucrats accountable. All too often, participation in any public forum that presents and challenges information could put people at risk—either via threats from powerful interests or by exposing their own involvement in corruption. The public sphere functionally serves openness, but at the same time also makes monitoring possible at the local level, which makes it problematic and hence resisted.

To understand the effects of social audits, we need to move beyond public meetings and look at how they enable private settlements.[11] The extent to which these private settlements are equitable depends on the type of prior relations of marginalized citizens with the state actors (Williams 2004). Further, ideas of the public sphere often assume direct participation, but we may have to imagine possibilities for indirect participation through proxies (Véron et al. 2003). In addition to communication (as in deliberation or speech), we also should acknowledge information (as in testimonies via documents) as a valid object in the public sphere. One possibility to explore is anonymized participation using documents as proxy, mediated by independent non-local actors, which allows for protection of the "participants" without undermining their local situation. In essence, we need to transform the imagination that is embodied in the public sphere from Habermasian idealism into an exercise of politics.

Citizens' capacity to use information to monitor the state depends on prior mobilization. As happened in the case of MKSS in Rajasthan and of JJSS in Bihar, the workers were politicized through engaging in protests demanding higher wages (Jenkins and Goetz 1999). As Jonathan Fox points out in his revisit of a field experiment of an Indonesian transparency study, sometimes the mobilization is not easily captured in narrowly defined field experiments (Olken 2007; Fox 2015). Anti-corruption interventions in Indonesia worked due to the prior mobilization of the community, which was then able to take advantage of information to put pressure on the state to be accountable (Fox 2015). Without that politicized history, it is unclear that the top-down effort from the state in Indonesia would have worked. The mobilization of Dalits in Andhra Pradesh through their involvement in social movements led them to those empowered to take advantage of the audit process, sometimes via private settlements. Inserting the power to monitor into the causal chain from transparency to accountability brings forth further questions. The intent and the capacity of citizens to monitor need to precede the distribution of the information to them.

Further, citizens are not monolithic; there is an inherent assumption in the literature that treats citizens as having relatively homogenous interests, goals, and power, which is not the case.[12] As we saw in Chapter 7, the willingness of workers to engage in the social audit process is further determined by the local political-economic context. Recently, there has been a rise in groups of activists under the banner of civic technology (Gigler and Bailur 2014; Peixoto et al. 2017). These activists focus on using technology, in particular social media, with the goal of inverting the directionality of James Scott's "seeing" to allow citizens to see the state rather than the other way around (Zuckerman 2014; Diamond 2010; Scott 1998). At first glance, it indeed seems to counter the Scottian analysis of giving the state the monopoly on seeing by allowing the citizens to see the state instead. However, Scott's concept of "seeing like a state" is symptomatic of a "high modernist" authoritarian state (Scott 1998). Ideally, the objective of seeing the state is to make it more democratic. But the civic technology movement suffers from considering the state largely as a monolith. In other words, while it seems to invert the directionality, it really reproduces the Scottian dichotomy by treating the state and citizens equally as monoliths. This "civic tech" movement also suffers from having monolithic vision not only of the state but also of the potential of the citizen to orchestrate the seeing. In my view, state and society must be disaggregated in order to recognize the possibilities of state-society synergies through patching development as I have explored it in this book (Evans 1996; Fox 2015).

The Andhra social audits case shows that for transparency to lead to accountability in the real world, it must be political and relational. This requires constant patching. A naïve understanding of transparency which fails to understand the political effects of openness often uses the metaphor of sunlight, an uncomplicated and universally illuminating force. A better metaphor through which to consider transparency is a "flashlight." The flashlight metaphor makes it possible to recognize and ask relational questions. For example, who is holding the flashlight? What is the object that is being illuminated? What is still in the dark? Who decides what is seen? How is the public seeing? And, what is the resistance to the flashlight? There is also the process of building a better flashlight through information technology to increase the ability to monitor. It is important to look at power in considering what is politically feasible, and what has opened, as these shift over time. The result is always a partial "openness." It is a terrain of struggle, facilitated by patching transparency.

To summarize, patching development at the last mile requires political will to create an enabling environment by providing the necessary autonomy for bureaucrats to rewrite their relationship with marginalized people. Social movement organizations, with their history of collective action, are necessary to empower marginalized citizens to be able to contest the actions of the local state through social audits or some other citizen-supported mechanism. Finally, and most crucially, upper-level bureaucrats must create mechanisms to ensure that those records will not be sabotaged at the local level. To do so, upper-level bureaucrats need to constantly innovate by embracing and adapting new technologies and evolving new processes to ensure that members of local political parties, local elites, and lower-level bureaucrats do not sabotage the delivery of programs at the last mile.

Going beyond the use of patching by a bureaucracy, as I have noted in this book, we need to develop a model for exercising citizenship over governmental platforms that focuses on small details at the level of patches. Creating such democratic engagement would require practices of documentation, transparency, and citizen engagement. It would also require civil society organizations to develop a new form of politics that pays attention to the mundane minutiae of technology—drop-down boxes, links, reports, and other details in governmental platforms (Hull 2012b). The framework for creating greater democratic engagement would also reform the design process to include patching of non-technical aspects such as designing institutions and processes for development.

With the increased global call to eliminate welfare programs because of perceived failures in implementation, it is important to demonstrate possibilities, as I hope I have done in this book, and a framework of patching development which focuses on overcoming challenges in the implementation. The last mile may be long, but as this book has shown, the struggles at the last mile can lead to the possibility of changing relations with the state as well as within society. To quote the great Indian jurist, economist, politician, and social reformer Babasaheb Ambedkar, "Progress by peaceful means is always a slow process and to impatient idealists like myself it is sometimes painfully slow. [. . .] No one need be disheartened by this. For to my mind, what matters is not so much the rate of progress as the nature of the outlook" (Ambedkar 1991, 103).

APPENDIX 1

Methodology: Using Ethnography to Study Political Economy of Information

> Happenstance shapes it as much as planning and foresight. *Numbing routine is as much a part of such work as living theater. Impulse is as important on the ground as rational choice, and mistakes are often as significant as accurate and wise choices. This may not be way fieldwork is reported, but it is the way it is carried out in reality.*
>
> —Van Maanen (2011, 2)

Patching Development is primarily based on an ethnographic investigation of government implementation of NREGA. My fieldwork was done in two states, Andhra Pradesh and Bihar, but I spent the majority of my time in Andhra Pradesh. The fieldwork was conducted over eighteen months in 2011 and 2012, with follow-up visits in 2016 and 2017. I used a variety of approaches to collect data, including participant observation, unstructured and semi-structured interviews, a survey administered in fifteen villages, content analysis of documents, and archival work in the assembly archives in Andhra Pradesh. I wanted my work to capture the situated essence of what was going on, not to suggest that what I discovered in Andhra Pradesh was true everywhere. Moreover, I was not merely interested in studying the impact of "solutions": I wanted to understand the mechanisms used to implement those solutions and why those mechanisms were chosen.

I had connections with the leaders of the Bihar social movement, Jan Jagaran Shakti Sanghatan (JJSS), through my work in the United States for The Association for India's Development. I have come across many activists in my decade of volunteering, so I had a good understanding and connections with some of the major groups working in development in India. Before beginning my fieldwork, I also briefly visited the Social Audit director of Andhra Pradesh. My permission to enter the scene came from the top, which helped me gain initial access to the audit teams and state bureaucracies. For the later stages of my work I used the snowballing technique to interview activists, political leaders, and bureaucrats.

My work in India can be divided into three phases. The first phase involved gaining an understanding of social audits in Bihar and Andhra Pradesh, which I carried out by participating as a social auditor. I volunteered as a social auditor for two months and shadowed an audit team while it conducted a door-to-door survey of workers. The second phase involved learning about the NREGA bureaucracy at the state, district, and mandal (subdistrict) levels. I attended several internal meetings of state-level bureaucrats and witnessed the day-to-day operations of the bureaucracy. I also attended more than twenty-five meetings (some of which were over twelve hours long), videoconferences, workshops, and political rallies at the village, mandal, and state levels.

The third phase was to understand the democratic process and the NREGA program from the perspective of the workers. To achieve this, I positioned myself among workers for a three-month period, in two different villages with different social structures, a tribal village and the other a large agricultural village. During this time, I worked as an unpaid daily wage laborer and interviewed a large number of workers and other residents in each village. I also attended the social audits in the village and retrieved documents from the Andhra Pradesh legislative assembly to analyze how the legislators discuss NREGA in their meetings. In the end, I conducted over 100 semi-structured interviews with individuals working at the village, regional, state, and national levels. I constantly solicited and received advice from my "subjects" themselves, filtering their responses through my own biases and abilities. Their comments ranged from epistemological concerns to advice about the mundane issues of where to stay and whom to talk to.

In Andhra Pradesh, I started by spending time in Chittoor, a region of Andhra Pradesh where the inhabitants speak Tamil, my mother tongue. I used the assistance of auditors who knew both Tamil and Telugu in the initial months. My interactions with bureaucrats were carried out predominantly in English. Eventually, thanks to this immersive experience in Telugu and to the close relation between Telugu and Tamil, I came to be relatively fluent in Telugu.

I hired a translator who spoke both Tamil and Telugu as both a traveling companion and a translator. This decision turned out to be invaluable, since he also gave me insights into the workers' quality of life and was able to share vignettes from his own village to compare with our experiences in the areas we visited. This man felt uncomfortable staying in a different place, although he spoke the language, so he did not perform the traditional role of guide and interpreter with the surrounding villagers. Instead, he remained in the background, serving as an excellent source of comparative information. Moreover, he was born in a Dalit caste and I was born in a Brahmin caste, and thus we were received differently. He was also a former lower-level bureaucrat, and his perspective helped me look at the perceptions from within the state in different ways. His stories from his own work and the challenges he faced from local elites were a rich source of insight.

Higher-level bureaucrats who had seen many survey-based researchers come and go were puzzled by my extended stay. In my first interview with a bureaucrat at this level, he asked, after discovering that I was going to be spending a year in Andhra Pradesh, "What will you do for so long in the field?" Like the bureaucrats, the workers did not know what to make of me. Our conversations often centered on whether or not I had come to police them. Was I a CIA agent sent from America? Had I run away from my family to take solace in the countryside? All this is to say that my method was a constant but often undirected search for patterns (Becker 2008). This is not a new method of doing ethnography, but it is a valuable one.

I was not the only active participant in the research process. Several of my "subjects" had an interest in promoting their own points of view. While the majority of the villagers in each case did not hesitate to talk to me about how NREGA works, my presence did change the reality. I did my best to blend in, but I was not always successful. Therefore, I took advantage of the effects of my presence to discover new material. I was thus far from a fly-on-the-wall researcher. I took the "participant" in "participant observation" seriously (Burawoy 1998). Instead of prioritizing consistency in my work, I chose to emphasize opportunistic diversity. With that said, I also took great care to remain neutral and to protect people's identities. One of the higher-level bureaucrats told me, "Of course you get access to only certain spaces. We let you see what we want you to see." It was a constant struggle to understand what was going on, and I developed several alternate strategies.

My outsider/observer/researcher status could provide only limited protection. If I worked with the auditors, it was very hard to gain the trust of the bureaucrats and the workers. In my work with the auditors I needed to vary my role. In one case I volunteered to serve as an active auditor, and in another case I stayed with the senior auditor supervising the auditing process. I was careful to vary the location where I performed each of these roles so that I could see and be seen in a new light in each case. I also attended several public hearings in different social, political, and geographic locations. I was alert to the possibility of different outcomes in the auditing process depending on the extent to which the meetings were politicized and exposed to protests.

When I was investigating the workers' experience at the village level, I did not want higher-level bureaucrats to keep track of me. I hoped to win the trust of the local bureaucrats and auditors so that they would talk to me sincerely, without feeling they had to perform for me.

Occasionally, of course, my strategy of neutrality failed. Activists worried that I would find NREGA to be corrupt and that my research would provide fodder for right-wing efforts to end the program. Bureaucrats did not want me to find that they were corrupt because they were afraid they might lose their jobs as a result. Similarly, the local auditors tried to either impress me by working harder than usual or to control and limit what I saw. Workers lingered at the field site to convince me that they were working longer hours. I tried both to take such distortions into account in my analysis and to exploit the effect for my own research purposes whenever possible. One lower-level bureaucrat accused me of being a "do-gooder" (*gandhi giri*) and asked me to not get involved in local issues. He was upset that I was delving into the land records of his village. In time I came to realize that the neutral position is not always a popular one. At one public meeting where I was taking a video of the proceedings, the auditors and the local bureaucrats, who were at odds with each other, all wanted a copy of the video. When I refused to yield to their demands, I was subjected to a great deal of harassment from the local elites. Nevertheless, my status as a researcher in the audit yielded many insights into the power of the audit process to penetrate the social space. I also received many testimonies of digressions that took place just beyond the reach of the auditors, and I learned of the lower-level bureaucrats' disdain for the auditors and the upper-level bureaucrats' bias against the lower-level bureaucrats.

In ethnography, the research site never leaves the researcher. It has been several years since I left Andhra Pradesh, but I return constantly in my mind as I sift through my data, interpret my experiences, and write up my analysis. The commitment to ethnography truly does not stop with fieldwork but continues long afterward. This project started as a dissertation, and has gone through several transformations before reaching this form. Finally, the method, if I can call it this, is a reflection of the processes that I uncover in the book: nothing is settled, there is a back and forth, some problems get patched and these patches create new problems, and so the journey continues.

APPENDIX 2

Explanatory Note on Comparing NREGA Performance across States

The discussion of NREGA performance across states in this book relies on NREGA performance indicators, as shown in Tables 2.1 and 2.2 in Chapter 2. The book uses those indicators that are known to be measured reliably in the NREGA Management and Information System (MIS). The indicators themselves have been compiled from the Ministry of Rural Development's annual reports. The population estimates are from the 2011 Census (Government of India 2013), and population projections published by the National Commission on Population (Government of India 2019). This section contains explanations about how these are calculated. The metadata of the table was inspired by (Drèze and Oldiges 2007). The indicators are for twenty large states, as described in the table notes. The indicators are:

(a) Proportion of expenditure on wages (%): Calculated by dividing expenditure for "unskilled wages" by "total actual expenditure."
(b) Wage expenditure per rural person (Rs.): Calculated as unskilled wage expenditure divided by the estimated rural population. The estimated rural population was compiled from the population projections.
(c) Proportion of expenditure on administration (%): Calculated by dividing expenditure on "administration" by "total actual expenditure."
(d) Administrative expenditure per rural person (Rs.): Calculated as total administrative expenditure divided by the estimated rural population. The estimated rural population was compiled from the population projections.
(e) Job cards as a proportion (%) of rural households: Calculated by dividing cumulative number of job cards issued by total number of rural households. Rural households were estimated from population projections; household size was estimated from the 2011 Census.
(f) Employment generated per rural household (days): Calculated by dividing total number of person-days generated by number of rural households. Rural households were estimated from population projections, and household size was estimated from the 2011 Census.
(g) Proportion of rural households who got work for 100 days (%): Calculated by dividing total number of households who worked for 100 days by the number of rural households. Rural households were estimated from population projections, and household size was estimated from the 2011 Census.
(h) Proportion of workdays by women (%): Calculated by dividing women workdays by total workdays.
(i) Average employment for a rural Dalit person (days): Calculated by dividing Dalit workdays by estimated rural Dalits population. Rural Dalit population was calculated by multiplying the 2011 Census rural Dalit population and the 2019 projected rural population.

(j) Average employment for a rural Adivasi person (days): Calculated by dividing Adivasi workdays by estimated rural Adivasi population. Rural Adivasi population was calculated by multiplying the 2011 Census Adivasi population and the 2019 projected rural population.

References

Government of India (2013): Census 2011—Primary Census Abstract. Office of the Registrar General and Census Commissioner of India: New Delhi.

Government of India (2019): Population Projections for India and States 2011–2036: Report of the Technical Group on Population Projections. National Committee on Population, Ministry of Health: New Delhi.

Drèze, Jean, and Christian Oldiges. 2007. "Commendable Act." *Frontline* 24 (14): 14–27.

Notes

Chapter 1

1. Andhra Pradesh is regarded as a model example of how to put the program into practice. Economists Clément Imbert and John Papp refer to it as a star state (Imbert and Papp 2012). Numerous sources identify the implementation of this program in Andhra Pradesh as a model to be imitated (Aiyar and Samji 2009; Imbert and Papp 2015; Maiorano 2014; Dasgupta et al., 2017; Mann et al. 2012; Muralidharan et al. 2016; Deininger and Liu 2013) and Andhra Pradesh's implementation of NREGA consistently ranks near the top among the states (Sukhtankar 2016).
2. Akhil Gupta's work on red tape argues that bureaucracies commit structural violence against the poor because of bureaucrats' apathy about the suffering of poverty-stricken people (Gupta 2012).
3. See also Fox (2020) for a summary of the literature that examines examples of bureaucracies that were forces for good under the rubrics of positive outliers or positive deviance. See also Du Gay (2005).
4. I do not mean to suggest that upper-level bureaucrats are always outside corrupt systems. They are often implicated as corruption trickles up, just as they often are when it trickles down. See Gupta (1995); Wade (1985).
5. This quote is from the remarks Ambedkar made at the Indian Constituent Assembly Debates in 1948 (Constituent Assembly Debates: Official Report, Volume VII, 39).
6. Jodhka (2002, 3343) argues that "for Gandhi the village was a site of authenticity, for Nehru it was a site of backwardness and for Ambedkar the village was the site of oppression."
7. Even in administering NREGA, not all practices were open, and it was a source of struggle between civil society activists, lower-level bureaucrats, politicians, and workers.
8. Most major banks do not allow a third party to operate an NREGA account. Accounts were maintained at local cooperative banks and post offices where possible. This anecdote is ten years old and the payment system in NREGA has gone through many changes in Bihar, as it has in the rest of the country.
9. As Kapur et al. (2017, 5) write, "contrary to the popular belief, the Indian state is one of the smallest among major nations on a per capita basis."
10. See Ravallion (1991) for a discussion of the political economy of rural public employment programs.
11. For a national program, where the center controls program funds, the political alignment between the ruling political party in the center and the subnational party was critical. Andhra Pradesh had that alignment when NREGA was introduced.

12. Gulzar and Pasquale (2017) show that when politicians are able to internalize benefits they are able to motivate bureaucrats to provide effective services.
13. Human rights activist Balagopal rejects the tendency to "clothe Y.S. Rajasekhara Reddy, an MBBS [a degree for a doctor,] with the image of the good doctor who has turned to politics to cure society" (Balagopal 2011, 326). He argues that "[YSR's] rise in politics has been accompanied by more bloodshed than that of any other politician in this state. Not bloodshed for some avowed 'higher cause,' but bloodshed for the narrowest possible cause—the rise of one individual to political power and prominence" (327). But as Maiorano (2014) argues, that political power enabled YSR to provide cover to bureaucrats to implement the NREGA without interference from members of his political party.
14. I thank Vivek Srinivasan for recommending that I look at documents archived at village police stations. These records reach back to colonial times.
15. As Evans and Heller (2015) point out, any statement about Indian government is suspect. The Indian state has been variously characterized as "soft" (Myrdal 1968), "exclusionary" (Heller and Mukhopadhyay 2015), "flailing" (Pritchett 2009), and as a "fragmented multi-class state" (Kohli 2004).
16. Further there are debates in the literature about how the state appears as a sovereign entity or whether the boundaries are porous (for example, see Gupta 2012 and Fuller and Harriss 2001).
17. The politics of agrarian history are complex and varied in the 600,000 villages of India. As Balagopal (2011, 165) notes, Indian agrarian history and politics defy summarization.
18. I met Raju in an office of the National Advisory Council in Delhi, where he was exploring how to replicate his success in the rest of the country. He was a soft-spoken man who was proud of his accomplishments. He showed me the numerous awards he had received during his years as a bureaucrat in Andhra Pradesh. At the time of my fieldwork, he had over thirty years of experience working at various levels in rural development in the state of Andhra Pradesh.
19. Interview with Koppula Raju, National Advisory Council, New Delhi, October 2011.
20. In the novel *A Suitable Boy*, Vikram Seth shows in detail how the local landlords (zamindars) controlled the local clerks who kept records in the 1950s and how the legal mandate to end the zamindari system had to contend with the power of the zamindars (Seth 1994). Thanks to Patrick Heller for bringing this to my attention.
21. For an analysis of how patching fits in the comparative state-society literature, see (Veeraraghavan and Pokharel, forthcoming).
22. As Patrick Heller writes, "In Kerala, the return to power of the CPM [Communist Party Marxist] in 1996 [that] saw the launching of the People's Campaign for Decentralized Planning . . . stands out as the boldest and most comprehensive decentralizing initiative yet to be undertaken in India. . . . In a single legislative act, money was devolved to Panchayats [local elected bodies] (35 to 40 percent of the plan expenditures) . . . and local-level planning was to be used as an instrument of social mobilization and as a means of creating a new civic culture" (Heller 2001, 139–41).

23. Durgam et al. (2017) argue that decentralization hinders effective implementation of NREGA in Karnataka because local elite actively subvert it through concerted action.
24. The process of patching development is fundamentally different from the concept of patchwork that McDonnell discusses in *Patchwork Leviathan* (2020). Patchwork refers to pockets of bureaucratic effectiveness in developing states. In contrast, *patching* as I use the term describes a sociotechnical process.
25. See Ahuja and Ostermann's (2018) work on the India's Election Commission, a bureaucracy that has taken advantage of moments of political opportunity to become one of the most powerful regulatory bodies.
26. Upper-level bureaucrats sought to eliminate the discretion of lower-level bureaucrats and attempted to restrict what they perceived as corrupt acts. However, as I will show later, not all actions by upper-level bureaucrats worked out in the best interest of workers. Workers wanted more flexibility to join and leave groups, which caused problems and delays.
27. Patching sometimes becomes recursive. A patch to fix an issue addresses the problem partially, but could create new problems, which then need a new patch to fix.
28. Finn (2018) develops the concept of public information infrastructures from the science and technology studies tradition.
29. But what causes infrastructure to change? There are two broad themes that drive change: the first, which is intrinsic to the human condition, is the inability to plan/design/foresee structures that last. The second incentives for change are those that are intrinsic to the technology caused by its affordances. They are characterized by "erosion, breakdown, and decay" and focus on repair of these infrastructures. Studies have looked at changes to infrastructures owing to "care," "grafting," "jugalbandi," "logistics," "breakdown," "everyday," and "values in repair" (Jack and Jackson 2016; Jackson et al. 2007; Jain 2020; Rosner and Ames 2014; Sanner et al. 2014; Houston et al. 2016). I extend this work by considering conflict and contestation as opposed to "organic growth" or "breakdown" as reasons for changes in infrastructure. The context of conflict that I study is the continuous political fighting that exists within the state bureaucracy. These conflicts manifest in the technologies of control used by the bureaucracy. See Veeraraghavan (2021).
30. Loveman (2005) traces the origins of the symbolic power that states possess and examines how historically contingent this power it is.
31. An influential study in Uganda, perhaps the most influential one that informed the 2004 World Development report, was based on the idea of "information for accountability" (Fox 2015; Reinikka and Svensson, 2004b). The study used statistical analysis to analyze an informational campaign focused on raising parental awareness of block grants for schools and the diversion of funds. It found a correlation between the distance from newspaper circulation to the school to argue that where parents are within reach of a newspaper, funds reach those schools. However, the data are not always on the side of openness. Several impact evaluations have shown that local dissemination of information has no impact on service provision (Banerjee et al., 2010; Keefer and Khemani, 2012; Lieberman et al., 2014; Ravallion et al., 2013). In fact, efforts to make government processes transparent and thus more equitable, can even backfire. For

example, another study of a government program in Bangalore called the Bhoomi project which sought to digitize and make open land records to prevent corruption found that digitization actually led to increased corruption, bribery, and facilitated large brokers in the land market to take advantage of the data (Benjamin et al., 2007).

32. Proponents of transparency often assume that public participation is unproblematic and that decision-making is democratic. This view is famously stated in Amartya Sen's finding that there have been no famines in countries with a functioning democracy (Sen and Drèze 1999). Sen was making an argument about the relationship between transparency and public pressure on a government. The underlying assumption is that once information about state action or inaction is in the public domain, problems such as famines will not reoccur because an informed citizenry will vote the political party responsible out of office. Sen relies on the power of democracy to diagnose and address problems in the bureaucratic functioning of the state.

    An essential support for the Senian vision of democratic deliberation is Jürgen Habermas's (1991) concept of the public sphere. Habermas was largely concerned with tracing the emergence and subsequent collapse of the bourgeois public sphere in Britain, France, and Germany in the eighteenth and nineteenth centuries. He defined the public sphere as an ideal speech situation where social issues are settled through rational deliberation even when inherent status and identity differences are present, the sphere where private people join together to deliberately form a public. He argues that the more deliberative the process, the more undistorted the communication and the more likely it is that consensus will be acceptable to all concerned. This model supports Sen's contention that citizens armed with information will mitigate the impact of major public disasters.

33. But the question that has challenged Habermas's account is whether those who are dominated by others can speak freely in an unequal world and thereby create the public deliberation that is needed to pressure the state to treat them fairly. Calhoun writes, "Habermas simply doesn't address the power relations, the networks of communication[,] . . . and the structure of influence of the public sphere except in general terms" (Calhoun 1992, 38).

34. In their study of the "social life of information," scholars Brown and Duguid (2017) argue that neither information nor the technologies used to transmit it are agents of radical social change. They argue against a belief that information will led to a positive end, and point out that there is no all-encompassing logic to or single dimension of social transformation.

35. A study examining the use of the United Kingdom's Open Government Data (OGD) finds that there is less use of open data for civic contexts (Davies 2010). There is also the question of who benefits from the open government data; OGD may reinforce existing inequalities between the "information-haves" and the "information-have-nots" (Gurstein 2012; Gurstein 2011).

36. This accountability strategy has worked in assemblies the Brazilian government has sponsored. Drawing on the Habermasian concept of the public sphere, Baiocchi (2003) studied public deliberations in two poor districts in Porto Alegre, Brazil. The participants were poor, were not formally educated, and had suffered under decades

of authoritarian rule. Baiocchi concluded that "even holding constant the definition of public sphere, its features are present in two poor districts in Porto Alegre, Brazil—a context that would be considered unlikely, given their citizens' material difficulties, their lack of education, and the lack of a liberal political culture" (Baiocchi 2003, 68). Baiocchi's main contributions to the Habermasian model were the concepts of mediation and state sponsorship, both of which raise important questions about the possibilities for accountability within the state when there is state action. These assemblies needed active support from the state, a form of affirmative action for the public sphere, in order to build and shape institutions in which marginalized citizens could participate freely.

37. See Mansuri and Rao (2012), a meta-analysis of the development literature.
38. As I argue elsewhere (Veeraraghavan 2017), the state-society literature relies implicitly on the concept of "joint intentionality," the notion that two parties, in this case state and societal actors, come together consciously and intentionally to work toward better outcomes. While outcomes in the synergy literature depend on the outcomes of power struggles between and within state and society, joint intentionality is a starting point for achieving such synergy. In the Indian context, Kerala stands out as a successful case of synergy; there, the developmental state was flexible in managing the competing demands of the landed class and landless laborers (Heller 2000). The coordinated outcomes of the synergy between the state and working-class parties in Kerala were labor market reform, legal and social protection enforced by the state, and the institutionalization of working-class power.
39. For example, in an agrarian context, if the working class has sufficient economic autonomy from the landed class, they are better able to demand social protection policies from the state (Heller 1996; Pattenden 2011; Roy 2020).
40. See (Ambedkar 1979).
41. See (Moffitt 2014) for an elaboration of "participatory bureaucracy" and its relationship with democratic accountability.
42. See Houtzager (2007) for an analysis of how the Brazilian state government in the city of São Paulo used an income guarantee program (Renda Minima) to build direct relations with citizens. The strategy of "manufacturing silence" by the Workers' Party (PT) is very similar to the creation of the social audit institution as a participatory bureaucracy in Andhra Pradesh, where organized civil society groups were left out of the implementation.
43. See also Sharma and Gupta (2009).
44. Hull traces the origins of bureaucratic writing to the desire of colonial powers to control local native functionaries. He writes, "British officers in India were frequently transferred among different posts. They lacked knowledge of the locales they administered and of the permanently posted native functionaries on whom they helplessly depended. In response to these uncertain loyalties, the British, building on the elaborate written procedures of the Mughals, expanded their graphic regime of surveillance and control" (Hull 2012b, 10).
45. See Veeraraghavan (forthcoming), which examines the question of whether information can make the subaltern speak through an examination of political theory.

46. An ethnographic study of a "school for digital kids" in a New York City public school documented how introducing tech-driven educational reform worsened the situation for the marginalized students the technology solution was supposed to benefit (Sims 2017). Another example is a study of US programs that digitize welfare payments, thus amplifying existing inequalities (Eubanks 2018).
47. The slogan "fail fast, fail often" celebrates success through rapid innovation and sees risk taking as a necessary component of achievement. Tech entrepreneurs frequently voice this mantra, and the mentality is spreading to "hackathons" and development thought (Irani 2019).
48. The law is named after Gordon Moore, one of the founders of Intel, who predicted that the power available on computer chips would approximately double every eighteen months. This has largely been the case. But as Brown and Duguid (2017) point out, the problem with such solutions is that "they take it on faith that more power will somehow solve the very problems that they have helped to create. Time alone, such solutions seem to say, with the inevitable cycles of the Law, will solve the problem. More information, better processing, improved data mining, faster connections, wider bandwidth, stronger cryptography—these are the answers. Instead of thinking hard, we are encouraged simply to 'embrace dumb power'" (16). What needs fixing is power in social relations, not power in computer chips.
49. Computer scientist Kentaro Toyama argues that technology merely amplifies human intentions and capacities (Toyama 2015; Toyama 2011). Brewer et al. (2005) make a case for technology-based interventions in the developing world. Further, some scholars, borrowing from the science and technology studies literature, argue that technology artifacts themselves embody politics (see, for example, Winner 1980; Pea 1985; Masiero 2018). This has particularly played out in artificial intelligence (machine learning), which encodes racial biases in data and technology (Buolamwini and Gebru 2018; Benjamin 2019; Noble 2018; Meredith 2018).
50. The ICTD field carries with it some of the problems of technology determinism and often these "tech for good" projects seem to be good for the researcher or the field rather than for marginalized citizens. See Pal (2017) for a reflective account. See Burrell (2012) for how internet enthusiasts in Accra, Ghana, have adapted the technological systems to their ends. See Kuriyan and Ray (2009b).
51. See Appendix 1 for more details about the method I used.

Chapter 2

1. Tamil Nadu is another southern state in India with NREGA performing well and with transformative outcomes. See Carswell and De Neve (2014) and Srinivasan (2015).
2. At a subnational state level, Maharashtra was the first state that guaranteed employment in 1976 (Bagchee 1984). Many of the provisions in NREGA has come from the experience of Maharashtra employment guarantee scheme (Khera 2011b).

3. Ambedkar pushed to include the words "directive" and "fundamental" in the Directive Policies of the constitution. He said, "It is not the intention to introduce in this part these principles as mere pious declarations. It is the intention of this Assembly that in future both the legislature and the executive should not merely pay lip service to these principles enacted in this part, but that they should be made the basis of all executive and legislative action that may be taken hereafter in the matter of the governance of the country." See Proceedings of the Constituent Assembly of India, November 19, 1948; available at https://www.constitutionofindia.net/constitution_assembly_debates/volume/7/1948-11-19.
4. This account is based on conversations with Vivek Srinivasan, the convener of the Right to Food campaign, in July 2019.
5. See Srinivasan (2005) for an extensive account of the history. Many of the original articles and pamphlets are archived at "Right to Food Campaign," n.d., http://www.righttofoodcampaign.in/.
6. To understand the connection between Public Action and Hunger, see Drèze and Sen (1989).
7. For example, Jean Drèze wrote an article titled "Starving the Poor" that stated that "if one sack of grain were placed on top of another it would reach the moon!" (Drèze 2001).
8. The Supreme Court issued a number of interim orders on the Right to Food case; see http://www.righttofoodcampaign.in/legal-action/supreme-court-orders. The hearings on this case started in April 2001 and have been held at regular intervals since then. According to the primer dated April 2005 in this website, forty-four interim orders have been issued. These interim orders serve as directions to both the central and state governments.
9. The campaign included the Bharat Gyan Vigyan Samiti (BGVS), Mazdoor Kisan Shakti Sangathan (MKSS), National Alliance of People's Movements (NAPM), Jan Swasthya Abhiyan (JSA), All India Democratic Women's Association (AIDWA), National Federation of Indian Women (NFIW), Human Rights Law Network (HRLN), National Conference of Dalit Organizations (NACDOR), National Campaign Committee for Rural Workers (NCCRW), and People's Union for Civil Liberties (PUCL) See Srinivasan (2015) for more details.
10. The act came to effect in February 2006 and was implemented in phases. In Phase I, in 2006, it was introduced in 200 of the most economically backward districts of the country. In Phase II, in 2007–2008, it was extended to an additional 130 districts. In Phase III, starting in April 1, 2008, the rest of the country was covered.
11. Their fears were not unfounded. Written testimonials often get withdrawn at the last minute and physical threats in retaliation for speaking out are part of the reality of social audits. A recent report estimates there have been fifty reported cases of deaths related to RTI Act audits (Pande 2015).
12. See Srinivasan (2015) for an extensive review of the literature.
13. Reddy and Patnaik (1993) document how the nexus between bureaucracy, police, and arrack (liquor) contractors conspired to stop the women's movement who were fighting to stop arrack sales in Andhra Pradesh. To mock the role of

the bureaucrats, they write, "No wonder, the district collectors engaged in such auction sales are sarcastically labelled as 'Indian arrack sellers' (IAS)" (Reddy and Patnaik 1993, 1065). "IAS" of course commonly stands for the Indian Administrative Service.

14. See Ahuja (2019). In his study spanning four states in India (UP, Bihar, Tamil Nadu, and Maharashtra), he argues that social mobilization between elections empowers every major party to accommodate the interests of Dalits. If Maharashtra launched the precursor to NREGA, the Employment Guarantee Scheme, Andhra Pradesh was chosen by Congress Party to launch the NREGA from Anantapur. It shows the power of social mobilization of Dalits to demand social programs that work.
15. The list represents the known incidents of murder or large-scale arson perpetrated against Dalits, Adivasis, and other marginalized people by caste Hindus in Andhra Pradesh. Karamchedu, a village in Prakasam district, was the location of the first recorded incident. Six Dalits were killed and three Dalit women were raped there in a mass assault by hundreds of men of the Kamma caste. See Balagopal (2011, 472–474) for the full list of incidents.
16. State attention also led to factions within Dalit groups, where some of the marginalized castes were demanding special attention. Madigas, a Dalit caste, claimed that Malas, another Dalit caste, had cornered all the benefits from the state and demanded preferential treatment.
17. In an appraisal of YSR, political scientist K. Srinivasulu writes, "The coexistence of benevolence and ruthlessness may appear to be paradoxical, but when seen in the proper historical and social context of the political culture that he had grown up in, their interlinkage would become apparent" (Srinivasulu 2009, 10). See also Balagopal (2011, 326–338) for a scathing commentary in his article titled "Beyond Media Images."
18. One of the reasons for the clout of YSR was his ability to supply funds to the Congress Party by channeling kickbacks through capturing government contracts (Maiorano 2014).
19. See Balagopal (2011, 332) for a critical interpretation of the rise of YSR and the politics of monopolizing the control of roads and public work contracts: "YSR was one of the pioneers of this change, which has terrorized and devastated the social and political life of the Rayalseema districts" in Andhra Pradesh.
20. I heard similar accounts from bureaucrats and politicians in my conversations during my field work.
21. YSR made it clear to his party men and cabinet colleagues that the MGNREGA and other welfare schemes could not be considered as a way to amass wealth and to finance political activities.
22. S. R. Sankaran came up in my interviews with bureaucrats as a model to be emulated. His name also came up in my interviews with civil society activists, as a "Gandhi" among the bureaucrats. Indeed, there is a two-volume book, edited by activists Saxena and Haragopal, on the life of S. R. Sankaran titled *Marginalization, Development and Resistance* (Saxena et al. 2014).
23. As Maiorano (2014) writes, this involved a lot of transfers.

24. Notably, Raju served in the post of a district collector (the highest administrative post in general administration of a district) at the forefront of the anti-arrack movement in Nellore, Andhra Pradesh.
25. This was not a YSR innovation, as in Andhra Pradesh bypassing the local panchayati system had a precedent right through its political history (Kohli 1988).
26. For a political history of change in Andhra Pradesh see Kohli (1988).
27. The creation of Mandals in 1986 was a political strategy by N. T. Rama Rao, who wanted to undermine any traces of Congress Party power, who were strong in districts and in the villages.
28. Though in practice, NREGA workers' requirement to stay the whole day at the worksite is not enforced. During my fieldwork, I noticed that NREGA workers wanted to linger longer at the worksite, because they had known that this was expected of them. This norm setting also led some workers to feel that they were not working as hard as they needed to get the full wages.
29. Interview at the National Advisory Council, New Delhi, October 2011.
30. Manor (2007) has shown how Chandrababu Naidu's attempt to extend his control was through by passing panchayati raj institutions. For example, his Janmabhoomi project was an attempt to build a huge network of contractors who served as a potent base for his political party.
31. The National Rural Employment Guarantee Act, 2005, Chapter 1V, 17(2). https://nrega.nic.in/amendments_2005_2018.pdf.
32. At the time of my fieldwork, the payment was processed first at the district level, then at the state level. Recently, the payment is processed by the central government in Delhi.
33. Andhra Pradesh experimented with biometrics payment, to ensure that workers get their payments directly and to prevent any theft of wages. The impact of biometrics payments has been documented; see Muralidharan et al. (2014); Srinivasan et al. (2018). The use of Aadhaar to authenticate workers have created great confusion and payment delays (Masiero 2020).
34. As Manor (2007) notes in his comparative research in different states in India, Andhra Pradesh has relatively a weak panchayati raj system, thanks to the unwillingness of the political parties in power. While the Congress Party never took it seriously, he traces the process of systematic dismantling of these structures to a conscious strategy starting from N. T. Rama Rao, who sought to undermine the power of the Congress Party.

Chapter 3

1. See Bovens and Zouridis (2002, 174), who show how technology improved transparency. As they argue, "Thanks to ICT, the implementation of the law has virtually being perfected," there is a direct line from the introduction to technology to effectively implementing the rule of law. On the contrary, in the Andhra Pradesh, the use

of technology was contested by the lower-level bureaucrats and politicians and was a struggle.

2. See Bussell (2012), who presents a comparative analysis of using computerization of public services across Indian states. She argues that the level and type of existing corruption generate the political will to effectively utilize digital technology to deliver public services. My analysis in the chapter is focused on explaining how the political will is translated by the bureaucrats to build the technical infrastructure and the challenges they had to overcome at the last mile.
3. See Mathur (2012), who describes how the implementation of NREGA failed in Uttarkhand partly because state-level administrators did not realize how much additional work lower-level bureaucrats would need to do to effectively implement NREGA's new transparency requirements. The automation of reports in Andhra Pradesh avoided that fate.
4. See Anand (2017), where he shows that in Mumbai the state works to make claims from some residents invisible.
5. See Gupta (2012), Hull (2012b), and Hetherington (2011), who describe how anthropologists studying the state have shown how everyday state documents play a central role in state making.
6. Interview on October 2011 with K. Raju at the National Advisory Council, New Delhi.
7. See Veeraraghavan (2021), who argues that conflict and contestation are a way to understand how changes in informational infrastructure can be understood.
8. Circulars are also patches in the sense that I am using the term, but what changed was the degree to which subordinates complied with changes rendered legible to upper-level bureaucrats.
9. Andhra Pradesh had a recent history of computerization of state operations. Chandrababu Naidu, the predecessor to the YSR government in Andhra, had prioritized computerization of state operations to improve government efficiency. Naidu aggressively promoted a move to modernize the state using computers and was often portrayed in the media working on his laptop.
10. The shift from labor to material component of corruption has been corroborated by other studies. See Aiyar and Mehta (2015); Afridi and Iversen (2014).
11. Anthropologist Ursula Rao, reflecting on the shift to use e-governance, observes that this disempowers bureaucrats as "mere computer clerks" without any say in decision-making, which they resist (Rao 2017).
12. https://egov.eletsonline.com/2012/01/mgovernance-initiative/
13. See Chaudhuri (2019) and Christin (2017), which depict a similar politics of "foot dragging" in other contexts.
14. The lower-level bureaucrats' lack of control over the algorithms actually gives them greater agency to not yield to demands from local politicians. Recent critical studies on "street-level algorithms" focus on the loss of agency of the street-level bureaucrats, but in some cases that loss of control gives them agency (Ali and Bernstein 2019).
15. MIS (Management Information System) is no panacea and has led to violate workers' legal entitlements. See Aggarwal (2017); Masiero (2017).

Chapter 4

1. I thank Rachel Brule for suggesting the phrase to me. See (Moffitt 2014) for an elaboration of "participatory bureaucracy" and its relationship with democratic accountability.
2. I use the phrase "joint intentionality" to describe the implicit assumption that exists in the scholarship when discussing state-society partnerships. They leave out possibilities where they do not have that tight intention to come together in a place (Veeraraghavan 2017).
3. I do not deny the role of social mobilization from the bottom. As Chapter 2 showed, political will does not come from thin air. In Andhra Pradesh, political will was a result of mobilization from the bottom over years of struggle at both the national and the state levels.
4. The state contracts with some of the auditors to manage the audit, renewing their contracts annually. Village-level auditors are hired on a per-audit basis and are paid a daily wage.
5. The enthusiasm for social audits in the bureaucracy has been high. Even after Raju left, the following principal secretaries and directors of NREGA until 2016 all have been supporters of the audit unit and have championed for their autonomy.
6. Interview at the National Advisory Council, New Delhi, October 2011.
7. For information on how the MKSS energized a certain section of senior bureaucratic circles in India to get the legislation passed, see Sharma (2015).
8. It was not clear whether he personally went or whether he sent his team.
9. The initial correspondence was a request from the ActionAid to send a resource person from MKSS. Eventually, they found Sowmya Kidambi to be the resource person, as she was already in Hyderabad.
10. Interview with Sowmya Kidambi over multiple days in Hyderabad, November 2011.
11. In the Food for Work Programme, citizens worked on public work projects and were paid in food grains in exchange for their work.
12. Interview in Chittoor with senior auditor, February 2011.
13. Interview in Chittoor with senior auditor, February 2011.
14. Interview in Hyderabad with senior auditor, February 2011.
15. Interview with Sowmya Kidambi, Hyderabad, November 2011.
16. I corroborated the events of the audit with conversations with three other auditors who were present during that time.
17. I was surprised by such vivid recollection of these audit meetings. But after spending time with the auditors and the bureaucrats who were involved in these meetings, I was convinced that the initial phase was an atmosphere of optimism and change. In a different conversation, a mid-level bureaucrat, who was a clerk, recalled how in the early days of NREGA in Andhra Pradesh, it was an all-hands effort to get this to work.
18. As told by Sowmya Kidambi during November 2011, in a series of taped interviews.
19. While this account largely is based on the narrative of the auditors in SSAAT, I had discussed this history with Raju when I met him in Delhi. He told an account which communicated how the bureaucracy had facilitated an autonomous institution from

the beginning. But the story was much more complicated and a result of contestation between the bureaucrats, politicians, NGOs, and the audit leadership, including Sowmya Kidambi.

20. As Dreze notes, the Anantapur audit was inspired by the Dungarpur [a district in Rajasthan where MKSS had done a mass audit] padayatra, while adding new dimensions to the exercise.
21. The number of civil society organizations that came together to do the social audits in one place was unprecedented. Here is the full list: Andhra Pradesh Vyavasaya Karmika Sangham, Vyavasaya Vruthidarula Union (APVVU), Dalitha Samakhya, Adisakthi, Podupu Sangham, Action Fraterna (RDT), Anantha Paryavan Parirakshana Samithi (APPS), Anantha Sramika Jana Sangharshana Samiti (ASJSS), Centre for Collective Development (CCD), Centre For Rural Action (CERA), Chaithanya, Centre For Rural Studies and Development (CRSD), Forum for Rural Development (FORD), Gutturu Rural Education Development Society (GREDS), Human and Natural Resource Development Society (HANDS), Jana Jagruthi, Kallumarri Rural Education Development Society (KREDS), Life and Nature Development Society (LANDS), Mahatma Gandhi Yuvajan Sangham (MGYS), Mass Education and Organisation Society (MEOS), MYRADA, Pragathi Mahila Macts, Peoples Monitoring Committee (PMC), Rural and Environment Development Society (REDS), Rural Integrated Development Society (RIDS), Social Action for Rural Development (SARD), Society for Action and Village Education (SAVE), Society for Rayalaseema Integrated Rural Education and Development (SRI RED), Sthri Samkshema Trust (SST), Timbaktu Collective, Voluntary Organisations for Integrated Community Emancipation (VOICE), Young India Project (YIP), Mazdoor Kisan Shakthi Sangathan, Rajasthan. The social audits came under the auspices of the ActionAid Strategy and performance Innovative Unit—Rural Department Government of Andhra Pradesh. (internal Anantapur Padayatra Report by SSAAT, Andhra Pradesh).
22. Internal report on Anantapur padayatra titled "Social Audit-Tool for Empowerment," compiled by SSAAT, Andhra Pradesh.
23. Workers of NREGA are supposed to get child care support while they work, shade to rest near the worksite, water, and unemployment allowances if they don't get paid on time.
24. Government order Lr. No. 17/SPIU/RD, dated July 21, 2006, by K. Raju, Principal Secretary of Rural Development to the District Collector, Anantapur.
25. Government order Lr. No. 17/SPIU/RD, dated July 21, 2006.
26. Internal audit report on Anantapur padayatra titled "Social Audit-Tool for Empowerment," compiled by SSAAT, Andhra Pradesh.
27. Interview with activist, Hyderabad, September 2011.
28. Internal audit report on Anantapur padayatra titled "Social Audit-Tool for Empowerment," compiled by SSAAT, Andhra Pradesh.
29. I refer to Sowmya Kidambi, who is the director of SSAAT in Telangana, after the state split in 2014.
30. Interview with Sowmya Kidambi, October 2011.

31. Interview with senior bureaucrat in Rural Development department, Hyderabad, October 2011.
32. Interview with Sowmya Kidambi, October 2011.
33. Interview with Sowmya Kidambi, October 2011.
34. Interview with NGO head, Anantapur, September 2011.
35. A group discussion with senior auditors at the SSAAT office, Hyderabad, November 2011.
36. Interview with NGO, Chittoor, September 2011.
37. Interview with NGO, Hyderabad, November 2011.
38. The government order was dated May 13, 2009.
39. Circular D.O.I.R., No. 143/SSAAT/2009, July 13, 2009.
40. There is precedence to the use of creating parallel structures. The Self Help Groups are a parallel structure whose members are in every village (Deshmukh-Ranadive 2004). Not all parallel institutional structures are equal. Naidu's Janmabhoommi committee is a parallel institution that gives more power the political party, by passing elected gram sabha institutions to manage local affairs.
41. The government order that created SSAAT in May 13, 2009, specified the composition of the governing body. The order said "the Society will be governed by a Governing Body not exceed 13 members. The Governing Body shall consist of 4 ex-officio members such as the Principal Secretary, RD (Rural Development), Commissioner, RD (Rural Development), Chief Executive Officer, Society for Elimination of Rural Poverty and the Secretary of the Society. 3–9 persons of eminence in their individual capacity shall be nominated by the ex-officio members for a term of 3 years. Criteria for such nomination shall be a minimum of 10 years of experience in rights-based approach, in working on the grassroot's peoples' issues and rural poverty eradication." It was clear that they had written the guidelines with MKSS activists in mind, and they are part of the governing board of SSAAT.
42. The demand for workers to recognized by the state as workers marked by state-certified identity cards has been a source of struggles by informal labor (see Agarwala 2013).
43. Interview with auditor, Chittoor, February, 2011.
44. This was a social audit in Medak district of Andhra Pradesh, now in Telangana,
45. An interview in Chittoor, February 2011.
46. Interview with the director social audit, November 2011.
47. A SSAAT report claimed that they had identified 1,358,074,870 rupees as "deviations" for the calendar year 2012–2013. As a result, the presiding officers in these audits accepted about 55 percent of this amount as accurate. This meant that the state accepted that these findings by the audit unit were real. Society for Social Audit, Accountability & Transparency, "Annual Report 2013–14."
48. Interview with an activist in Srikakulam, March 2012.
49. From 2005, the start of NREGA, until 2014, when Andhra Pradesh split into Telangana, Andhra Pradesh was the only state that implemented social audits, as specified. From 2014, SSAAT was responsible for both states. Since 2017, a separate unit for Andhra Pradesh, with a different director was set up. The rest of the states

had started setting up social audit units around 2016, although at the time of this writing it is not clear how active they are in practice, except in a handful of states like Meghalaya, Bihar.

50. For an example, see Ali's (2020) argument that how perception of bureaucrats could negatively affect the success of "participatory" reforms.
51. The ultimate test of the social audit process is whether as Fox (2015, 356) writes, "the main determinant of a subsequent pro-accountability power shift is whether or not pro-change actors in one domain can empower the others—thereby triggering a virtuous circle." See also Fox (1996).

Chapter 5

1. The legitimacy of khap panchayats is increasingly being questioned in the Indian media. Many view them as a regressive force primarily involved in moral policing and supporting anachronistic causes. For example, khap panchayats are allegedly involved in the "honor killings" of people of different religions or caste who decide to marry.
2. While I had full access to many of the meetings, I was not allowed to attend some private meetings. This was true at all levels of the bureaucracy.
3. At this mandal, the observing team of senior bureaucrats consisted of the vigilance officer of the mandal, the school headmaster, the panchayati secretary, and the local head of the veterinary department.
4. For a description of a similar unplanned meeting the bureaucrats had to administer and how these unplanned meetings are actually par for the course (and are thus planned), see Akhil Gupta's discussion of a health camp (Gupta 2012).
5. In the next section, I discuss a meeting where this same issue was raised.
6. About 500 people showed up for the rachabanda I attended. Only about ten to twenty people show up for regular gram sabhas.
7. The role of participant observer entails more than "fly on the wall" work where the observer merely records events. But it is not clear to what extent the participant can and should affect the work he or she is observing and to what extent the work is affected simply by his or her presence. The process presents a dilemma to the practical researcher, but it also gives new insights into the agency of the observer and the biases and limitations inherent in such encounters. While I was careful to be consistent in how I approached the audits, the extent to which I was able to exert agency in the audit varied. I discuss more of my rationale in Appendix 1.
8. The complexity is determined by the extent of problems a mandal has encountered in previous audits. Mandals that require more support receive a greater number of district resource persons and are often assigned more skilled auditors, although all of these decisions are made informally.
9. Even though the identities of the district resource persons assigned to a particular audit are not known ahead of time and it is not guaranteed that the same set of district

resource persons will always work together, they often know each other, and any district resource person's attitude toward the work is easy to glean through discussions.

10. One circular addressed the issue of accommodation by decreeing that women auditors should stay in the office of the mandal program development officer, the most "luxurious" office in the mandal headquarters.
11. The abysmal public transport system further ensures that the auditors are dependent on field assistants for their travel needs. The motorbikes the field assistants so often use cannot be purchased by someone who earns only a field assistant's salary; thus, they are an indication of the ubiquitous minor corruption.
12. While the social audit is mandated every six months, it took the state some time to organize regular audits. The time between audits typically varies from six months (the target) to a year. In some mandals, audits happen only once every two years. The reasons range from local resistance to the struggles of bureaucrats at a higher level.
13. The documents also let the workers know how much they should expect to be paid for their work. The payment slips act as a physical record that their work has been measured.
14. Senior village social auditors participate in more audits than the other village social auditors, but only a few village social auditors become senior village social auditors.
15. Local bureaucrats exploit such ambiguities at gram sabhas and at public meetings.
16. They are supposed to make another visit, but often there is no time.
17. When I first observed an audit and saw the auditors filling their notebooks after the surveys were over, I mistakenly thought that they were involved in a massive fraud, filling out the documents in the office instead of doing their work.
18. B. R. Ambedkar was a social reformer and the architect of the Indian Constitution. Throughout his life, he fought for the annihilation of castes and campaigned in particular against discrimination against Dalits. Ambedkar is a major inspiration for Dalits in contemporary India.
19. Dalits who see Ambedkar as their role model are fiercely modernist and consider the West to be very progressive. Ambedkar is often seen in statues dressed in Western clothes. Thus it is natural that this worker would be impressed by my US affiliation.
20. I had many discussions with senior auditors and bureaucrats about the superficiality of the current audit process. I used every opportunity to advocate for including qualitative in addition to quantitative audits. Indirectly, I was advocating for the state to store information about each village so that they could develop a robust vision of the political situation in that village. Later I found that the local police record (or used to record) such data (see Chapter 7).
21. This was the first time this district resource person had been in this village; that is why he wasn't aware of where previous meetings had been held.
22. There have been objections to this timing, and a new process has now been issued that brings special officers in to preside at these meetings.
23. In practice the number of workdays allowed per family changes based on the year and season.
24. The media in Andhra Pradesh are very politicized. There is a mouthpiece for each party, and each media outlet portrays its party in the best possible light.

Chapter 6

1. Andhra Pradesh split into two states on June 2, 2014: Andhra Pradesh and Telangana. The social audit unit, SSAAT, had a Telangana unit.
2. I was a participant observer in the audits, and I traveled with, worked with, and lived with the team for the entire audit. Usually I was able to retain my identity as a researcher when I was not shadowing the auditors. However, when I accompanied the auditors, villagers sometimes assumed that I was part of the audit team. This confusion often led to productive conversations that I exploited in the interest of learning as much as possible about the auditing process. While I was careful to be consistent in how I approached the audits, the extent to which I was able to exert agency in each audit varied.
3. They are supposed to make another visit, but often there is not enough time.
4. Local bureaucrats exploit such ambiguities at gram sabhas and at public meetings.
5. In practice, the household survey is not totally private, and people nearby assemble, but care is taken to ensure that the field assistant is not nearby.
6. As Durgam et al. (2013) in their study in Karnataka show, the social audit process flounders if they are not able to contest the actions of the local elites.
7. See Sowmya Sivakumar, *The Hindu*, October 2, 2010, "No Guarantees Anymore."
8. Zuckerman has deployed Schudson's term of "monitorial citizenship" to discuss, as he puts it, the "post-informed citizen" (Schudson 1996; Zuckerman 2014).
9. See Aiyar and Mehta (2005) for more on the exceptionality of Andhra Pradesh's bureaucratic implementation, as opposed to implementing them via local elected bodies.
10. A report from SSAAT claimed that upper-level NREGA administrators accepted about 55 percent of this amount as accurate.
11. Aiyar and Mehta (2015) report that Rs. 230 million had been recovered in 2013; about 16.5 percent of what was found, and action was taken on 40 percent of the officials who were implicated.

Chapter 7

1. I heard this from many people, including activists and government bureaucrats, who thought that field research was too expensive and brought no real returns for anybody.
2. See Pattenden (2017) for a class-relational approach in Karnataka.
3. Here I am excluding the tribal villages, which were not segregated based on caste.
4. Personal communication with Vivek Srinivasan. See also Srinivasan (2010).
5. I was told that the complete records were in the archives in the district headquarters. The police constable needed some coaching from the inspector to help him find the records. He returned with a pile of dusty notebooks; I was clearly the first person to consult them in years. When I asked the police inspector who used them, he told me

that they were important in introducing the village to a new inspector. The police are transferred often and the records provide a way to get up to speed on what is going on in the village. Yet this practice of recording detailed surveillance has stopped in this area and the notes have not been updated for several years. The police told me that this was because the factionalism problem has gone away.

6. Apart from information about local conflicts, the notes contained basic statistics about the village: population, caste composition, temples, water sources, crimes, names of prostitutes, the important people in the village and their political affiliations, and the number and status of court cases. They categorized the factions in the village and listed the types of threats each posed, identifying the faction leaders, their main associates, and the people who made bombs by name.
7. Surveillance is not panoptic; it is always targeted against the dominated (Browne 2015).
8. The Mala and Madiga divisions among Dalits were present in these villages. Normally a Madiga isn't allowed to eat at a Mala's house. One Mala woman told me that on the rare occasion when Madigas eat in Mala homes, the Malas vigorously wash their plates to preserve their "purity." This "trickling down" of caste feelings has been referred to as the "Sanskritization" of society (Srinivas 1956). Even though Dalits have now embraced Christianity, I did not notice changes with respect to these deep-rooted caste divisions.

   See Balagopal (2000) to understand the conflict among the Dalit reservation (affirmative action) between Malas and the Madigas and how they escalated when the legal system got involved.
9. While I am not aware of any studies that examine a reduction in agricultural productivity since the NREGA became law, members of NGOs and activists who work in sustainable agriculture echo the view that the NREGA has indeed affected farming. Some of them told me that farming was hard work and that farming is suffering because the laborers are not interested in working for the low wages that farmers pay. While politically and ideologically they side with the laborers and wish for higher wage rates, they also wonder whether the smaller farmers are able to afford the higher wages and whether the laborers are willing to do hard work.
10. If NREGA were consistently confined to certain months of the year, the farmers would be able to plan around the schedule. As the system stands, however, the arbitrary schedule affects workers and Reddies alike. When I asked upper-level bureaucrats about the intermittent nature of NREGA work, they told me that NREGA is an on-demand program and that it was within their rights to start and stop the program. According to the NREGA legislation, the demand should come from the workers, but in reality the workers seemed to have very little, if any, influence on when NREGA work was offered. Scholars who do aggregate analysis debate about whether or not NREGA has affected wages (Imbert and Papp 2012; Jha and Ramaswami 2012; see also Mookerjhee 2014). A 2019 study in Andhra Pradesh found that the mean income of NREGA workers had increased by 12.7 percent and that 90 percent of that increase came from increased agricultural wages (Muralidharan et al. 2019). Data I gathered during my fieldwork supports this finding. One piece of evidence is the

"crop holidays" farmers declared elsewhere, keeping their land fallow as a form of protest (Vakulabharanam et al. 2011). They were signaling that the government should not ignore the needs of farmers. A local Telugu-language newspaper tied these protests to NREGA, and the state's rural development department sent teams to examine these claims in the district where farmers had declared crop holidays. Although the investigators concluded that the strikes were not related to NREGA, that conclusion is too convenient for the existing government system to be believed without corroboration.

11. The NREGA's rules specify that if no public work is included in the list from the central office, work should be done first on Dalit land, then on land belonging to the caste immediately above the Dalits, and so on. The Reddies' land would thus come last. I did not see any work being done on Dalit land, although I did hear about a survey to identify Dalit lands for cultivation. I also heard murmurs that the process of identifying land belonging to Dalits was fraught with problems and that more often than not upper-caste lands were identified as Dalit lands.
12. Balagopal finds fault with the Left parties because they do not appreciate the non-economic angle. He documents how the Left has lost support over the years because it has ignored issues of caste and other social issues (Balagopal 2011).
13. With only 100 days per household guaranteed as part of NREGA, in practice, the dependency with the Reddies and the landed class has not withered away. The point is that NREGA gives them an additional option. But Dalits still need to maintain cordial relationships with the landed Reddies.
14. Among many other stories, I heard of a two-glass system to separate cups for Dalits from cups for Reddies. I also heard accounts of the first time Dalits were allowed to enter the Hindu temples, a date the Dalits remembered as an epochal moment, and of the debate about whether Dalits should be allowed to drink water from the common well.
15. During my fieldwork, I saw the technical assistant and the field assistant visit worksites, but I never saw them measuring the work completed. Instead, the field assistant collected the muster rolls from the mates each week and took them to be entered in the computer system.
16. In 2012, workers who were appointed as mates were paid INR 2 more than regular workers.
17. Chapter 3 discusses how the upper-level bureaucrats built a technology system to remotely control the program.
18. These time-and-motion studies came to NREGA by experiments conducted by an NGO to determine the cost estimates for the various types of work that was done under NREGA by accounting for different types of terrain, different soil types, and other features to replace archaic notions of how much work needed to be done before the government would pay a worker.
19. Interview with a senior bureaucrat in Hyderabad, November 2011.
20. Some of that negligence can be traced to apathy at the mandal level, which meant that work was available inconsistently, but some could be traced to the more centralized control in Hyderabad. The work could be stopped at the mandal level due to several reasons. This could be because of lack of field assistants to open up works, or

the ability of the local farmers to force the lower-level bureaucrats to stop the work locally.

21. The NREGA is paid for largely from funds provided by the central Indian government in Delhi, as opposed to local state governments. Rural development bureaucrats in Delhi tried to protest the raising of minimum wages by the local state governments like Andhra Pradesh by fixing the amount of the NREGA wage and urging the state governments to make up the difference.
22. P. Sainath, an avid and rare commentator on rural issues in India in English-language newspapers, pointed out in an interview with me that NREGA could be a blessing for small farmers (those who own less than five acres of land) because it does not exclusively target the poor. Small farmers can work for NREGA in lean seasons to supplement their income. While I could not find any farmers who were willing to admit that the program helped them, all of the small farmers I encountered had job cards and seemed to have benefited from NREGA.
23. The first thing the mandal program development officer did was describe the NREGA setup to me. He drew some diagrams on a piece of paper and described the district's administrative hierarchy. Eventually he gave me a document called the "At-a-Glance Report," which can easily be downloaded from the Internet thanks to the extensive computerization of NREGA reports. I tried to resist this time-wasting tactic, telling him that I already knew the basic structure of the system. He chided me for not being patient and continued to tell me facts I already knew.

    I then told him that I wanted to hear about the pressure he was receiving from the Reddies to stop NREGA work. He told me that I should find out such things on my own. I asked for more details about the land survey that was done to identify private lands to be developed for cultivation. He was surprised that I knew about the survey and said that it would take time to explain the details and that I should return later, perhaps in the evening, when he would have them ready. As I suspected, when I returned in the evening he was not there. He refused requests for another meeting, saying that the office was busy preparing for the village audits.
24. One of the disadvantages of the current auditing system is that it limits the potential for effective change before the audit has even begun.
25. I have made a comparison of how local social structures affect local implementation in NREGA, by comparing a Dalit village with a Tribal village (Veeraraghavan 2017).
26. The union was formed to fight for the rights of field assistants. During my fieldwork, the field assistants were organizing to fight for job security and an increase in wages. They eventually got the increase in salary.
27. I discuss this issue from the auditors' perspective in Chapter 4.
28. See Chapter 4 for the discussion of the politics associated with what needs to be read out by the social auditors in the village social audit meeting.

Chapter 8

1. In 2013, Andhra Pradesh split into Andhra Pradesh and Telangana. The bulk of the field work was done when the state was Andhra Pradesh.

2. See Mosse (2004, 241) for the importance of studying processes to understand "how the work of implementation, especially, was shaped by administrative and political agency."
3. See also Gitelman (2013).
4. Chauchard (2017) shows how caste-based affirmative action has an effect, even if it is not seen in narrowly defined material benefits.
5. The committee would examine the feasibility of using the employment generated under the Mahatma Gandhi National Rural Employment Guarantee Act (MNREGA) in agriculture related activities both pre-harvest and post-harvest. "Committee to Examine Using NREGA in Agriculture," *Financial Times*, June 17, 2018. https://www.financialexpress.com/india-news/committee-to-examine-using-mnrega-in-agriculture/1209786/
6. Diego Maiorano and Chakrhadar Buddha, "Using MGNREGA Funds to Subsidise Farm Labour is a Recipe for Disaster," *The Wire*, July 4. https://thewire.in/labour/using-mgnrega-funds-to-subsidise-farm-labour-is-a-recipe-for-disaster
7. As Appadurai (2001, 43) notes, "like all serious exercises in democratic practice, it is not automatically reproductive. It has particular conditions of possibility and conditions under which it grows weak or corrupt."
8. Costanza-Chock (2020) offers a paradigm of "design justice."
9. Duguid (2005) argues that the "art of knowing" is a lot more challenging than simplistic but popular notions that posits "information facilitates action."
10. However, Ivan Krastev gives the strongest critique of the citizen monitoring, when he argues: "The movement aims to build a reverse panopticon whereby it is not government that will monitor society but society that will monitor those in power. The totalitarian utopia of people spying for the government is now replaced by the progressive utopia of people spying on the government" (Krastev 2013). https://www.eurozine.com/the-transparency-delusion/
11. As Scott points out, resistance can take many forms, and often are in the form of "hidden transcripts" (Scott 1992).
12. See Fox (2015).

References

Aakella, Karuna Vakati, and Sowmya Kidambi. 2007a. "Challenging Corruption with Social Audits." *Economic and Political Weekly* 42 (5): 345–47.

Aakella, Karuna Vakati, and Sowmya Kidambi. 2007b. "Social Audits in Andhra Pradesh: A Process in Evolution." *Economic and Political Weekly* 42 (47): 18–19.

Abers, Rebecca. 2001. "Practicing Radical Democracy." *The Planning Review* 37 (147): 32–38.

Acemoglu, Daron, Simon Johnson, and James A. Robinson. 2001. "The Colonial Origins of Comparative Development: An Empirical Investigation." *American Economic Review* 91 (5): 1369–401.

Adhikari, Anindita, and Kartika Bhatia. 2010. "NREGA Wage Payments: Can We Bank on the Banks?" *Economic and Political Weekly* 45: 30–37.

Afridi, Farzana, and Vegard Iversen. 2014. "Social Audits and MGNREGA Delivery: Lessons from Andhra Pradesh." In *India Policy Forum 2013–14*, edited by Arvind Panagariya, Barry Bosworth, and Shah Shekhar, Vol. 10: 297–341. National Council of Applied Economic Research: SAGE Publications India.

Afridi, Farzana, Vegard Iversen, and M. R. Sharan. 2017. "Women Political Leaders, Corruption, and Learning: Evidence from a Large Public Program in India." *Economic Development and Cultural Change* 66 (1): 1–30.

Agarwala, Rina. 2013. *Informal Labor, Formal Politics, and Dignified Discontent in India*. Illustrated edition. Cambridge Studies in Contentious Politics. Cambridge: Cambridge University Press.

Aggarwal, Ankita. 2017. "Tyranny of MGNREGA's Monitoring System." *Economic and Political Weekly* 52 (37): 24–26.

Agre, Philip E., and Marc Rotenberg. 1998. *Technology and Privacy: The New Landscape*. Cambridge, MA: MIT Press.

Ahuja, Amit. 2019. *Mobilizing the Marginalized: Ethnic Parties without Ethnic Movements*. New York: Oxford University Press.

Ahuja, Amit, and Susan L. Ostermann. 2018. "From Quiescent Bureaucracy to 'Undocumented Wonder': Explaining the Indian Election Commission's Expanding Mandate." *Governance* 31 (4): 759–76.

Aiyar, Yamini, and Soumya Kapoor Mehta. 2015. "Spectators or Participants? Effects of Social Audits in Andhra Pradesh." *Economic & Political Weekly* 50 (7): 66–71.

Aiyar, Yamini, S. Mehta, and S. Sami. 2011. "Strengthening Public Accountability: Lessons From Implementing Social Audits in Andhra Pradesh." Accountability Initiative Working Paper Series. Accountability Initiative, Centre for Policy Research, New Delhi. https://accountabilityindia.in/sites/default/files/working-paper/strengthening_public_accountability.pdf.

Aiyar, Yamini, and Salimah Samji. 2009. "Transparency and Accountability in NREGA: A Case Study of Andhra Pradesh." Centre for Policy Research, New Delhi, Engaging Accountability: Working Paper Series No. 1, February, 28.

Ali, Sameen A. Mohsin. 2020. "Driving Participatory Reforms into the Ground: The Bureaucratic Politics of Irrigation Management Transfer in Pakistan." *World Development* 135 (November): 105056.

Alkhatib, Ali, and Michael Bernstein. 2019. "Street-Level Algorithms: A Theory at the Gaps between Policy and Decisions." In *Proceedings of the 2019 CHI Conference on Human Factors in Computing Systems*, 1–13. CHI '19. New York: Association for Computing Machinery.

Ambedkar, B. R. 1979. "Castes in India: Their Mechanism, Genesis and Development." In *Dr. Babasaheb Ambedkar: Writings and Speeches*, 1: 3–22. Bombay: Government of Maharashtra.

Ambedkar, B. R. 1991. *Writing and Speeches*. Vol. 10. Bombay: Government of Maharashtra.

Anand, Nikhil. 2017. *Hydraulic City: Water and the Infrastructures of Citizenship in Mumbai*. Illustrated edition. Durham, NC; London: Duke University Press.

Appadurai, Arjun. 2001. "Deep Democracy: Urban Governmentality and the Horizon of Politics." *Environment and Urbanization* 13 (2): 23–43.

Appu, P. S. 1997. *Land Reforms in India: A Survey of Policy, Legislation and Implementation*. 1st edition. New Delhi: Vikas.

Auerbach, Adam Michael. 2019. *Demanding Development: The Politics of Public Goods Provision in India's Urban Slums*. Cambridge; New York: Cambridge University Press.

Bagchee, Sandeep. 1984. "Employment Guarantee Scheme in Maharashtra." *Economic and Political Weekly* 19 (37): 1633–38.

Baiocchi, Gianpaolo. 2003. "Emergent Public Spheres: Talking Politics in Participatory Governance." *American Sociological Review* 68 (1): 52–74.

Baiocchi, Gianpaolo. 2005. *Militants and Citizens: The Politics of Participatory Democracy in Porto Alegre*. 1st edition. Stanford, CA: Stanford University Press.

Baiocchi, Gianpaolo, Patrick Heller, and Marcelo Silva. 2011. *Bootstrapping Democracy: Transforming Local Governance and Civil Society in Brazil*. 1st edition. Stanford, CA: Stanford University Press.

Balagopal, Kandalla. 2000. "A Tangled Web: Subdivision of SC Reservations in AP." *Economic and Political Weekly* 35 (13): 1075–81.

Balagopal, Kandalla. 2006. "Maoist Movement in Andhra Pradesh." *Economic and Political Weekly* 41 (29): 3183–87.

Balagopal, Kandalla. 2011. *Ear to the Ground: Writings on Class and Caste*. New Delhi: Navayana.

Banerjee, Abhijit, Rema Hanna, Jordan C. Kyle, Benjamin A. Olken, and Sudarno Sumarto. 2016. "Contracting Out the Last-Mile of Service Delivery: Subsidized Food Distribution in Indonesia." w21837. Cambridge, MA: National Bureau of Economic Research.

Banerjee, Abhijit V., Rukmini Banerji, Esther Duflo, Rachel Glennerster, and Stuti Khemani. 2010. "Pitfalls of Participatory Programs: Evidence from a Randomized Evaluation in Education in India." *American Economic Journal. Economic Policy* 2 (1): 1–30.

Banerjee, Abhijit V., and Esther Duflo. 2009. "The Experimental Approach to Development Economics." *Annual Review of Economics* 1 (1): 151–78.

Bardhan, Pranab. 1980. "Interlocking Factor Markets and Agrarian Development: A Review of Issues." *Oxford Economic Papers* 32 (1): 82–98.

Bardhan, Pranab. 1999. *The Political Economy of Development in India*. 2nd edition. Oxford; New York: Oxford University Press.

Bardhan, Pranab. 2002. "Decentralization of Governance and Development." *Journal of Economic Perspectives* 16 (4): 185–205.

Bardhan, Pranab K., and Dilip Mookherjee, eds. 2006. *Decentralization and Local Governance in Developing Countries: A Comparative Perspective*. Cambridge: MIT Press.

Bates, Robert H. 2005. *Markets and States in Tropical Africa: The Political Basis of Agricultural Policies: With a New Preface*. 2nd edition. Berkeley: University of California Press.

Baviskar, Amita. 2013. "Winning the Right to Information in India: Is Knowledge Power?" In *Citizen Action and National Policy Reform: Making Change Happen*, edited by John Gaventa and Rosemary McGee, 130–52. London: Zed Books.

Bayly, Susan. 2001. *Caste, Society and Politics in India from the Eighteenth Century to the Modern Age*. Vol. 3. Cambridge: Cambridge University Press.

Becker, Howard S. 2008. *Tricks of the Trade: How to Think about Your Research While You're Doing It*. Chicago: University of Chicago Press.

Benjamin, Solomon, Ramkumar Bhuvaneswari, and P. Rajan. 2007. "Bhoomi: 'E-Governance,' or, an Anti-Politics Machine Necessary to Globalize Bangalore?" *CASUM-m Working Paper*, 1–53.

Bernstorff, Dagmar. 1973. "Eclipse of 'Reddy-Raj'? The Attempted Restructuring of the Congress Party Leadership in Andhra Pradesh." *Asian Survey* 13 (10): 959–79.

Bhatia, Amiya, and Jacqueline Bhabha. 2017. "India's Aadhaar Scheme and the Promise of Inclusive Social Protection." *Oxford Development Studies* 45 (1): 64–79.

Bourdieu, Pierre. 1973. *Cultural Reproduction and Social Reproduction. Knowledge, Education, and Cultural Change*. 1st edition. London: Routledge.

Bourdieu, Pierre, Loic J. D. Wacquant, and Samar Farage. 1994. "Rethinking the State: Genesis and Structure of the Bureaucratic Field." *Sociological Theory* 12 (1): 1–18.

Bovens, Mark, and Stavros Zouridis. 2002. "From Street-Level to System-Level Bureaucracies: How Information and Communication Technology Is Transforming Administrative Discretion and Constitutional Control." *Public Administration Review* 62 (2): 174–84.

Brewer, Eric, Michael Demmer, Bowei Du, Melissa Ho, Matthew Kam, Sergiu Nedevschi, Joyojeet Pal, Rabin Patra, Sonesh Surana, and Kevin Fall. 2005. "The Case for Technology in Developing Regions." *IEEE Computer Society, Perspectives*, 38 (6): 25–38.

Brown, John Seely, and Paul Duguid. 1991. "Organizational Learning and Communities-of-Practice: Toward a Unified View of Working, Learning, and Innovation." *Organization Science* 2 (1): 40–57.

Brown, John Seely, Paul Duguid 2017. *The Social Life of Information: Updated, with a New Preface*. Revised edition. Boston: Harvard Business Review Press.

Browne, Simone. 2015. *Dark Matters: On the Surveillance of Blackness*. Illustrated edition. Durham, NC: Duke University Press Books.

Brulé, Rachel E. 2020a. "Reform, Representation, and Resistance: The Politics of Property Rights' Enforcement." *The Journal of Politics* 82 (4): 1390–1405.

Brulé, Rachel E. 2020b. *Women, Power, and Property: The Paradox of Gender Equality Laws in India*. Cambridge, MA: Cambridge University Press.

Buolamwini, Joy, and Timnit Gebru. 2018. "Gender Shades: Intersectional Accuracy Disparities in Commercial Gender Classification." In *Conference on Fairness,*

Accountability and Transparency, 77–91. New York: Association for Computing Machinery.

Burawoy, Michael. 1998. "The Extended Case Method." *Sociological Theory* 16 (1): 4–33.

Burrell, Jenna. 2012. *Invisible Users: Youth in the Internet Cafés of Urban Ghana*. Cambridge, MA: MIT Press.

Bussell, Jennifer. 2012. *Corruption and Reform in India: Public Services in the Digital Age*. New York: Cambridge University Press.

Bussell, Jennifer. 2019. *Clients and Constituents: Political Responsiveness in Patronage Democracies*. New York: Oxford University Press.

Bussell, Jennifer L. 2010. "Why Get Technical? Corruption and the Politics of Public Service Reform in the Indian States." *Comparative Political Studies* 43 (10): 1230–57.

Byres, Terence James, Karin Kapadia, and Jens Lerche. 2013. *Rural Labour Relations in India*. 1st edition. London: Routledge.

Calhoun, Craig J. 1992. *Habermas and the Public Sphere*. 1st edition. Cambridge, MA: MIT Press.

Carswell, Grace, and Geert de Neve. 2014. "MGNREGA in Tamil Nadu: A Story of Success and Transformation?" *Journal of Agrarian Change* 14 (4): 564–85.

Chadwick, Andrew. 2003. "Bringing E-Democracy Back In: Why It Matters for Future Research on E-Governance." *Social Science Computer Review* 21 (4): 443–55.

Chambers, Robert. 1994. "The Origins and Practice of Participatory Rural Appraisal." *World Development* 22 (7): 953–69.

Chandra, Kanchan. 2004. *Why Ethnic Parties Succeed: Patronage and Ethnic Head Counts in India*. Illustrated edition. Cambridge; New York: Cambridge University Press.

Chatterjee, Partha. 2004. *The Politics of the Governed: Reflections on Popular Politics in Most of the World*. New York: Columbia University Press.

Chauchard, Simon. 2017. *Why Representation Matters: The Meaning of Ethnic Quotas in Rural India*. Cambridge; New York: Cambridge University Press.

Chaudhuri, Bidisha. 2014. *E-Governance in India: Interlocking Politics, Technology and Culture*. 1st edition. London; New York: Routledge.

Chaudhuri, Bidisha. 2019. "Paradoxes of Intermediation in Aadhaar: Human Making of a Digital Infrastructure." *South Asia: Journal of South Asian Studies* 42 (3): 572–87.

Chaudhuri, Bidisha. 2021. "Distant, Opaque and Seamful: Seeing the State through the Workings of Aadhaar in India." *Information Technology for Development* 27 (1): 37–49.

Chopra, Deepta. 2011a. "Policy Making in India: A Dynamic Process of Statecraft." *Pacific Affairs* 84 (1): 89–107.

Chopra, Deepta. 2011b. "Interactions of 'Power' in the Making and Shaping of Social Policy." *Contemporary South Asia* 19 (2): 153–71.

Christens, Brian, and Paul W. Speer. 2006. "Review Essay: Tyranny/Transformation: Power and Paradox in Participatory Development." *Forum, Qualitative Social Research* 7 (2). https://doi.org/10.17169/fqs-7.2.91.

Christin, Angèle. 2017. "Algorithms in Practice: Comparing Web Journalism and Criminal Justice." *Big Data & Society* 4 (2): 1–14.

Chu, Julie Y. 2014. "When Infrastructures Attack: The Workings of Disrepair in China." *American Ethnologist* 41 (2): 351–67.

Cohen, Lawrence. 2019. "The 'Social' De-Duplicated: On the Aadhaar Platform and the Engineering of Service." *South Asia: Journal of South Asian Studies* 42 (3): 482–500.

Constituent Assembly of India. 1948. "Constituent Assembly of India Debates (Proceedings), Volume VII." Constitution of India. November 19, 1948.

Cooke, Bill, and Uma Kothari. 2001. *Participation: The New Tyranny?* London: Zed Books.

Corbridge, Stuart, and Manoj Srivastava. 2013. "Mapping the Social Order by Fund Flows: The Political Geography of Employment Assurance Schemes in India." *Economy and Society* 42 (3): 455–79.

Corbridge, Stuart, Glyn Williams, Manoj Srivastava, and René Véron. 2005. *Seeing the State: Governance and Governmentality in India*. Vol. 10. Contemporary South Asia. Cambridge: Cambridge University Press.

Coslovsky, Salo, Roberto Pires, and Renato Bignami. 2017. "Resilience and Renewal: The Enforcement of Labor Laws in Brazil." *Latin American Politics and Society* 59 (2): 77–102.

Costanza-Chock, Sasha. 2020. *Design Justice: Community-Led Practices to Build the Worlds We Need*. Cambridge, MA: MIT Press.

Dada, Danish. 2006. "The Failure of E-Government in Developing Countries: A Literature Review." *The Electronic Journal of Information Systems in Developing Countries* 26 (1): 1–10.

Dandeker, Christopher. 1994. *Surveillance, Power and Modernity: Bureaucracy and Discipline from 1700 to the Present Day*. Cambridge: Polity.

Dasgupta, Aditya, Kishore Gawande, and Devesh Kapur. 2017. "(When) Do Antipoverty Programs Reduce Violence? India's Rural Employment Guarantee and Maoist Conflict." *International Organization* 71 (3): 605–32.

Dasgupta, Aditya, and Devesh Kapur. 2020. "The Political Economy of Bureaucratic Overload: Evidence from Rural Development Officials in India." *American Political Science Review* 114 (4): 1316–34.

Davies, Tim. 2010. *Open Data, Democracy and Public Sector Reform*. Master's thesis: University of Oxford.

Deininger, Klaus, and Yanyan Liu. 2013. "Welfare and Poverty Impacts of India's National Rural Employment Guarantee Scheme: Evidence from Andhra Pradesh." The World Bank, Policy Research Working Paper No. 6543: 1–29. Washington, DC: The World Bank.

Desai, Sonalde, Prem Vashishtha, and Omkar Joshi. 2015. "Mahatma Gandhi National Rural Employment Guarantee Act: A Catalyst for Rural Transformation." Working Paper 7259. New Delhi: National Council of Applied Economic Research.

Deshingkar, Priya, Craig Johnson, and John Farrington. 2005. "State Transfers to the Poor and Back: The Case of the Food-for-Work Program in India." *World Development* 33 (4): 575–91.

Deshmukh-Ranadive, Joy. 2004. "Women's Self-Help Groups in Andhra Pradesh: Participatory Poverty Alleviation in Action." In *Conference on Scaling Up Poverty Reduction, Shanghai*. https://documents1.worldbank.org/curated/en/442521468752429977/pdf/308310IN0Andhra0SHGs01see0also0307591.pdf.

Diamond, Larry. 2010. "Liberation Technology." *Journal of Democracy* 21 (3): 69–83.

Drèze, Jean. 2004. "Democracy and Right to Food." *Economic and Political Weekly* 39 (17): 1723–31.

Drèze, Jean. 2007. "NREGA: Dismantling the Contractor Raj." *The Hindu* 20. https://www.thehindu.com/todays-paper/tp-opinion/NREGA-Dismantling-the-contractor-raj/article14878947.ece.

Drèze, Jean. 2010. "Employment Guarantee and the Right to Work." In *Oxford Companion to Indian Politics*, edited by Niraja Gopal Jayal and Pratap Bhanu Mehta. New Delhi: Oxford University Press.

Drèze, Jean. 2019. *Sense and Solidarity: Jholawala Economics for Everyone*. Oxford: Oxford University Press.

Drèze, Jean, Nikhil Dey, and Reetika Khera. 2006. "NREGA: A Primer, New Delhi." *Right to Food Campaign*.

Drèze, Jean, and Reetika Khera. 2017. "Recent Social Security Initiatives in India." *World Development* 98 (C): 555–72.

Drèze, Jean, and Amartya Sen. 1989. *Hunger and Public Action*. Revised edition. Oxford: Oxford University Press.

Drèze, Jean, and Amartya Sen. 2013. *An Uncertain Glory: India and Its Contradictions*. Princeton, NJ: Princeton University Press.

Duguid, Paul. 2005. "'The Art of Knowing': Social and Tacit Dimensions of Knowledge and the Limits of the Community of Practice." *The Information Society* 21 (2): 109–18.

Durgam, Rajasekhar, Salim Lakha, and Manjula Ramachandra. 2013. "How Effective Are Social Audits under MGNREGS? Lessons from Karnataka." *Sociological Bulletin* 62 (3): 431–55.

Durgam, Rajasekhar, Salim Lakha, and Manjula Ramachandra. 2017. "Is Decentralisation Promoting or Hindering the Effective Implementation of MGNREGS? The Evidence from Karnataka." *Institute for Social and Economic Change.*, Working Paper Series 395, July 22.

Escobar, Arturo. 2011. *Encountering Development: The Making and Unmaking of the Third World*. Revised edition. Vol. 1. Princeton, NJ: Princeton University Press.

Eubanks, Virginia. 2018. *Automating Inequality: How High-Tech Tools Profile, Police, and Punish the Poor*. New York: St. Martin's Press.

Evans, Peter. 1996. "Government Action, Social Capital and Development: Reviewing the Evidence on Synergy." *World Development* 24 (6): 1119–32.

Evans, Peter. 1997. "State-Society Synergy: Government and Social Capital in Development." *World Development* 24 (6): 1119–32.

Evans, Peter. 2004. "Development as Institutional Change: The Pitfalls of Monocropping and the Potentials of Deliberation." *Studies in Comparative International Development* 38 (4): 30–52.

Evans, Peter. 2012. *Embedded Autonomy: States and Industrial Transformation*. Princeton, NJ: Princeton University Press.

Evans, Peter B. 1989. "Predatory, Developmental, and Other Apparatuses: A Comparative Political Economy Perspective on the Third World State." *Sociological Forum* 4 (4): 561–87.

Evans, Peter, and Patrick Heller. 2015. "Human Development, State Transformation, and the Politics of the Developmental State." In *The Oxford Handbook of Transformations of the State*, edited by Stephan Leibfried, Evelyne Huber, Matthew Lange, Jonah D. Levy, and John D. Stephens, 691–713. Oxford: Oxford University Press.

Ferguson, James. 1990. *The Anti-Politics Machine: "Development", Depoliticization and Bureaucratic Power in Lesotho*. Minneapolis, MN: CUP Archive.

Finn, Megan. 2018. *Documenting Aftermath: Information Infrastructures in the Wake of Disasters*. Illustrated edition. Cambridge, MA: MIT Press.

Finn, Megan, Janaki Srinivasan, and Rajesh Veeraraghavan. 2014. "Seeing with Paper: Government Documents and Material Participation." In *Proceedings of the 2014 47th Hawaii International Conference on System Sciences*, 1515–24. HICSS '14. : IEEE Computer Society.

Flanagin, Andrew J., Craig Flanagin, and Jon Flanagin. 2010. "Technical Code and the Social Construction of the Internet." *New Media & Society* 12 (2): 179–96.

Foucault, Michel. 1977. *Discipline and Punish: The Birth of the Prison*. Translated by Alan Sheridan. New York: Pantheon Books.

Fox, Jonathan. 1993. *The Politics of Food in Mexico: State Power and Social Mobilization*. Ithaca, NY: Cornell University Press.

Fox, Jonathan. 1996. "How Does Civil Society Thicken? The Political Construction of Social Capital in Rural Mexico." *World Development* 24 (6): 1089–103.

Fox, Jonathan. 2007. "The Uncertain Relationship between Transparency and Accountability." *Development in Practice*, Center for Global, International and Regional Studies, Working Paper Series, 17 (4): 663–71.

Fox, Jonathan. 2015. "Social Accountability: What Does the Evidence Really Say?" *World Development* 72 (0): 346–61.

Fox, Jonathan. 2020. "Contested Terrain: International Development Projects and Countervailing Power for the Excluded." *World Development* 133 (September): Article number: 104978.

Frankel, Francine R. 1978. *India's Political Economy, 1947–1977, the Gradual Revolution*. 1st edition. Princeton, NJ: Princeton University Press.

Frankel, Francine R., and M. S. A. Rao, eds. 1990. *Dominance and State Power in Modern India: Decline of a Social Order*. Vol. 1. Delhi; New York: Oxford University Press.

Fuller, C. J., and John Harriss. 2001. "For an Anthropology of the Modern Indian State." In *The Everyday State and Society in Modern India*, edited by C. J. Fuller and Veronique Bénéï, 1–30. London: Hurst.

Fung, Archon, and Eric Olin Wright. 2001. "Deepening Democracy: Innovations in Empowered Participatory Governance." *Politics and Society* 29 (1): 5–41.

Fung, Archon, Mary Graham, and David Weil. 2007. *Full Disclosure: The Perils and Promise of Transparency*. Illustrated edition. New York: Cambridge University Press.

Furlong, Kathryn. 2014. "STS Beyond the 'Modern Infrastructure Ideal': Extending Theory by Engaging with Infrastructure Challenges in the South." *Technology in Society* 38 (August): 139–47.

Gandhi, Rikin, Rajesh Veeraraghavan, Kentaro Toyama, and Vanaja Ramprasad. 2009. "Digital Green: Participatory Video and Mediated Instruction for Agricultural Extension." *Information Technologies & International Development* 5 (1): 1–15.

Gaventa, John. 2006. "Triumph, Deficit or Contestation? Deepening the 'Deepening Democracy' Debate," IDS Working Paper 264, 1–34. Brighton. Institute of Development Studies.

Gay, Paul du, ed. 2005. *The Values of Bureaucracy*. Oxford; New York: Oxford University Press.

Gigler, Bjorn-Soren, and Savita Bailur, eds. 2014. *Closing the Feedback Loop: Can Technology Bridge the Accountability Gap?* Washington, DC: The World Bank.

Gitelman, Lisa. 2013. *"Raw Data" Is an Oxymoron*. Cambridge, MA: MIT Press.

Gulzar, Saad, and Benjamin J. Pasquale. 2017. "Politicians, Bureaucrats, and Development: Evidence from India." *American Political Science Review* 111 (1): 162–83.

Gupta, Akhil. 1995. "Blurred Boundaries: The Discourse of Corruption, the Culture of Politics, and the Imagined State." *American Ethnologist* 22 (2): 375–402.

Gupta, Akhil. 2012. *Red Tape: Bureaucracy, Structural Violence, and Poverty in India*. Durham, NC: Duke University Press Books.

Gurstein, Michael. 2011. "Open Data: Empowering the Empowered or Effective Data Use for Everyone?" *First Monday* 16 (2). https://journals.uic.edu/ojs/index.php/fm/article/view/3316/2764.

Gurstein, Michael. 2012. "Two Worlds of Open Government Data: Getting the Lowdown on Public Toilets in Chennai and Other Matters." *The Journal of Community Informatics* 8 (2).

Habermas, Jurgen. 1991. *The Structural Transformation of the Public Sphere: An Inquiry Into a Category of Bourgeois Society*. Translated by Thomas Burger and Frederick Lawrence. Sixth edition. Cambridge, MA: MIT Press.

Harari, Yuval Noah. 2018. "Why Technology Favors Tyranny." *The Atlantic Monthly* 322 (3): 64–70.

Harriss, John. 2001. *Depoliticizing Development: The World Bank and Social Capital*. 1st edition. London: Anthem Press.

Harriss, John. 2003. "Do Political Regimes Matter? Poverty Reduction and Regime Differences across India." In *Changing Paths: International Development and the New Politics of Inclusion*, edited by Peter P. Houtzager and Mick Moore, 204–32. Ann Arbor: University of Michigan Press.

Harriss, John. 2012. "Reflections on Caste and Class, Hierarchy and Dominance." *Seminar* 633 (May): 19–22. https://www.india-seminar.com/2012/633/633_john_harriss.htm.

Harriss-White, Barbara. 2003. *India Working: Essays on Society and Economy*. 8. Cambridge, MA: Cambridge University Press.

Hasan, Zoya. 2018. *Agitation to Legislation: Negotiating Equity and Justice in India*. New Delhi: Oxford University Press India.

Hayek, F.A. 1944. *The Road to Serfdom*. 1st edition. Chicago: University of Chicago Press.

Hayes, Michael. 2017. "Incrementalism and Public Policy-Making." *Oxford Research Encyclopedia of Politics*, April. https://oxfordre.com/politics/view/10.1093/acrefore/9780190228637.001.0001/acrefore-9780190228637-e-133.

Heeks, Richard. 1999. "Information Technology and the Management of Corruption." *Development in Practice* 9 (1–2): 184–89.

Heeks, Richard. 2003. "Most EGovernment-for-Development Projects Fail: How Can Risks Be Reduced?" iGovernment Working Paper No. 14. Oxford, UK. https://papers.ssrn.com/sol3/papers.cfm?abstract_id=3540052.

Heeks, Richard, and Savita Bailur. 2007. "Analyzing E-Government Research: Perspectives, Philosophies, Theories, Methods, and Practice." *Government Information Quarterly* 24 (2): 243–65.

Heller, Patrick. 2000. *The Labor of Development: Workers and the Transformation of Capitalism in Kerala, India*. 1st edition. Ithaca, NY: Cornell University Press.

Heller, Patrick. 2011. "Binding the State: State Capacity and Civil Society in India." In *State Building Workshop*, 12. New Delhi: Center for Policy Research.

Heller, Patrick. 2012. "Democracy, Participatory Politics and Development: Some Comparative Lessons from Brazil, India and South Africa." *Polity* 44 (4): 643–65.

Heller, Patrick. 2013. "Challenges and Opportunities: Civil Society and Social Movements in a Globalizing World." New York: United Nations Development Programme, UNDP Human Development Report Office Occasional Paper 6.

Heller, Patrick, and Partha Mukhopadhyay. 2015. "State-Produced Inequality in an Indian City." *Seminar* 672: 51–55.

Helmke, Gretchen, and Steven Levitsky. 2004. "Informal Institutions and Comparative Politics: A Research Agenda." *Perspectives on Politics* 2 (4): 725–40.

Herring, Ronald J. 1983. *Land to the Tiller: The Political Economy of Agrarian Reform in South Asia*. New Haven, CT: Yale University Press.

Herring, Ronald J., and Rex M. Edwards. 1983. "Guaranteeing Employment to the Rural Poor: Social Functions and Class Interests in the Employment Guarantee Scheme in Western India." *World Development* 11 (7): 575–92.

Hetherington, Kregg. 2011. *Guerrilla Auditors: The Politics of Transparency in Neoliberal Paraguay*. Durham, NC: Duke University Press.

Hetherington, Kregg. 2012. "Promising Information: Democracy, Development, and the Remapping of Latin America." *Economy and Society* 41 (2): 127–50.

Houston, Lara, Steven J. Jackson, Daniela K. Rosner, Syed Ishtiaque Ahmed, Meg Young, and Laewoo Kang. 2016. "Values in Repair." In *Proceedings of the 2016 CHI Conference on Human Factors in Computing Systems*, 1403–14. New York: Association for Computing Machinery.

Houtzager, Peter P. 2007. "The Silent Revolution in Anti? Poverty Programmes: Minimum Income Guarantees in Brazil." *IDS Bulletin* (Brighton. 1984) 38 (6): 56–63. Oxford, UK: Blackwell Publishing Ltd.

Hull, Matthew S. 2012a. "Documents and Bureaucracy." *Annual Review of Anthropology* 41 (1): 251–67.

Hull, Matthew S. 2012b. *Government of Paper: The Materiality of Bureaucracy in Urban Pakistan*. 1st edition. Berkeley: University of California Press.

Imbert, Clément, and John Papp. 2012. "Equilibrium Distributional Impacts of Government. Employment Programs: Evidence from India's Employment Guarantee." *Paris School of Economics*, Working Paper Series, 2012 (14), March, 1–75.

Imbert, Clément, and John Papp. 2015. "Labor Market Effects of Social Programs: Evidence from India's Employment Guarantee." *American Economic Journal: Applied Economics* 7 (2): 233–63.

Irani, Lilly. 2019. *Chasing Innovation: Making Entrepreneurial Citizens in Modern India*. Princeton, NJ: Princeton University Press.

Irani, Lilly, Janet Vertesi, Paul Dourish, Kavita Philip, and Rebecca E. Grinter. 2010. "Postcolonial Computing: A Lens on Design and Development." In *Proceedings of the SIGCHI Conference on Human Factors in Computing Systems*, 1311–20. New York: Association for Computing Machinery.

Jack, Margaret, and Steven J. Jackson. 2016. "Logistics as Care and Control: An Investigation into the UNICEF Supply Division." In *Proceedings of the 2016 CHI Conference on Human Factors in Computing Systems*, 2209–19. New York: Association for Computing Machinery.

Jackson, Steven J., Paul N. Edwards, Geoffrey C. Bowker, and Cory P. Knobel. 2007. "Understanding Infrastructure: History, Heuristics and Cyberinfrastructure Policy." *First Monday* 12 (6).

Jaffrelot, Christophe. 2003. *India's Silent Revolution: The Rise of the Lower Castes in North India*. New York: Columbia University Press.

Jain, Sanjay. 2020. "From Jugaad to Jugalbandi: Understanding the Changing Nature of Indian Innovation." *Asia Pacific Journal of Management*, 1–26.

Jakimow, Tanya. 2014. "'Breaking the Backbone of Farmers': Contestations in a Rural Employment Guarantee Scheme." *The Journal of Peasant Studies* 41 (2): 263–81.

Janssen, Katleen. 2012. "Open Government Data and the Right to Information: Opportunities and Obstacles." *The Journal of Community Informatics* 8 (2). https://doi.org/10.15353/joci.v8i2.3042.

Jenkins, Rob. 2016. "A Grassroots Revolution." *The Hindu Business Line*.

Jenkins, Rob, and Anne Marie Goetz. 1999. "Accounts and Accountability: Theoretical Implications of the Right-to-Information Movement in India." *Third World Quarterly* 20 (3): 603–22.

Jenkins, Rob, and James Manor. 2017. *Politics and the Right to Work: India's National Rural Employment Guarantee Act*. Oxford; New York: Oxford University Press.

Jha, Shikha, and Bharat Ramaswami. 2012. "The Percolation of Public Expenditure: Food Subsidies and the Poor in India and Philippines." Indian Statistical Institute, Planning Unit, New Delhi Discussion Papers 11–14, Indian Statistical Institute, New Delhi.

Jodhka, Surinder S. 2002. "Nation and Village: Images of Rural India in Gandhi, Nehru and Ambedkar." *Economic and Political Weekly* 37 (32): 3343–53.

Joshi, Anuradha, and Peter P. Houtzager. 2012. "Widgets or Watchdogs? Conceptual Explorations in Social Accountability." *Public Management Review* 14 (2): 145–62.

Kapur, Devesh, Pratap Bhanu Mehta, and Milan Vaishnav. 2017. *Rethinking Public Institutions in India*. Oxford; New York: Oxford University Press.

Keefer, Philip, and Stuti Khemani. 2012. "Do Informed Citizens Receive More . . . or Pay More? The Impact of Radio on the Government Distribution of Public Health Benefits." Policy Research Working Papers, No. WPS 5952. Washington, DC: The World Bank.

Keniston, Kenneth, and Deepak Kumar, eds. 2004. *IT Experience in India: Bridging the Digital Divide*. 1st edition. New Delhi; Thousand Oaks, CA: SAGE Publications.

Khan, Sarah. 2019. "Personal Is Political: Prospects for Women's Substantive Representation in Pakistan." Working Paper.

Khera, Reetika. 2005. "Bringing Grass Roots Democracy to Life: MKSS Campaign in Rajasthan." *Economic and Political Weekly* 40 (8): 725–28.

Khera, Reetika. 2011a. "The UID Project and Welfare Schemes." *Economic and Political Weekly* 46 (9): 38–43.

Khera, Reetika, ed. 2011b. *The Battle for Employment Guarantee*. Illustrated edition. New Delhi: Oxford University Press.

Khera, Reetika. 2018a. "The Aadhaar Debate: Where Are the Sociologists?" *Contributions to Indian Sociology* 52 (3): 336–42.

Khera, Reetika. 2018b. *Dissent on Aadhaar: Big Data Meets Big Brother*. Hyderabad, Telangana: Orient Blackswan.

Khera, Reetika, and Vineeth Patibandla. 2020. "Information Technology (IT) and Welfare in India: Does IT Work?" In *Proceedings of the 3rd ACM SIGCAS Conference on Computing and Sustainable Societies*, 284–85. COMPASS '20. New York: Association for Computing Machinery.

Kohli, Atul. 1987. *The State and Poverty in India. The Politics of Reform*. New York: Cambridge University Press.

Kohli, Atul. 1988. "The NTR Phenomenon in Andhra Pradesh: Political Change in a South Indian State." *Asian Survey* 28 (10): 991–1017.

Kohli, Atul. 1998. "India Defies the Odds: Enduring Another Election." *Journal of Democracy* 9 (3): 7–20.

Kohli, Atul. 2004. *State-Directed Development: Political Power and Industrialization in the Global Periphery*. Illustrated edition. Cambridge; New York: Cambridge University Press.

Kohli, Atul. 2012. *Poverty Amid Plenty in the New India*. 1st edition. Cambridge; New York: Cambridge University Press.

Krastev, Ivan. 2013. "The Transparency Delusion." *Eurozine*. https://www.eurozine.com/the-transparency-delusion/.

Kruks-Wisner, Gabrielle. 2018. *Claiming the State: Active Citizenship and Social Welfare in Rural India*. Cambridge: Cambridge University Press.

Kuriyan, Renee, Savita Bailur, Bjorn-Soren Gigler, and Kyung Park. 2011. *Technologies for Transparency and Accountability: Implications for ICT Policy and Implementation*. Open Development Technology Alliance. Washington, DC: The World Bank.

Kuriyan, Renee, and Isha Ray. 2009a. "Outsourcing the State? Public-Private Partnerships and Information Technologies in India." *World Development* 37 (10): 1663–73.

Kuriyan, Renee, and Isha Ray. 2009b. "E for Express: Seeing the Indian State through ICTD." In *2009 International Conference on Information and Communication Technologies and Development (ICTD)*, 66–73. Doha.

Lakha, Salim, Durgam Rajasekhar, and Ramachandra Manjula. 2015. "Collusion, Co-Option and Capture: Social Accountability and Social Audits in Karnataka, India." *Oxford Development Studies* 43 (3): 330–48.

Lavalle, Adrian Gurza, Arnab Acharya, and Peter P. Houtzager. 2005. "Beyond Comparative Anecdotalism: Lessons on Civil Society and Participation from Sao Paulo, Brazil." *World Development* 33 (6): 951–64.

Lessig, Lawrence. 1999. *Code: And Other Laws Of Cyberspace*. 1st edition. New York: Basic Books.

Li, Tania Murray. 2007. *The Will to Improve: Governmentality, Development, and the Practice of Politics*. Durham, NC: Duke University Press.

Lieberman, Evan S., Daniel N. Posner, and Lily L. Tsai. 2014. "Does Information Lead to More Active Citizenship? Evidence from an Education Intervention in Rural Kenya." *World Development* 60 (C): 69–83.

Lindblom, Charles E. 1959. "The Science of 'Muddling Through.'" *Public Administration Review* 19 (2): 79–88.

Lindblom, Charles E. 1979. "Still Muddling, Not Yet Through." *Public Administration Review* 39 (6): 517–26.

Lipsky, Michael. 1980. *Street-Level Bureaucracy: Dilemmas of the Individual in Public Services*. 1st edition. New York: Russell Sage Foundation.

Loveman, Mara. 2005. "The Modern State and the Primitive Accumulation of Symbolic Power." *American Journal of Sociology* 110 (6): 1651–83.

Lyon, David. 1994. *Electronic Eye: The Rise of Surveillance Society*. 1st edition. Minneapolis: University of Minnesota Press.

MacAuslan, Ian. 2008. "India's National Rural Employment Guarantee Act: A Case Study for How Change Happens." *From Poverty to Power*. Case Study. Oxford: Oxfam International. https://oxfamilibrary.openrepository.com/bitstream/handle/10546/112481/fp2p-cs-india's-national-rural-employment-guarantee-act-140608-en.pdf?sequence=1.

Madon, Shirin. 2005. "Governance Lessons from the Experience of Telecentres in Kerala." *European Journal of Information Systems* 14 (4): 401–16.

Madon, Shirin. 2011. "E-Governance for Development: A Focus on Rural India." *Progress in Development Studies* 11 (1): 81–82.

Maiorano, Diego. 2014. "The Politics of the Mahatma Gandhi National Rural Employment Guarantee Act in Andhra Pradesh." *World Development* 58 (C): 95–105.

Mander, Harsh, and Abha Joshi. 1999. "The Movement for the Right to Information in India. People's Power for the Control of Corruption." In *Conference on Pan Commonwealth Advocacy*, 46. Harare. http://rtiworkshop.pbworks.com/f/1999-01-IN-The-Movement-for-RTI-in-India-Mander-Joshi.pdf.

Mangla, Akshay. 2018. "Elite Strategies and Incremental Policy Change: The Expansion of Primary Education in India." *Governance* 31 (2): 381–99.

Mann, Michael. 1984. "The Autonomous Power of the State: Its Origins, Mechanisms and Results." *European Journal of Sociology* 25 (2): 185–213.

Mann, Neelakshi, Varad Pande, and Mihir Shah, eds. 2012. *MGNREGA Sameeksha: An Anthology of Research Studies on the Mahatma Gandhi National Rural Employment Guarantee Act, 2005, 2006–2012.* Ministry of Rural Development, Government of India. New Delhi: Orient Blackswan.

Manor, James. 2007. "Successful Governance Reforms in Two Indian States: Karnataka and Andhra Pradesh." *Commonwealth & Comparative Politics* 45 (4): 425–51.

Mansuri, Ghazala, and Vijayendra Rao. 2012. "Localizing Development: Does Participation Work?" Policy Research Report. Washington, DC: The World Bank.

Mansuri, Ghazala, and Vijayendra Rao. 2013. "Can Participation Be Induced? Some Evidence from Developing Countries." *Critical Review of International Social and Political Philosophy* 16 (2): 284–304.

Marathe, Megh, and Priyank Chandra. 2020. "Officers Never Type: Examining the Persistence of Paper in E-Governance." In *Proceedings of the 2020 CHI Conference on Human Factors in Computing Systems*, 1–13. New York: Association for Computing Machinery.

Masiero, Silvia. 2015. "Redesigning the Indian Food Security System through E-Governance: The Case of Kerala." *World Development* 67 (C): 126–37.

Masiero, Silvia. 2017. "Digital Governance and the Reconstruction of the Indian Anti-Poverty System." *Oxford Development Studies* 45 (4): 393–408.

Masiero, Silvia. 2020. "Biometric Infrastructures and the Indian Public Distribution System." *South Asia Multidisciplinary Academic Journal* 23 (September): 1–21.

Masiero, Silvia, and Soumyo Das. 2019. "Datafying Anti-Poverty Programmes: Implications for Data Justice." *Information, Communication & Society* 22 (7): 916–33.

Masiero, Silvia, and Diego Maiorano. 2018. "MGNREGA, Power Politics, and Computerization in Andhra Pradesh." *Forum for Development Studies* 45 (1): 1–24.

Mathur, Nayanika. 2012. "Transparent-Making Documents and the Crisis of Implementation: A Rural Employment Law and Development Bureaucracy in India." *PoLAR: Political and Legal Anthropology Review* 35 (2): 167–85.

Mathur, Nayanika. 2015. *Paper Tiger: Law, Bureaucracy and the Developmental State in Himalayan India*. Delhi: Cambridge University Press.

McCartney, Matthew, and Indrajit Roy. 2016. "A Consensus Unravels: NREGA and the Paradox of Rules-Based Welfare in India." *The European Journal of Development Research* 28 (4): 588–604.

McDonnell, Erin Metz. 2020. *Patchwork Leviathan: Pockets of Bureaucratic Effectiveness in Developing States*. Princeton, NJ: Princeton University Press.

Mendelsohn, Oliver. 1993. "The Transformation of Authority in Rural India." *Modern Asian Studies* 27 (4): 805–42.

Meyer, David S., and Sidney Tarrow, eds. 1997. *The Social Movement Society*. Lanham, MD: Rowman & Littlefield.

Migdal, Joel S. 2001. *State in Society: Studying How States and Societies Transform and Constitute One Another*. Cambridge Studies in Comparative Politics. Cambridge: Cambridge University Press.

Mitchell, Timothy. 2002. *Rule of Experts: Egypt, Techno-Politics, Modernity*. 1st edition. Berkeley: University of California Press.

Moffitt, Susan L. 2014. *Making Policy Public: Participatory Bureaucracy in American Democracy*. Cambridge: Cambridge University Press.

Mohan, Giles, and Kristian Stokke. 2000. "Participatory Development and Empowerment: The Dangers of Localism." *Third World Quarterly* 21 (2): 247–68.

Mooij, Josephine Esther. 2002. *Welfare Policies and Politics: A Study of Three Government Interventions in Andhra Pradesh, India*. London: ODI.

Mookerjhee, Dilip. 2014. "MNREGA: Populist Leaky Bucket or Successful Anti-Poverty Programme?" Blog. Ideas for India, May 28, 2014. https://www.theigc.org/blog/mnrega-populist-leaky-bucket-or-anti-poverty-success/.

Morozov, Evgeny. 2014. *To Save Everything, Click Here: The Folly of Technological Solutionism*. Reprint edition. New York: PublicAffairs.

Mosse, David. 2004. *Cultivating Development: An Ethnography of Aid Policy and Practice*. 1st edition. London; Ann Arbor, MI: Pluto Press.

Mukherji, Rahul, and Seyed Hossein Zarhani. 2020. "Governing India: Evolution of Programmatic Welfare in Andhra Pradesh." *Studies in Indian Politics* 8 (1): 7–21.

Mukherji, Rahul, Seyed Hossein Zarhani, and K. Raju. 2018. "State Capacity and Welfare Politics in India: Implementing the Mahatma Gandhi National Rural Employment Guarantee Scheme in Undivided Andhra Pradesh." *Indian Journal of Human Development* 12 (2): 282–97.

Mukhopadhyay, Piali, Kathik Muralidharan, Paul Niehaus, and Sandip Sukhtankar. 2013. "Implementing a Biometric Payment System: The Andhra Pradesh Experience." AP Smartcard Impact Evaluation Project Policy Report. La Jolla, CA.

Murali, Akunuri. 2013. "India: Technological Innovation for Effective Management Information Systems." In *Public Works as a Safety Net: Design, Evidence, and Implementation*, edited by Kalanidhi Subbarao, Carlo del Ninno, Colin Andrews, and Claudia Rodríguez-Alas, 233–49. Washington, DC: The World Bank.

Muralidharan, Karthik, Paul Niehaus, and Sandip Sukhtankar. 2014a. "Payments Infrastructure and the Performance of Public Programs: Evidence from Biometric Smartcards in India." Working Paper 19999. National Bureau of Economic Research.

Muralidharan, Karthik, Paul Niehaus, and Sandip Sukhtankar. 2014b. "Building State Capacity: Evidence from Biometric Smartcards in India." *American Economic Review* 106 (10): 2895–929.

Muralidharan, Karthik, Paul Niehaus, and Sandip Sukhtankar. 2017. "General Equilibrium Effects of (Improving) Public Employment Programs: Experimental Evidence from India." Working Paper 23838. National Bureau of Economic Research.

Muralidharan, Karthik, Abhijeet Singh, and Alejandro J. Ganimian. 2019. "Disrupting Education? Experimental Evidence on Technology-Aided Instruction in India." *American Economic Review* 109 (4): 1426–60.

Myrdal, Gunnar. 1968. *Asian Drama: An Inquiry into the Poverty of Nations*. 1st edition. New York: Pantheon Books.

Nilsen, Alf Gunvald. 2018. "India's Turn to Rights-Based Legislation (2004–2014): A Critical Review of the Literature." *Social Change* 48 (4): 653–65.

Noble, Safiya Umoja. 2018. *Algorithms of Oppression: How Search Engines Reinforce Racism*. Illustrated edition. New York: New York University Press.

North, Douglass C. 1991. *Institutions, Institutional Change and Economic Performance*. Cambridge: Cambridge University Press.

North, Douglass C., and Barry R. Weingast. 1989. "Constitutions and Commitment: The Evolution of Institutions Governing Public Choice in Seventeenth-Century England." *The Journal of Economic History* 49 (4): 803–32.

O'Donnell, Guillermo. 1993. "On the State, Democratization and Some Conceptual Problems: A Latin American View with Glances at Some Postcommunist Countries." *World Development* 21 (8): 1355–69.

Olken, Benjamin A. 2007. "Monitoring Corruption: Evidence from a Field Experiment in Indonesia." *Journal of Political Economy* 115 (2): 200–49.

Ostrom, Elinor. 1990. *Governing the Commons: The Evolution of Institutions for Collective Action*. New York: Cambridge University Press.

Ostrom, Elinor. 1996. "Crossing the Great Divide: Coproduction, Synergy, and Development." *World Development* 24 (6): 1073–87.

Ostrom, Vincent. 1994. *The Meaning of American Federalism: Constituting a Self-Governing Society*. San Francisco, CA: ICS Press.

Pande, Suchi. 2014. *The Right to Know, the Right to Live: Grassroots Struggle for Information and Work in India*. Doctoral dissertation, University of Sussex.

Pande, Suchi. 2015. "Dying for Information: Right to Information and Whistleblower Protection in India." *U4 Brief* 3. https://www.cmi.no/publications/5539-dying-for-information.

Pande, Suchi. n.d. "The Non-Party Left's Looming 'War of Position.'" https://india-seminar.com/2016/677/677_suchi_pande.htm. Accessed March 8, 2021.

Pande, Suchi, and Rakesh R. Dubbudu. 2017. "Citizen Oversight and India's Right to Work Program: What Do the Social Auditors Say?" Accountability Working Paper No. 1. Accountability Research Center.

Pattenden, Jonathan. 2011. "Social Protection and Class Relations: Evidence from Scheduled Caste Women's Associations in Rural South India." *Development and Change* 42 (2): 469–98.

Pattenden, Jonathan. 2017. "Class and Social Policy: The National Rural Employment Guarantee Scheme in Karnataka, India." *Journal of Agrarian Change* 17 (1): 43–66.

Pea, Roy. 1985. "Beyond Amplification: Using the Computer to Reorganize Mental Functioning." *Educational Psychologist* 20 (4): 167–82.

Peixoto, Tiago. 2013. "The Uncertain Relationship between Open Data and Accountability: A Response to Yu and Robinson's The New Ambiguity of 'Open Government.'" *UCLA Law Review*, Discourse 60: 200–48.

Peixoto, Tiago, Micah L. Sifry, Andrew Jonathon Mellon, and Fredrick Matias Sjoberg. 2017. *Civic Tech in the Global South: Assessing Technology for the Public Good*. Washington, DC: World Bank and Personal Democracy Press.

Pires, Roberto R. C. 2011. "Beyond the Fear of Discretion: Flexibility, Performance, and Accountability in the Management of Regulatory Bureaucracies." *Regulation & Governance* 5 (1): 43–69.

Piven, Frances Fox, and Richard Cloward. 1978. *Poor People's Movements: Why They Succeed, How They Fail*. New York: Vintage.

Prakash, Amit, Anjali Karol Mohan, and Bidisha Chaudhuri. 2015. "What Do Citizens Value in E-Governance?" *Economic and Political Weekly* 54 (10): 41–49.

Prillaman, Soledad Artiz. 2018. "Strength in Numbers: How Women's Groups Close India's Political Gender Gap." Working Paper. Harvard University, John F. Kennedy School of Government: 1–92. https://www.povertyactionlab.org/sites/default/files/research-paper/StrengthingNumbers_Oct2017.pdf.

Pritchett, Lant. 2009. "Is India a Flailing State? Detours on the Four Lane Highway to Modernization." Faculty Research Working Paper Series rwp09-13: 1–47. Harvard University, John F. Kennedy School of Government,

Rajadhyaksha, Ashish. 2011. "The Last Cultural Mile." *The Centre for Internet and Society*, 1–216. https://cis-india.org/raw/histories-of-the-internet/last-cultural-mile.pdf.

Rajasekhar, Durgam, Salim Lakha, and R. Manjula. 2013. "How Effective Are Social Audits under MGNREGS? Lessons from Karnataka." *Sociological Bulletin* 62 (3): 431–55.

Ramesh, Randeep. 2004. "Shock Defeat for India's Hindu Nationalists." *The Guardian*, May 14, 2004. https://www.theguardian.com/world/2004/may/14/india.randeepramesh.

Rao, Ursula. 2017. "Writing, Typing and Scanning: Distributive Justice and the Politics of Visibility in the Era of E-Governance." In *Media as Politics in South Asia*, edited by Sahana Udupa and Stepher D. McDowell, 127–40. Oxford: Routledge.

Rao, Ursula. 2019. "Response to 'The Aadhaar Debate: Where Are the Sociologists?'" *Contributions to Indian Sociology* 53 (3): 431–40.

Rao, Ursula, and Vijayanka Nair. 2019. "Aadhaar: Governing with Biometrics." *South Asia: Journal of South Asian Studies* 42 (3): 469–81.

Rao, Vijayendra, and Paromita Sanyal. 2010. "Dignity through Discourse: Poverty and the Culture of Deliberation in Indian Village Democracies." *The Annals of the American Academy of Political and Social Science* 629 (1): 146–72.

Rao, Y. Chinna. 2015. "Dalit Movement in Andhra Pradesh: A Historical Outline of a Hundred Years." *Indian Historical Review* 42 (1): 113–39.

Ratnam, K. Y. 2008. *The Dalit Movement and Democratization in Andhra Pradesh.* Working Papers No. 13, December. East-West Center, Washington.

Ravallion, Martin. 1991. "Reaching the Rural Poor through Public Employment: Arguments, Evidence, and Lessons from South Asia." *The World Bank Research Observer* 6 (2): 153–75.

Ravallion, Martin, Dominique van der Walle, Puja Dutta, and Rinku Murgai. 2013. "Testing Information Constraints on India's Largest Antipoverty Program." The World Bank, Policy Research Working Paper No. 6598: 1–29. Washington, DC: The World Bank.

Ravi, Shamika, and Monika Engler. 2015. "Workfare as an Effective Way to Fight Poverty: The Case of India's NREGS." *World Development* 67 (C): 57–71.

Reddy, D. Narasimha, and Arun Patnaik. 1993. "Anti-Arrack Agitation of Women in Andhra Pradesh." *Economic and Political Weekly* 28 (21): 1059–66.

Reddy, Narasimha. 2013. "Functioning of NREGS in Andhra Pradesh." In *The Long Road to Social Security: Assessing the Implementation of National Social Security Initiatives for the Working Poor in India*, edited by K. P. Kannan and Jan Breman, 117–63. New Delhi: Oxford University Press.

Reinikka, Ritva, and Jakob Svensson. 2004a. "Local Capture: Evidence from a Central Government Transfer Program in Uganda." *The Quarterly Journal of Economics* 119 (2): 679–705.

Reinikka, Ritva, and Jakob Svensson. 2004b. "The Power of Information: Evidence from a Newspaper Campaign to Reduce Capture." The World Bank, Policy Research Working Paper Series No. 3239: 1–37. Washington, DC: The World Bank.

Rosner, Daniela K., and Morgan Ames. 2014. "Designing for Repair? Infrastructures and Materialities of Breakdown." In *Proceedings of the 17th ACM Conference on Computer Supported Cooperative Work & Social Computing*, 319–31. CSCW '14. New York: Association for Computing Machinery.

Roy, Aruna, and Nikhil Dey. 2001. "The Right to Information: Facilitating People's Participation and State Accountability." Mimeo, paper presented at the *Asia-Pacific Workshop at the 10th IACC Prague*.

Roy, Aruna, MKSS Collective. 2018. *The RTI Story: Power to the People*. New Delhi: Lotus Collection/Roli Books.

Roy, Indrajit. 2014. "Reserve Labor, Unreserved Politics: Dignified Encroachments Under India's National Rural Employment Guarantee Act." *The Journal of Peasant Studies* 41 (4): 517–45.

Roy, Indrajit. 2018. *Politics of the Poor: Negotiating Democracy in Contemporary India*. Delhi: Cambridge University Press.

Roy, Indrajit. 2020. "Class Coalitions and Social Protection: The Labouring Classes and the National Rural Employment Guarantee Act in Eastern India." *The Journal of Development Studies* 0 (0): 1–19.

Sainath, Palagummi. 1996. *Everybody Loves a Good Drought: Stories from India's Poorest Districts*. 1st edition. New Delhi; New York: Penguin Books.

Sanner, Terje Aksel, Tiwonge Davis Manda, and Petter Nielsen. 2014. "Grafting: Balancing Control and Cultivation in Information Infrastructure Innovation." *Journal of the Association for Information Systems* 15 (4): 25.

Sanyal, Paromita, and Vijayendra Rao. 2018. *Oral Democracy: Deliberation in Indian Village Assemblies*. Cambridge: Cambridge University Press.

Sassen, Saskia. 2002. "Towards a Sociology of Information Technology." *Current Sociology* 50 (3): 365–88.

Saxena, K. B., G. Haragopal, S. R. Sankaran, and Council for Social Development (India). 2014. *Marginalization, Development and Resistance: Essays in Tribute to S. R. Sankaran*. Delhi: Aakar Books.

Schudson, Michael. 1996. "What if Civic Life Didn't Die?" *The American Prospect* 25: 17–20.

Scott, James C. 1985. *Weapons of the Weak: Everyday Forms of Peasant Resistance*. New Haven, CT: Yale University Press.

Scott, James C. 1992. *Domination and the Arts of Resistance: Hidden Transcripts*. Revised edition. New Haven, CT: Yale University Press.

Scott, James C. 1996. "State Simplifications: Nature, Space, and People." *Nomos* 38: 42–85.

Scott, James C. 1998. *Seeing like a State: How Certain Schemes to Improve the Human Condition Have Failed*. New Haven, CT: Yale University Press.

Sen, Amartya. 2000. *Development as Freedom*. Illustrated edition. New York: Anchor.

Sen, Amartya, and Jean Drèze. 1999. *The Amartya Sen and Jean Drèze Omnibus: (Comprising) Poverty and Famines; Hunger and Public Action; and India: Economic Development and Social Opportunity*. New Delhi; New York: Oxford University Press.

Seth, Vikram. 1994. *A Suitable Boy*. New Delhi: Penguin Books India.

Shankar, Shylashri. 2010. "Can Social Audits Count?" ASARC Working Paper 2010 (09). The Australian National University, Australia South Asia Research Centre.

Shankar, Shylashri, Raghav Gaiha, and Raghbendra Jha. 2011. "Information, Access and Targeting: The National Rural Employment Guarantee Scheme in India." *Oxford Development Studies* 39 (1): 69–95.

Sharma, Aradhana. 2013. "State Transparency after the Neoliberal Turn: The Politics, Limits, and Paradoxes of India's Right to Information Law." *PoLAR: Political and Legal Anthropology Review* 36 (2): 308–25.

Sharma, Prashant. 2015. *Democracy and Transparency in the Indian State: The Making of the Right to Information Act*. 1st edition. London: Routledge.

Sims, Christo. 2017. *Disruptive Fixation: School Reform and the Pitfalls of Techno-Idealism*. Princeton, NJ: Princeton University Press.

Singh, Prerna. 2017. *How Solidarity Works for Welfare: Subnationalism and Social Development in India*. Reprint edition. Cambridge: Cambridge University Press.

Singh, Ranjit. 2019b. "Give Me a Database and I Will Raise the Nation-State." *South Asia: Journal of South Asian Studies* 42 (3): 501–18.

Singh, Ranjit. 2020. "The Living Dead." *Public* 30 (60): 92–104.

Singh, Ranjit, and Steven J. Jackson. 2017. "From Margins to Seams: Imbrication, Inclusion, and Torque in the Aadhaar Identification Project." In *Proceedings of the 2017 CHI Conference on Human Factors in Computing Systems*, 4776–824. CHI '17. New York: Association for Computing Machinery.

Singh, Shekhar. 2005. "The Notion of Transparency." In *Speaking Truth to Power: A Symposium on People's Right to Information*. https://www.india-seminar.com/2005/551/551%20shekhar%20singh.htm

Srinivas, Mysore Narasimhachar. 1956. "A Note on Sanskritization and Westernization." *The Far Eastern Quarterly* 15 (4): 481–96.

Srinivasan, Janaki. 2011. *The Political Life of Information: "Information" and the Practice of Governance in India*. Doctoral dissertation, University of California, Berkeley.

Srinivasan, Janaki, Megan Finn, and Morgan Ames. 2017. "Information Determinism: The Consequences of the Faith in Information." *The Information Society* 33 (1): 13–22.

Srinivasan, Vivek. 2010. *Understanding Public Services in Tamil Nadu: An Institutional Perspective*. Doctoral dissertation, Syracuse University.

Srinivasan, Vivek. 2015. *Delivering Public Services Effectively: Tamil Nadu and Beyond. Delivering Public Services Effectively*. Oxford: Oxford University Press.

Srinivasan, Vivek, Rajendran Narayanan, Dipanjan Chakraborty, Rajesh Veeraraghavan, and Vibhore Vardhan. 2018. "Are Technology-Enabled Cash Transfers Really 'Direct'?" *Economic and Political Weekly* 53 (30): 58–64.

Srinivasan, Vivek, and Sudha Narayanan. 2009. "Food Policy and Social Movements: Reflections on the Right to Food Campaign in India (11-1)." *Case Studies in Food Policy for Developing Countries: Policies for Health, Nutrition, Food Consumption, and Poverty* 1: 247.

Srinivasulu, K. 2009. "Y S Rajasekhara Reddy: A Political Appraisal." *Economic and Political Weekly* 44 (38): 8–10.

Stiglitz, Joseph E. 2002. "Transparency in Government." In *The Right to Tell: The Role of Mass Media in Economic Development*, edited by Roumeen Islam, 1st edition, 27–44. Washington, DC: World Bank Publications.

Strathern, Marilyn. 2000. *Audit Cultures: Anthropological Studies in Accountability, Ethics and the Academy*. 1st edition. London; New York: Routledge.

Sukhtankar, Sandip. 2016. "India's National Rural Employment Guarantee Scheme: What Do We Really Know about the World's Largest Workfare Program?" *India Policy Forum* 13: 2009–10.

Tarlau, Rebecca. 2013. "Coproducing Rural Public Schools in Brazil Contestation, Clientelism, and the Landless Workers' Movement." *Politics & Society* 41 (September): 395–424.

Tarlau, Rebecca. 2019. *Occupying Schools, Occupying Land: How the Landless Workers Movement Transformed Brazilian Education*. Illustrated edition. New York: Oxford University Press.

Tendler, Judith. 1998. *Good Government in the Tropics*. Baltimore, MD: Johns Hopkins University Press.

Thachil, Tariq. 2020. "Does Police Repression Spur Everyday Cooperation? Evidence from Urban India." *The Journal of Politics* 82 (4): 1474–89.

Toyama, Kentaro. 2011. "Technology as Amplifier in International Development." In *Proceedings of the 2011 IConference*, 75–82. IConference '11. New York: Association for Computing Machinery.

Toyama, Kentaro. 2015. *Geek Heresy: Rescuing Social Change from the Cult of Technology*. 1st edition. New York: Public Affairs.

Tsoukas, Haridimos. 1997. "The Tyranny of Light: The Temptations and the Paradoxes of the Information Society." *Futures* 29 (9): 827–43.

Vakulabharanam, Vamsi, N. Purendra Prasad, K. Laxminarayana, and Sudheer Kilaru. 2011. "Understanding the Andhra Crop Holiday Movement." *Economic and Political Weekly* 46 (50): 13–16.

Van Maanen, John. 2011. *Tales of the Field: On Writing Ethnography*. 2nd edition. Chicago: University of Chicago Press.

Varshney, Ashutosh. 2000. "Is India Becoming More Democratic?" *The Journal of Asian Studies* 59 (1): 3–25.

Varshney, Ashutosh. 2014. *Battles Half Won: India's Improbable Democracy*. Delhi: Penguin Publishing Group.

Veeraraghavan, Rajesh. 2013. "Dealing with the Digital Panopticon: The Use and Subversion of ICT in an Indian Bureaucracy." In *Proceedings of the Sixth International Conference on Information and Communication Technologies and Development: Full Papers*, Vol. 1, 248–55. ICTD '13. New York: Association for Computing Machinery.

Veeraraghavan, Rajesh. 2017. "Strategies for Synergy in a High Modernist Project: Two Community Responses to India's NREGA Rural Work Program." *World Development* 99 (C): 203–13.

Veeraraghavan, Rajesh. 2021. "Cat and Mouse Game: Patching Bureaucratic Work Relations by Patching Technologies." *PACM on Human-Computer Interaction* 5 (No. CSCW1, Article #186): 21.

Veeraraghavan, Rajesh, Naga Yasodhar, and Kentaro Toyama. 2009. "Warana Unwired: Replacing PCs with Mobile Phones in a Rural Sugarcane Cooperative." *Information Technologies & International Development* 5 (1): 81–95.

Véron, René, Stuart Corbridge, Glyn Williams, and Manoj Srivastava. 2003. "The Everyday State and Political Society in Eastern India: Structuring Access to the Employment Assurance Scheme." *The Journal of Development Studies* 39 (5): 1–28.

Visvanathan, Shiv. 2008. "The Necessity of Corruption." In *Seminar*. http://www.india-seminar.com/2008/590/590_shiv_visvanathan.htm.

Wade, Robert. 1985. "The Market for Public Office: Why the Indian State Is Not Better at Development." *World Development* 13 (4): 467–97.

Walle, Dominique van der, Martin Ravallion, Puja Dutta, and Rinku Murgai. 2012. "Does India's Employment Guarantee Scheme Guarantee Employment?" *Economic and Political Weekly* 47 (16): 7–8.

Weil, David, Mary Graham, and Archon Fung. 2013. "Targeting Transparency." *Science* 340 (6139): 1410–11.

Weinstein, Jeremy, and Joshua Goldstein. 2012. "The Benefits of a Big Tent: Opening up Government in Developing Countries: A Response to Yu & Robinson's the New Ambiguity of Open Government." *UCLA Law Review*, Discourse, 60 (38): 38–48.

Wilkinson, Steven I. 2004. *Votes and Violence: Electoral Competition and Ethnic Riots in India*. Cambridge Studies in Comparative Politics. Cambridge: Cambridge University Press.

Williams, Glyn. 2004. "Evaluating Participatory Development: Tyranny, Power and (Re) Politicisation." *Third World Quarterly* 25 (3): 557–78.

Winner, Langdon. 1980. "Do Artifacts Have Politics?" *Daedalus* 109 (1): 121–36.

World Bank Staff. 2004. *World Development Report 2004: Making Services Work for Poor People*. Washington, DC: The World Bank.

Wyche, Susan, and Charles Steinfield. 2015. "Why Don't Farmers Use Cell Phones to Access Market Prices? Technology Affordances and Barriers to Market Information Services Adoption in Rural Kenya." *Information Technology for Development* 22 (2): 320–33.

Zuckerman, Ethan. 2014. "New Media, New Civics?" *Policy & Internet* 6 (2): 151–68.

Index

For the benefit of digital users, indexed terms that span two pages (e.g., 52–53) may, on occasion, appear on only one of those pages.

Note: Tables and figures are indicated by *t* and *f* following the page number

Aadhaar, 173–74, 193n.33
accountability, 172–73
 of bureaucrats, 16, 21, 163, 164
 sarpanches and, 82
 state supporting, 188–89n.36
 transparency challenges for, 114–15, 174–75, 177
Action AID, 73
activists, 2
 auditors as, 88–89
 on independence, 83–84, 84*t*
 on social audits, 81–82
 SSAAT and bureaucrats as, 22–23, 89–90
 for transparency, 85, 89
Adivasis
 caste, dominant on, 12
 comparisons on, 184
 NREGA employing, 29, 36, 36*t*, 37*t*
 violence against, 192n.15
AID. *See* Association for India's Development
Aiyar, Yamini, 115–16, 160, 200n.11
algorithm, 19, 61, 64–65, 66, 194n.14
Ambedkar, Bhimrao Ramji
 Ambedkar Association and, 106–8, 109–10, 111
 on caste consciousness, 3, 39
 Dalits on, 3, 199n.18
 India constitution from, 3, 178, 191n.3, 199n.18
 on local power, 22, 185n.6
 for marginalized citizens, 3
 on rights, 30
Ambedkar Association, 106–8, 109–10, 111
Anantapur, 71–72, 76–77, 78, 79–80, 81, 192n.14, 196n.20, 196n.24, 196n.26, 196n.21, 197n.34
Andhra Pradesh
 caste relations in, 38
 data collection in, 26
 for democracy, 26
 development programs in, 13–14
 digital technology and, 18, 66, 194n.9
 hierarchy structure of, 42–43
 information infrastructure in, 3–4, 16, 20
 last mile and, 11, 45*f*
 lower-level vs. auditors in, 124–25
 marginalized groups in, 38–39
 with mass social audits, 76–79
 NREGA in, 2, 7, 35–37, 36*t*, 37*t*, 170, 185n.1, 197–98n.49, 203n.1
 with participatory audits, 69
 patching in, 19
 politics and audits in, 71–72, 185n.11, 193n.25
 power redistribution in, 14–15
 Raju in, 148, 186n.18
 social audit by, 36–38, 89–90
 social audit units for, 80–82, 200n.1
 social mobilization in, 195n.3
 SSAAT by, 44–45
 upper-level bureaucrats and legibility in, 51–52
anti-arrack moment, 38–39, 191–92n.13, 193n.24
"anti-politics machine," 111–12, 175
anti-worker nexus
 Drèze on, 1–2, 11, 196n.20
 local power system as, 1–2, 11–14
 upper-level bureaucrats in, 2–3
Antonio, Gramsci, 174
appeal process, 133–34, 138
Association for India's Development (AID), 179
auditors, 172–73, 179
 as activists, 88–89
 Andhra Pradesh with lower-level vs., 124–25
 as director, 83, 85, 88–89, 105–6, 179
 documents for, 118, 162
 field assistants for local, 101–2
 findings summary by, 123–24
 hiring of, 85–86, 195n.4

auditors, (*cont.*)
- independence of, 83–84, 84*t*, 101, 157
- on landed class, 167–68
- languages and, 180
- on local elites, 167*t*, 200n.6
- mates bribing, 156
- minimum wage for, 85–86
- NREGA record access by, 118
- for paper muster rolls, 62
- perception of, 87–88, 89, 90, 103, 104, 157
- on politics, 122
- politics avoided by, 86, 167–68
- public hearings with lower-level vs., 128, 129
- as rewriting records, 117, 167*t*, 168–69, 199n.17
- roles of, 86, 167–68, 167*t*
- settlements on, 156
- on social audits, 195n.17
- village opinion on, 103–4
- as villagers, 84*t*, 85, 86, 101–3
- village support of, 108
- village time by, 123
- as women, 102, 199n.10
- on worksites, 118–19, 167*t*

audits. *See* social audits

backlash
- by gram panchayats, 34
- by sarpanches, 34, 125
- on social audits, 79, 175–76, 191n.11
- social audits with intimidation and, 107, 168
- worker fear of, 138, 148

Balagopal, Kandalla, 38–39, 186n.13, 192n.19, 201n.8, 202n.12

Bardhan, Pranab, 12

bargaining power, 39, 157
- workers with, 35, 134–35, 137, 138–39, 142, 160, 165, 166*t*, 169, 170

Bharatiya Janata Party, 31–32

Bihar
- JJSS in, 165, 175–76, 179
- NREGA challenges in, 11, 21, 68–69, 75–76, 122, 172
- NREGA implementation in, 74, 75, 82, 124, 170–71, 179, 185n.8, 192n.14, 197–98n.49

biometric authentication, 148–49, 173–74, 193n.33

Bourdieu, Pierre, 20, 21–22, 23

Brahmin caste, 87–88, 180

bureaucracy
- accountability of, 16, 21, 163, 164
- as activists, 22–23, 89–90
- on anti-worker resistance, 2–3
- ethnography of everyday, 2–3
- last mile and, 9–10, 162
- patching documents on, 23–24
- power lost by, 44, 107–8
- power system of, 1–2
- Raju and, 43, 44–45, 51–53, 72–73, 76
- service delivery by, 186n.12
- on social audits, 195n.5, 195–96n.19
- social audits as protests and, 90
- social movements and state, 68, 89–90

bureaucrats. *See also* lower-level bureaucrats; upper-level bureaucrats
- central, 1, 39–40
- district level, 58, 60–61, 64, 88, 133–34
- lower-level, 16, 43, 44, 66–67
- state level, 9–10, 39–40, 43, 61, 151
- upper-level, 2–8, 13, 14–15, 18, 21, 22–23, 24, 26–27, 42–43, 48, 49, 50, 51–55, 56–57, 60–67, 72–89, 125–28, 132–34, 137, 140, 143, 148–60, 164–20, 181, 185n.4, 187n.26, 201–2n.10, 202n.17
- village level, 42–43, 47, 69–70, 71–72, 85–86, 87, 91, 97, 101–2, 111–12, 131, 158, 162, 181

caste
- on Adivasis, 12
- Ambedkar on, 3, 39
- Brahmin as, 87–88, 180
- class and, 39, 136, 186n.15
- cruelty of, 146
- on Dalits, 12, 39, 65–66, 96–97, 139, 202n.14
- discrimination in, 141, 199n.18
- "feelings" and, 65–66, 96–97, 145, 146, 201n.8
- gram sabhas with lower, 75–76, 92–93, 96–97, 115
- hiring as ignoring, 65–66
- in India, 38
- as Kamma, 139, 192n.15
- Kapu as, 65
- Madigas as, 139, 141, 192n.16, 201n.8
- Malas as, 139, 141, 192n.16, 201n.8
- meat eating and, 87–88
- NREGA on, 1–2, 138, 204n.4
- oppression, 3, 141, 146, 185n.6
- politics by low-, 38
- politics on, 202n.12
- power system of, 1–2
- SC and Dalit in, 65
- segregation by, 42, 103, 109, 139, 200n.3
- social audit locations and, 108–9
- tribal villages without, 200n.3

Central bureaucrats, 1, 39–40

Chatterjee, Partha, 8
circular, 54–55, 56, 78, 82–83, 94, 152, 194n.8, 197n.39, 199n.10
citizens participation, 20, 21, 22, 24, 28, 92–93, 100, 101, 109, 112–13, 114, 127, 141
Civic Tech, 176–77
class. *See also* landed class
  caste and, 39, 136, 186n.15
  compromise in, 103–4, 151–52
  divisions, 13–14, 26–27, 38, 97
  equality and, 8, 10, 22–23
  power system of, 1–2, 11–12
  as working, 189n.38
Clément Imbert and John Papp., 35, 151–52, 185n.1, 201–2n.10
collusion, 14, 52, 63, 86, 167–68
computers. *See* digital technologies
Congress, 31–32, 39–41, 79, 99, 125, 139, 192n.14, 192n.18, 193n.27, 193n.34
Constitutional amendment, 43, 91, 92, 124
contractors
  ban and, 52, 150–51
  corruption from, 14
  machinery used by, 14, 52, 75, 119
  NREGA and, 14, 52
control
  by colonial powers, 189n.44
  digital technologies for, 49, 166, 169–70
  legibility for, 51
  parallel structures and, 83
  patching for, 169–70
  Reddies on Dalits and, 145, 202n.13
  of social audits, 80–81, 89–90
  social movements on state, 70
Corbridge, Stuart, 13, 115
corruption. *See also* fraud
  from contractors, 14
  digital payments on, 50
  elite capture on audits and, 55, 158
  engineers and, 14, 52, 155
  field assistants and, 199n.11
  Food for Work program with, 14, 39–40, 44, 52, 72–77
  JJSS as wary on, 7, 68–69
  land records digitization on, 25, 34
  last mile and, 74, 77–78, 130, 134, 148, 153–56, 160, 169
  from local elites, 6–7, 14, 44, 52
  by local politicians, 14, 55
  of lower-level bureaucrats, 73, 160
  with materials, 59–60, 150–51, 155–56, 194n.10
  mates and, 155, 156
  MKSS on, 32, 33
  NREGA with, 78–79, 125–26, 150–51
  political parties on, 122
  public hearings on, 33–34, 68, 175–76
  rachabanda meetings and, 100
  as redistribution, 155
  sarpanches and, 44, 73–74, 75–76, 107
  social audits on, 22–23, 74, 77–78, 89, 125–26, 133, 153–56, 158, 160, 169, 199n.11
  technology on, 173
  upper-level bureaucrats and, 148–49, 177, 185n.4, 200n.10
cricket, 103–4, 107–8

Dalit Mahasabha, 39
Dalits, 192n.14, *See also* marginalized citizens
  Ambedkar and, 3, 199n.18
  caste on, 12, 39, 65–66, 139, 202n.14
  comparisons on, 183
  cross-caste marriages and, 96–97
  food or cash to, 147
  landed class and freedom of, 140, 148
  landless workers and, 139
  land of, 202n.11
  local landlords on, 1–2, 13–14, 137, 186n.20, 189n.38, 202n.13
  as Madigas, 139, 141, 192n.16, 201n.8
  as Malas, 139, 141, 192n.16, 201n.8
  on NREGA, 145–48
  NREGA employing, 29, 36, 36*t*, 37*t*
  police surveillance on, 140
  power for, 138–39
  on public meetings, 160
  Reddy control of, 145, 202n.13
  violence against, 192n.15
data, 26, 50, 53–54, 56, 57, 58, 59–64, 66–67, 74, 84*t*, 118–19, 121–22, 123, 126, 138, 153, 155, 172–73, 179, 181, 188n.35, 190n.48, 190n.49, 199n.20, 201–2n.10
data collection, 26, 61–64
Delhi, 57, 58, 186n.18, 186n.19, 193n.29, 193n.32, 194n.6, 195n.6, 195–96n.19, 203n.21
Deshingkar, Priya, 13–14, 35, 44, 52, 57, 73–74, 75
development, 1
  in Andhra Pradesh, 13–14
  digital technology and, 25–26
  as freedom, 170
  for marginalized citizens, 13–14, 115
  NREGA patching, 17
  on power, 163
development literature, 13, 15–17

digital payments platform, 47–48, 50, 173, 193n.32
digital technologies
  Andhra Pradesh and, 16, 66, 194n.9
  for control, 49, 166, 169–70
  design of, 174
  development and, 25–26
  for field assistant hiring, 64–65
  for land records, 25, 34
  for last mile, 49, 148–52, 173
  on local resistance, 24–25
  muster rolls in, 58
  on NREGA work projects, 55, 66
  patching and, 49–50, 56, 166
  politics and, 50, 59–60, 166
  on positioning and fraud, 63–64
  solutionism and, 19, 171–72, 190n.48, 190n.50
  YSR for, 44–45
directive principles of State policy, 30
District level bureaucrats, 58, 60–61, 64, 88, 133–34
district resource persons, 45–46, 46*f*, 84–86, 84*t*, 87–88
  in audit meeting, 101–2, 103, 104–5, 106, 107, 108–9, 126, 198–99n.9
  mandals and, 198n.8
documents, 194n.5
  auditors requesting, 118, 162
  audits with household survey and, 117–21, 200n.5
  "benami" work in, 62, 118–19, 120
  bureaucracy and patching, 23–24
  challenges with, 168–69
  last mile and non-local language, 131
  marginalized citizens and, 116–17, 122–23, 134, 162, 169
  metadata files as, 56, 58, 63
  muster rolls as work, 47–48, 57, 202n.15
  patching and, 164
  power from, 23–24, 116, 169
  reading of, 23, 114–35, 117*t*, 157–58
  RTI for access and, 5, 28
  seeing of, 50, 51, 117, 117*t*, 121–22
  social audits on, 116, 152–53
  SSAAT and worker, 117–21
  by state, 23, 116
  transparency and, 188n.35
  upper-level bureaucrats on rewriting of, 117, 168–69
  visibility and, 176–77, 200n.8
  wages and, 199n.13
  writing of, 23, 39, 79, 81, 116, 131, 132, 154, 189n.44
Drèze, Jean, 1–2, 11, 196n.20
Dubbudu, Rakesh, 114

elected representative, landholder. *See* mukhiya
elected village council leaders. *See* sarpanches
elite capture, 8, 21, 168
  auditor corruption and, 55, 158
  inequality producing, 91, 163
  politics allowing, 126, 163
  social audits and, 158, 168
eMuster, 61–62
  Action AID, 73
  Anantapur, 71–72, 76–77, 78, 79–80, 81, 192n.14, 196n.20, 196n.24, 196n.26, 197n.34
  anti-politics machine, 111–12, 175
engineers
  as consultants, 42*f*, 43
  corruption and, 14, 52, 155
  on muster rolls, 17
  NREGA on local, 14
  social audit with, 158
  upper-level interviewing, 64
ethnography
  of everyday bureaucrats, 2–3
  of NREGA implementation, 26, 179
  participant observer in, 198n.7, 200n.2
  on politics and information, 179–81
  on technology and education, 190n.46
  upper-level bureaucrats on, 180
Evans, Peter, 2, 21, 186n.15
everyday resistance, 2–3, 18–19
everyday state, 2–4, 194n.5

Ferguson, James, 13–14, 175
field assistants, 103, 157–58, 203n.26
  bias and, 106–8, 109–10
  corruption and, 199n.11
  fund skimming by, 155–56
  hiring of, 64–65
  for local auditors, 101–2
  mates and, 159, 169
  testimony against, 121–23
financial audits, 74, 75, 89, 114
first mile, 48, 163
  last mile and, 8–11, 133–34
flashlight metaphor, 177
follow-through, 71–72, 133–34, 160, 166, 166*t*, 175–76
Food for Work Program
  corruption in, 14, 39–40, 44, 52, 72–77
  grain payments in, 195n.11
  NREGA predecessor as, 13–14, 44, 195n.11

Fox, Jonathan, 11, 16, 70, 176, 198n.51
fraud. *See also* corruption
  detection and investigation of, 114
  digital technologies on, 63–64
  by field assistants, 155–56
  on labor and materials, 194n.10
  last mile record tampering as, 131–32
  by lower-level bureaucrats, 59
  muster rolls and, 11, 17–18, 44, 57, 62, 162
  patches on, 150–51
  as settlements and auditors, 156
  social audits deterring, 89, 125–26, 133, 153, 156
  SSAAT on, 197n.47
  technical assistant and, 125, 155
  by village, 154–55
  worker responses on, 119–21

Gandhi, Mahatma, 78, 185n.6, 192n.22, 204n.5
Gandhi, Sonia, 31–32
gender, 1–2, 12, 60–61, 102–3, 164
good design, 10, 163
gram panchayats (village councils), 10–11, 14, 48, 91, 163, 186n.22, 198n.1
  backlash by, 34
  mandals and, 42, 43
  panchayati secretary of, 95, 198n.3
  president of, 6
  public hearings and, 92, 141
gram sabhas
  discovery of, 94, 95
  locations of, 95, 97
  lower caste at, 75–76, 92–93, 96–97, 115
  lower-level bureaucrats on, 94–96
  political parties absent from, 97–98
  rachabanda as "real," 97–98, 111–12
  social audits with, 85, 91, 93, 108
  upper-level bureaucrats on, 95
  as village meeting, 44–45, 47, 75–76, 87, 91, 92–98
Gramsci Antonio, 174
Guillermo O Donnell, 12
Gupta, Akhil, 14, 23, 116, 185n.2

Habermas, Jürgen, 176, 188n.32, 188n.33, 188–89n.36
Hayek, Frederick, 15
Heller, Patrick, 9–10, 13, 70, 186n.22
Hetherington, Kregg, 168–69, 194n.5
high modernism, 18, 61, 176–77
hiring
  castes ignored in, 65–66
  compromises on, 64–65
  technology for, 64–65
household survey, 117–21, 133, 200n.5
Hull, Mathew, 23, 116, 189n.44

ICTD. *See* Information and Communication Technologies for Development
Imbert, Clément, 35, 151–52, 185n.1, 201–2n.10
India, 185n.9, 186n.15, 186n.17
  activists of, 2
  Ambedkar and constitution of, 3, 178, 191n.3, 199n.18
  caste relations in, 38
  development literature on, 13
  NREGA by, 1, 203n.21
  rights-based approach and constitution of, 1, 28, 30, 142, 197n.41
  RTI by, 1
India shining, 31–32, 39–40
information, 3–4, 7, 14–17, 20–21, 23, 43, 53–54, 58, 104, 119, 121–22, 162, 163, 175–76, 188n.32, 188n.35, 190n.48
Information and Communication Technologies for Development (ICTD), 25–26, 175, 190n.50
information asymmetries, 20–21, 163
information infrastructure, 187n.28, 204n.9
  in Andhra Pradesh, 3–4, 16, 20
  for audit rulings, 133–34
  ethnography on politics and, 179–81
  local discretion and, 171
  marginalized citizens and, 21
  NREGA for, 29
  patching of, 18–19, 171
  solutionism and, 171–72
  technology and, 174–76, 188n.34
  transparency and, 20–21, 23, 24
  by upper-level bureaucrats, 3–4, 20, 24, 44–45, 194n.2
  for visibility and participation, 20
intermediary, 101, 148–49

Jan Jagaran Shakti Sanghatan (JJSS)
  in Bihar, 165, 175–76, 179
  on corruption, 7, 68–69
  as landless labor union, 162
  on muster role and worker, 175–76
  on NREGA, 4–5, 68
  public hearing and audit by, 4–6, 7–8, 24, 68–69, 82, 162
  for transparency, 68

Jenkins, Rob, 1, 29, 134
job cards, 131, 183, 197n.42

Kamma caste, 139, 192n.15
Kapu caste, 65
khap panchayats, 198n.1
Kidambi, Sowmya, 73, 80–81, 82, 89–90, 195n.9

laborer, 1–2, 13–14, 26, 35, 38–41, 75, 87, 88–89, 137, 138, 139, 142, 143–45, 147–48, 151–52, 170, 179–80, 189n.38, 201n.9. *See also* workers, landless
labor union, 4–7, 162
landed class, 12
 auditors on, 167–68
 Dalits freedom from, 140, 148
 landless workers vs., 1–2, 13–14, 137, 189n.38, 202n.13
 as Reddies, 137, 139, 142
last mile, 52, 163. *See also* lower-level bureaucrats
 Andhra Pradesh and, 11, 45*f*
 bureaucracy and, 9–10, 162
 corruption and, 74, 77–78, 130, 134, 148, 153–56, 160, 169
 digital technologies on power and, 49, 148–52, 173
 expense transparency and, 131
 first aid and, 131
 first mile limiting, 8–11, 133–34
 implementation challenges in, 9
 legibility for, 53–55
 local power in, 1
 lower-level bureaucrats implementing, 3
 monitoring of, 152–60
 NREGA job card lack in, 131
 NREGA on, 172–73
 patching and, 20, 114, 165–69, 166*t*, 167*t*, 177, 178
 records and non-local language in, 131
 record tampering in, 131–32
 social audit and, 22–23, 74, 77–78, 153–56, 160, 169
 technology for, 9, 49, 53–55, 174
 transparency and, 91, 131
 wage underpayment, 129–30
 worker wages and, 132, 148–49
 work measurement and, 130–31, 147, 154, 202n.15
 work projects withheld by, 131
 wrong worker payment, 130
legibility
 in Andhra Pradesh, 51–52
 for control, 51
 data collection and, 61–64
 of lower-level actions, 57
 states using, 50–53
 technology patches for last-mile, 53–55
Lessig, Lawrence, 49
local elites
 auditors and, 167*t*, 200n.6
 corruption and politicians as, 14, 55
 corruption from, 6–7, 14, 44, 52
 patching as assistance and, 172
 power lost by, 44, 107–8
 upper-level bureaucrats on, 167*t*, 177
 on worker testimonies, 126–28
local power system. *See also* power
 Ambedkar on, 22, 185n.6
 as anti-worker nexus, 1–2, 11–14
 challenge to, 6–7
 landlords in, 1–2, 13–14, 137, 186n.20, 189n.38, 202n.13
 in last mile, 1
 patching on, 163–64
 power lost by, 44, 166*t*, 171
 against public records access, 14
 resistance by, 1, 3, 107–8, 163
lower-level bureaucrats, 43, 44, 66–67, 172–73. *See also* last mile
 accountability for, 16, 21, 163, 164
 Andhra Pradesh legibility on, 51–52
 Andhra Pradesh with auditors vs., 124–25
 avoidance strategies by, 59, 67
 corruption of, 73, 160
 exploitation by, 199n.14, 200n.4
 fraud shifts by, 59
 on gram sabhas, 94–96
 last-mile implementation and, 3
 legibility of, 57
 patching and, 18–19, 49
 politician pressure on, 52, 55, 67, 141, 151, 166*t*, 167*t*, 170, 194n.14
 private settlements among workers and, 107–8, 134–35, 157, 167*t*, 169
 public hearings with auditors vs., 128, 129
 Reddies on, 143
 "sandwich" strategies on, 22, 70
 social audits and, 78–79
 social audits manipulated by, 158, 168
 on transparency, 67
 upper-level monitoring, 49, 51–52, 56–57, 60–63, 66–67, 83, 114, 124–26, 166*t*, 167*t*, 169–70, 177, 187n.26
Lower-level bureaucrats, 16, 43, 44, 66–67

Madigas, 139, 141, 192n.16, 201n.8
Maharashtra, 190n.2, 192n.14

Mahatma Gandhi National Rural Employment Guarantee Act (MNREGA), 204n.5
Maiorano, Diego, 10–11, 41, 186n.13, 192n.23, 204n.6
Malas, 139, 141, 192n.16, 201n.8
Management and Information System (MIS), 183, 194n.15
mandal program development officer (MPDO)
  public hearings and, 128–34, 133*t*
  work projects by, 42*f*, 42–43, 203n.23
mandals, 42, 58, 86, 93–94, 193n.27
  district resource persons and, 198n.8
  observing team at, 198n.3, 198n.8
  technical assistant of, 43
Mann, Michael, 20
marginalized citizens, 1, 20. *See also* Dalits
  Ambedkar for, 3
  in Andhra Pradesh, 38–39
  development programs for, 13–14, 115
  document access and corrections by, 116–17, 122–23, 134, 162, 169
  information infrastructure and, 21
  monitoring by, 175–77
  participatory bureaucracies engaging, 91, 163
  politicians ignoring, 8
  social movements for, 68, 177
  technology and, 173
  YSR on rural poor, 39–41
mass social audits, 80–82. *See also* social audits
  Andhra Pradesh with, 76–79
  NGOs criticizing, 80–82, 195–96n.19
  of villages, 84, 84*t*
materiality, 18–19, 74
materials
  corruption with, 59–60, 150–51, 155–56, 194n.10
  fraud on labor and, 194n.10
mates
  auditors bribed by, 156
  complicated relationships and, 149, 157
  corruption and, 155, 156
  field assistants and, 159, 169
  on social audits, 153–54
  wages of, 202n.16
  as worker representative, 149
  on workers, 153–55
Mathur, Nayanika, 23, 53, 116
Mazdoor Kisan Shakti Sangathan (MKSS)
  on corruption, 32, 33
  on public hearings, 33–35
  Roy and, 32–34, 89–90
  RTI Act and, 34
  on social audits, 32–35
measurements, 130–31, 147, 154, 202n.15
Meghalaya, 170–71, 197–98n.49
Mehta, S., 115–16, 160, 200n.11
minimum wage, 44, 77
  for auditors, 85–86
  manual labor and, 10, 29
  nonpayment of, 32–33
  piece-rate system and, 57
  as raised, 40, 151
MIS. *See* Management Information System
MKSS. *See* Mazdoor Kisan Shakti Sangathan
MNREGA. *See* Mahatma Gandhi National Rural Employment Guarantee Act
mobile phones, 45, 53–54, 59, 61, 63
monitoring
  programs, 41, 44–45, 45*f*, 57, 59–60, 62–63, 84, 85, 169–70, 175–76
  reform, 127–28, 149, 166, 170, 172–73, 176, 177, 200n.8
  state action, 1, 3–4, 7–8, 20–21, 34, 36–37, 45–46, 51–52, 53–54, 56, 58, 63, 80–81, 167–68, 167*t*, 169, 175
Morozov, Evgeny, 19, 171–72
Movimento dos Trabalhadores Sem Terra (MST), 70
MPDO. *See* mandal program development officer
MST. *See* Movimento dos Trabalhadores Sem Terra
mukhiya (elected representative, landholder), 6, 7, 11–12
muster rolls
  auditors for paper, 62
  definition of, 47–48
  digitization of, 58
  engineers on, 17
  as falsified, 11, 17–18, 44, 57, 62, 162
  JJSS on, 175–76
  legibility and data collection on, 61–64
  as not seen, 5, 46–47
  software and, 58–59, 60–61, 62, 118
  in SSAAT audits, 117–18
  upper-level bureaucrats on, 60–61
  as work documentation, 47–48, 57, 202n.15
  workers cheated with, 5, 32–33, 44

Naidu, Chandrababu, 31–32, 44, 193n.30, 194n.9
National Common Minimum Program, 31–32
National Democratic Alliance, 31–32
National Food for Work program. *See* Food for Work Program
National Human Rights Commission, 39

National Rural Employment Guarantee Act (NREGA). *See also* last mile
Adivasis employed by, 29, 36, 36*t*, 37*t*
administration of, 185n.7
in Andhra Pradesh, 2, 35–37, 36*t*, 37*t*, 170, 185n.1, 197–98n.49, 203n.1
auditors and record access of, 118
Bihar challenges in, 11, 21, 68–69, 75–76, 122, 172
Bihar implementation by, 74, 75, 82, 124, 170–71, 179, 185n.8, 192n.14, 197–98n.49
on caste, 1–2, 138, 204n.4
challenges for, 48
consequences of, 151
with corruption, 78–79, 125–26, 150–51
for Dalits, 29, 36, 36*t*, 37*t*
Dalits on, 145–48
decentralization and, 187n.23
development patched by, 17
digital technologies on projects and, 55, 66
Drèze on, 1–2, 11, 196n.20
engineers and, 14
ethnography on, 26, 179
as Food for Work program and, 13–14, 44, 195n.11
implementation of, 191n.10
India enacting, 1, 203n.21
for infrastructure work, 29
JJSS on, 4–5, 68
for landless workers, 28, 35, 38–41, 137, 138, 170
large Reddies not affected by, 143–44
last mile and job card lack of, 131
in Meghalaya, 170–71, 197–98n.49
payment system of, 47–48
on politics and contractors, 14, 52
politics for, 14, 31–32
Reddies manipulating, 151–52
Reddy on assistance and, 142, 143–45
right-to-food campaign on, 30–31, 32
RTI Act in, 34–35
social audit from, 1, 10, 28, 70–71, 77–78, 108–9
software for, 44, 53–55
state comparisons in, 183–84
Tamil Nadu with, 190n.1, 192n.14
on technology, 25–26, 42*f*, 43, 50
in Telangana, 170–71, 197–98n.49, 203n.1
time-and-motion studies for, 202n.18
transparency from, 1, 3, 28, 44–45, 50, 52–53, 62, 131, 137, 145
in Uttarkhand, 194n.3
village work in, 138
on wages, 201–2n.10
women employed by, 29, 35, 36, 36*t*, 37*t*, 109, 110
worker bargaining power from, 35, 134–35, 137, 138–39, 142, 160, 165, 166*t*, 169, 170
workers on, 145–48, 169
work project creation in, 42*f*, 42–43, 165
work types by, 10, 29
YSR on, 41–42, 192n.21
nongovernmental organization (NGO)
audits and, 69, 71–74, 77–78, 85–86
audits criticized by, 80–82, 195–96n.19
on farming wages, 201n.9
SSAAT and, 45–46, 81
NREGA. *See* National Rural Employment Guarantee Act
political will, 31–32, 38, 114, 133–34, 168, 170–71, 175–76

O'Donnell, Guillermo, 12
on-demand employment
comparisons on, 183
NREGA on, 201–2n.10
work types in, 1, 29, 84*t*, 131, 142, 145–46, 150–51, 152, 201–2n.10
openness (open data/open government), 20–21, 121, 168, 174–76, 177

panchayati raj, 193n.30, 193n.34
panchayati secretary, 95, 198n.3
Pande, Suchi, 114
Papp, John, 35, 151–52, 185n.1, 201–2n.10
Partha, Chatterjee, 8
participation
citizens, 20, 21, 22, 24, 28, 92–93, 100, 101, 109, 112–13, 114, 127, 141
workers, 3, 4, 29, 36*t*, 37*t*, 69, 89, 91, 92, 93, 94, 97, 160, 175–76
participatory bureaucratic institution
Andhra Pradesh and, 69
audits of, 82–89, 84*t*, 91, 114
marginalized citizen engagement in, 91, 163
patching for, 22–23, 173–74
as SSAAT, 22, 24, 26, 69, 71, 89–90, 114, 163, 166, 189n.42
patching development. *See also specific subjects*
ambiguity for, 71, 83, 89–90
definition of, 17, 18–19
limitations of, 171–72, 187n.27
as sociotechnical process, 187n.24
as technological and administrative, 19
for updates, 56–57
payment infrastructure, 47–48, 173–74

People's Union for Civil Liberties (PUCL), 30–31, 191n.9
police, 12, 13, 139–40, 186n.14, 199n.20, 200–1n.5
  station of, 130, 140
political party, 1, 8, 31–32, 39, 41–42, 59–60, 71–72, 79, 80, 83, 91–92, 97–98, 99, 100, 101, 102, 105, 107, 108, 110, 111–13, 122, 125, 167–68, 185n.11, 186n.13, 188n.32, 193n.30, 197n.40
  Bharatiya Janata Party, 31–32
  Congress, 31–32, 39–41, 79, 99, 125, 139, 192n.14, 192n.18, 193n.27, 193n.34
  National Democratic Alliance, 31–32
  Telugu Desam Party, 31–32, 39–40, 98, 139
  United Progressive Alliance, 31–32
political will
  designing development programs, 1–2, 8, 9, 10–11, 17, 100, 163, 194n.2, 195n.3
  NREGA, 31–32, 38, 114, 133–34, 168, 170–71, 175–76
  patching, 164, 165, 172, 177
politics
  Andhra Pradesh audits and, 71–72, 185n.11, 193n.25
  auditors avoiding, 86, 167–68
  auditors on, 122
  on caste, 202n.12
  citizen monitoring and, 175–77
  on corruption, 122
  corruption and local, 14, 55
  Dalit Mahasabha and, 39
  decentralization and, 186n.22
  digital technologies and, 50, 59–60, 166
  economic and social rights with, 30
  for elite capture, 126, 163
  ethnography on information and, 179–81
  gram sabhas without parties of, 97–98
  by low-caste groups, 38
  lower-level bureaucrats pressured by, 52, 55, 67, 141, 151, 166*t*, 167*t*, 170, 194n.14
  on marginalized citizens, 8
  media and, 199n.24
  NREGA and, 14, 31–32
  NREGA on contractors and, 14, 52
  patching development and, 18–19, 171
  rachabanda as power, 98, 113
  rachabanda meeting as, 91–92, 98–100, 112–13
  resistance and informational, 26
  social audits and village, 103–4, 105, 107–8, 109–10, 111
  technology neutralizing, 67, 190n.49
  transparency and, 171, 177
  upper-level avoidance of, 124–26
  YSR and, 192n.17
polycentricity, 15
post offices, 148–49
power
  Andhra Pradesh and redistribution of, 14–15
  Bourdieu on, 20, 21–22, 23
  of bureaucracy, 1–2
  of caste, gender, and bureaucracy, 1–2
  on citizen monitoring, 175–77
  class and, 1–2, 11–12
  coercive state-society and, 12, 13
  Dalits gaining, 138–39
  development programs on, 163
  digital technologies on last mile and, 49, 148–52, 173
  from documents, 23–24, 116, 169
  elite capture from inequality and, 91, 163
  local bureaucrats losing, 44, 107–8
  local power system losing, 44, 166*t*, 171
  patching and exercise of, 19
  patch iteration over, 24–25
  public hearing as democratizing, 24, 116–17
  public hearings and, 24, 126–27
  public hearings for losing, 24
  rachabanda meetings and political, 98, 113
  Reddies on loss and, 142, 143, 144
  of Reddy, 148
  of sarpanches, 97–98, 126
  social audits and, 24, 116–17, 198n.51
  state and, 20, 188n.33
  transparency and, 20–21
  upper-level bureaucrats centralizing, 98
  workers and bargaining, 35, 134–35, 137, 138–39, 142, 160, 165, 166*t*, 169, 170
  worker testimony as, 122
principal secretary, 17, 51–52, 58, 77, 82–83
Pritchett, Lant, 9–10, 140
programs monitoring, 41, 44–45, 45*f*, 57, 59–60, 62–63, 84, 85, 169–70, 175–76
public hearings
  auditors vs. lower-level at, 128, 129
  on complaints, 166–67
  on corruption, 33–34, 68, 175–76
  Dalits on, 160
  on field assistants, 121–23
  JJSS and, 4–6, 7–8, 24, 68–69, 82, 162
  on local elite intimidation, 126–28
  at mandal-level, 128–34, 133*t*
  MKSS on, 33–35
  MPDO and, 128–34, 133*t*
  patching and, 75

public hearings (*cont.*)
power and, 24, 126–27
as power democratization, 24, 115
power lost at, 24
social audits stage of, 75, 87, 123–28, 166–67
structure of mandal, 129
transparency and, 122–23, 126, 188n.32
upper-level bureaucrats with mandal, 132–33, 133*t*
on village council decisions, 141
public records access
dangers in, 114
local bureaucrats against, 14
record digitization for, 25, 34
upper-level bureaucrats for, 3–4
PUCL (People's Union for Civil Liberties), 30–31

rachabanda meetings
attendance at, 98, 100, 198n.6
corruption and, 100
as politics meeting, 91–92, 98–100, 112–13
as power politics, 98, 113
as "real" gram sabhas, 97–98, 111–12
Rajadhyaksha, Ashish, 9
Rajasthan, 196n.20
Raju, Koppula, 14, 41
in Andhra Pradesh, 148, 186n.18
on arrack, 193n.24
social audit and, 72–73, 76, 80, 186n.18
as state bureaucrat, 43, 44–45, 51–53, 72–73, 76
technology and, 53–54
Rao, Biju, 75–76, 92–94, 98, 115, 141, 175
Rao, N. T. Rama, 39–40, 193n.27, 193n.34
Rao, Ursula, 194n.11
Ravallion, Martin, 185n.10
record digitization, 25, 34
Reddies
on audits, 158
on Dalits and control, 145, 202n.13
Kamma and, 139, 192n.15
landed class as, 137, 139, 142
as large farmers, 143–44
on lower-level bureaucrats, 143
for NREGA assistance, 142, 143–45
NREGA work manipulated by, 151–52
police surveillance on, 140
on power loss, 142, 143, 144
power of, 148
quasi-feudal clientelism and, 145–46
as small farmers, 144, 201n.9, 203n.22
workers watched by, 137, 145–46, 147
work types manipulated by, 151–52
Reddy, Y. S. Rajasekhar (YSR), 76–77, 148, 186n.13, 192n.21, 193n.25, 194n.9
for computers and social audits, 44–45
digital technologies and, 44–45
on marginalized rural poor, 39–41
on NREGA, 41–42, 192n.21
politics and, 192n.17
reform monitoring, 127–28, 149, 166, 170, 172–73, 176, 177, 200n.8
reprisal. *See* backlash
resistance
bureaucrats on anti-worker, 2–3
digital technology on local, 24–25
informational politics for, 26
by local power system, 1, 3, 107–8, 163
on patching, 172
rights-based approach, 1, 28, 30, 142, 197n.41
Right to Food, 30–31, 32, 191n.4, 191n.7
Right to Information (RTI) Act
bureaucrat accountability in, 16, 21, 163, 164
document access by, 5, 28
by India, 1
MKSS and, 34
in NREGA, 34–35
social audits and, 162
transparency from, 28
right to work, 1, 28, 30–32, 34–35, 162
Roy, Aruna, 32–34, 89–90
RTI. *See* Right to Information Act

Sainath, P., 11, 203n.22
sampling, 104–5, 118
"sandwich" strategies, 22, 70
Sankaran, S. R., 41, 192n.22
Sanyal, Paromita, 75–76, 92–94, 98, 115, 141
sarpanches (elected village council leaders)
accountability and, 82
audits and, 103, 107, 108–9, 110–11, 114, 124–25, 128–29
backlashes and, 34, 125
corruption and, 44, 73–74, 75–76, 107
government jobs with, 52
power of, 97–98, 126
SC. *See* scheduled caste
scheduled caste (SC), 65
Scott, James, 15, 18, 50–52, 61, 68, 176–77, 204n.11
segregation, by caste, 42, 103, 109, 139, 200n.3
Sen, Amartya, 170, 188n.32
settlements
from appeals, 133–34
on auditors, 156
fraud as, 156

lower-level and workers with private, 107–8, 134–35, 157, 167*t*, 169
social audits and private, 134–35, 160–61, 176
73rd amendment to India's Constitution, 43
small farmers, 144, 201n.9, 203n.22
social audits, 179, 199n.22, 203n.24, *See also* mass social audits
activists on, 81–82
Andhra Pradesh politics on, 71–72, 185n.11, 193n.25
Andhra Pradesh units for, 80–82, 200n.1
Andhra Pradesh with, 36–38, 89–90
auditors on, 195n.17
backlash on, 79, 175–76, 191n.11
bureaucracy on, 195n.5, 195–96n.19
caste and location of, 108–9
as citizen oversight mechanism, 1
control of, 80–81, 89–90
on corruption, 22–23, 74, 77–78, 89, 125–26, 133, 153–56, 158, 160, 169, 199n.11
decisions on, 69–70
directors of, 105–6, 179
district resource persons and, 101–2, 103, 104–5, 106, 107, 108–9, 126, 198–99n.9
documents and, 116, 152–53
elite capture and, 158, 168
with engineers, 158
financial audits vs., 75
follow-through on, 71–72, 133–34, 160, 166, 166*t*, 175–76
as fraud deterrence, 89, 125–26, 133, 153, 156
with gram sabhas, 85, 91, 93, 108
household survey and document access in, 117–21, 200n.5
information infrastructure and rulings of, 133–34
intimidation in, 107, 168
JJSS and, 4–6, 7–8, 24, 68–69, 82, 162
Kidambi and, 73, 80, 82, 89–90, 195n.9
by labor union, 4–7
on last mile, 22–23, 74, 77–78, 153–56, 160, 169
lower-level bureaucrats and, 78–79
lower-level manipulation of, 158, 168
as manual, 74
mates on, 153–54
MKSS on, 32–35
NGOs and, 69, 71–74, 77–78, 85–86
NREGA and, 1, 10, 28, 70–71, 77–78, 108–9
participatory bureaucratic institution and, 82–89, 84*t*, 91, 114
patching and, 69, 71–72, 75, 85, 89–90
politics of village and, 103–4, 105, 107–8, 109–10, 111
power and, 24, 116–17, 198n.51
as power democratization, 24, 116–17
private settlements and, 134–35, 160–61, 176
process of, 46–47, 71–72, 74–75, 104–7
as protests and bureaucracy, 90
with public hearings, 75, 87, 123–28, 166–67
Raju and, 72–73, 76, 80, 186n.18
Reddies on, 158
RTI Act and, 162
sarpanches and, 103, 107, 108–9, 110–11, 114, 124–25, 128–29
schedules of, 199n.12
SSAAT and, 45–46, 82–83, 197–98n.49
stages of, 86–87, 117, 117*t*
for state record rewriting, 133
state resource persons in, 45–46, 46*f*, 84, 84*t*, 85–86, 108–9, 110
state support for, 77–78
Telangana and units for, 200n.1
training for, 73–74
transparency and, 114–15, 122–23, 127–28, 174–78
uncontrolled participation in, 100–11
upper-level bureaucrats using, 3–4, 66–67, 71–72, 75–76, 78–79, 81, 82, 167–68, 167*t*
village base for, 103, 104
village meetings in, 87, 123–28
villager cooperation in, 106–7, 157–58
for worker leverage, 158–61, 167*t*
workers on, 138
YSR for, 44–45
social movements
for audits, 70–71
for marginalized citizens, 68, 177
MST and, 70
"sandwich strategy" and, 22, 70
state bureaucrats and, 68, 89–90
on state control, 70
upper-level bureaucrats and, 69
Society for Social Audit and Transparency (SSAAT), 79, 85, 90, 124, 127, 129, 158
by activist bureaucrats, 22–23, 89–90
as activists, 22–23, 89–90
Andhra Pradesh creating, 44–45
on auditor and activist independence, 83–84, 84*t*
audits and, 45–46, 82–83, 197–98n.49
audits and worker documents by, 117–21
on fraud, 197n.47
muster rolls and audits of, 117–18
NGOs and, 45–46, 81

Society for Social Audit and Transparency (SSAAT) (*cont.*)
  participatory bureaucratic institution as, 22, 24, 26, 69, 71, 89–90, 114, 163, 166, 189n.42
  reports from, 200n.10
  specter of, 154
  structure of, 46*f*, 197n.41
  for transparency, 22
  units of, 200n.1
  upper-level bureaucrats creating, 82–83
  villagers on, 83
socio-technical, 49, 163
software, 17–19, 53–55, 56–57, 82, 118, 150, 151, 166
  for inspections, 63–64
  muster rolls and, 58–59, 60–61, 62, 118
  for NREGA, 44, 53–55
  patching and, 4, 17, 49–50, 55–57, 150, 151
  for "write access," 82, 166
solutionism, 19, 171–72, 190n.48, 190n.50
Srinivasan, Vivek, 38, 52, 186n.14
Srivastava, Manoj, 115
SSAAT. *See* Society for Social Audit and Transparency
state action monitoring, 1, 3–4, 7–8, 20–21, 34, 36–37, 45–46, 51–52, 53–54, 56, 58, 63, 80–81, 167–68, 167*t*, 169, 175
State level bureaucrats, 9–10, 39–40, 43, 61, 151
state resource persons
  in audit team, 45–46, 46*f*, 84, 84*t*, 85–86, 108–9, 110
  information from, 105, 106, 110–11
state-society, 168, 186n.16, 187n.30
  for accountability, 188–89n.36
  actors for, 167*t*
  bargaining power with, 157
  cooperation in, 77–79
  definition of, 13
  documents by, 23, 116
  as everyday, 3–4, 194n.5
  first mile as, 8
  household survey for, 133
  India and, 185n.9, 186n.15
  legibility for, 50–53
  literature of, 22, 189n.38
  marginalized citizens writing documents of, 116–17, 122–23, 134, 162, 169
  marginalized people seeing, 1, 115
  partnerships, 15–16, 70, 195n.2
  police as coercive, 12, 13
  power and, 20, 188n.33
  right-to-food campaign on, 30–31, 32
  for social audits, 77–78
  social movements on control and, 70
  synergies and, 176–77
  transparency challenges for, 174–75
Supreme Court, 30–31, 191n.8
surveillance, 61, 104, 116, 139, 140, 189n.44, 200–1n.5, 201n.7
  in audit, 104
  by colonial powers, 116, 189n.44, 201n.7
  by digital technology, 61
  by police, 139, 140, 200–1n.5
  by Reddy landlords, 145–46

Tamil Nadu, 190n.1, 192n.14
Tata Consultancy Services (TCS), 53–54, 58
technical assistant
  fraud and, 125, 155
  of mandals, 43
  on measurements, 130–31, 147, 154, 202n.15
  misappropriation and, 125, 155
technocracy, 173–78
technology, 187n.28
  avoidance of, 173–74
  on corruption, 173
  for democracy, 178
  drop-down boxes in, 178
  ethnography on, 190n.46
  information infrastructure and, 174–76, 188n.34
  last mile and, 9
  for last-mile legibility, 53–55
  marginalized citizens and, 173
  mobile phones in, 45, 53–54, 59, 61, 63
  on monolithic citizens and states, 176–77
  NREGA on, 25–26, 42*f*, 43, 50
  patching and, 19, 53–55
  politics and, 67, 190n.49
  on rapid innovation, 190n.47
  on transparency, 64, 174, 193–94n.1
  upper-level bureaucrats with, 3–4, 49, 202n.17
techno-utopians, 173
Telangana, 170–71, 197–98n.49, 200n.1, 203n.1
Telugu Desam Party, 31–32, 39–40, 98, 139
transparency, 176
  accountability and, 114–15, 174–75, 177
  activists for, 85, 89
  democracy and, 188n.32
  documents and, 188n.35
  flashlight metaphor in, 177
  information expansion from, 20–21, 23, 24

information infrastructure and, 20–21, 23, 24
JJSS for, 68
last mile and, 91, 131
lower-level bureaucrats on, 67
Mathur on, 23, 53, 116
NREGA and, 1, 3, 28, 44–45, 50, 52–53, 62, 131, 137, 145
patching and, 174–78
politics and, 171, 177
power and, 20–21
public hearings and, 122–23, 126, 188n.32
from RTI, 28
social audits and, 114–15, 122–23, 127–28, 174–78
Society for Social Audit and Transparency for, 22
state-society and, 174–75
technology on, 64, 174, 193–94n.1
tribal villages, 150, 179–80, 203n.25

United Progressive Alliance, 31–32
upper-level bureaucrats
as administrators, 3, 200n.10
on Andhra Pradesh legibility, 51–52
anti-worker system and, 2–3
on caste and hiring, 65–66
circulars and patches from, 194n.8
corruption and, 148–49, 177, 185n.4, 200n.10
on document rewriting, 117, 167*t*, 168–69, 199n.17
engineers interviewed by, 64
on ethnography, 180
on field assistant hiring, 64–65
follow-through by, 71–72, 133–34, 160, 166, 166*t*, 175–76
on gram sabhas, 95
information infrastructure by, 3–4, 20, 24, 44–45, 194n.2
on local power elites, 167*t*, 177
on lower-level collusion, 14, 52, 63
lower-level monitored by, 49, 51–52, 56–57, 60–63, 66–67, 83, 114, 124–26, 166*t*, 167*t*, 169–70, 177, 187n.26
mandal public hearings for, 132–33, 133*t*
on muster rolls, 60–61
patching by, 18–19, 19, 51–52, 164
on politics avoidance, 124–26
on post offices and corruption, 148–49
power centralization by, 98
with records access, 3–4
social audit and, 3–4, 66–67, 71–72, 75–76, 78–79, 81, 82, 167–68, 167*t*
social movements and, 69
SSAAT by, 82–83
with technology, 3–4, 49, 202n.17
Uttarkhand, 194n.3

Veron, Rene, 115
village
auditors and, 84*t*, 85, 86, 101–4, 108, 123
fraud by, 154–55
gram sabhas as meeting and, 44–45, 47, 75–76, 87, 91, 92–98
mass social audits of, 84, 84*t*
NREGA work in, 138
social audits and, 87, 103–4, 105, 106–8, 109–10, 111, 123–28, 157–58
village councils. *See* gram panchayats
village level bureaucrats, 42–43, 47, 69–70, 71–72, 85–86, 87, 91, 97, 101–2, 111–12, 131, 158, 162, 181

wages
Aadhaar and, 173–74, 193n.33
comparisons on, 183
consequences of guaranteed, 151
Dalits with food or, 147
documents and, 199n.13
in Food for Work Program, 195n.11
increase of, 40, 58, 138–39, 142, 148, 151, 160, 165, 201–2n.10
last mile and worker, 132, 148–49
last mile underpayment on, 129–30
of mates, 202n.16
as minimum, 10, 29, 32–33, 40, 44, 57, 77, 85–86, 151
NGO on farming, 201n.9
NREGA on, 201–2n.10
patching and payment of, 148–49, 150, 185n.8, 193n.33
payment infrastructure for, 47–48, 173–74
worker and wrong, 130
Weber, 20, 41–42, 71
Williams, Glyn, 115
Winner, Langdon, 49
Witsoe, Jeffrey, 48
women
anti-arrack moment by, 38–39, 191–92n.13
auditors as, 102, 199n.10
comparisons on, 183
NREGA employing, 29, 35, 36, 36*t*, 37*t*, 109, 110

workers, landless, 172–73
on audits, 138
audits and documents for, 117–21, 167*t*
backlash fears of, 138, 148
bargaining power for, 35, 134–35, 137, 138–39, 142, 160, 165, 166*t*, 169, 170
benefits for, 196n.23
Dalits as, 139
on fraud, 119–21
fraud by village and, 154–55
group interactions of, 121–23
JJSS labor union of, 162
landed class vs., 1–2, 13–14, 137, 189n.38, 202n.13
last mile and wage payments of, 132, 148–49
last mile work withheld on, 131
local elites and testimonies by, 126–28
Maharashtra and, 190n.2, 192n.14
mandal public hearings without, 128–29
mates on, 149, 153–55
mukhiya on, 6, 7, 11–12
muster rolls for cheating, 5, 32–33, 44
on NREGA, 145–48, 169
NREGA for, 28, 35, 38–41, 137, 138, 170
private settlements among lower-level and, 107–8, 134–35, 157, 167*t*, 169
Reddies as quasi-feudal on, 145–46
Reddies watching, 137, 145–46, 147
social audits and leverage of, 158–61, 167*t*
social protection for, 189n.39
state identity cards and, 197n.42
testimony as power, 122
wage increases for, 40, 58, 138–39, 142, 148, 151, 160, 165, 201–2n.10
working with, 136–37
on work sites, 193n.28
work types and, 149–50, 151, 167*t*
wrong payments for, 130
workers participation, 3, 4, 29, 36*t*, 37*t*, 69, 89, 91, 92, 93, 94, 97, 160, 175–76
work projects, 202–3n.20
by MPDO, 42*f*, 42–43, 203n.23
NREGA creating, 42*f*, 42–43, 165
work types
creation of, 149–50, 151, 167*t*
on government land, 150
by NREGA, 10, 29
as "on demand," 1, 29, 84*t*, 131, 142, 145–46, 150–51, 152, 199n.23, 201–2n.10
patching and, 149, 150
Reddies manipulating, 151–52

YSR. *See* Reddy, Y. S. Rajasekhar